Becoming a
Professional Pilot

Becoming a Professional Pilot

Robert Mark

TAB Books
Division of McGraw-Hill, Inc.
Blue Ridge Summit, PA 17294-0850

FIRST EDITION
FIRST PRINTING

© 1994 by **TAB Books**.
TAB Books is a division of McGraw-Hill, Inc.

Library of Congress Cataloging-in-Publication Data

Mark, Robert (Robert Paul)
   Becoming a professional pilot / by Robert Mark.
     p. cm.
   Includes index.
   ISBN 0-8306-4145-9   ISBN 0-8306-4146-7 (pbk.)
   1. Air pilot. 2. Aeronautics—Vocational guidance. I. Title.
TL561.M37 1993
629.132'52'023—dc20   93-32866
                                          CIP

Acquisitions Editor: Jeff Worsinger
Editor: Sally Anne Glover
Production Team: Katherine G. Brown, Director
                Susan E. Hansford, Coding
                Wendy L. Small, Layout
                Lorie L. White, Proofreading
Design Team: Jaclyn J. Boone, Designer
              Brian Allison, Associate Designer   AV1
Cover Design and Illustration: Denny Bond, East Petersburg, Pa.   4236

For Nancy.

Contents

Foreword

CONGRATULATIONS! You hold in your hand a book that could be the starting point for a very exciting, professionally rewarding, and challenging career. Becoming a professional pilot takes a lot of work, but the rewards, both personal and financial, are well worth the investment.

Our astronauts talked about having the "right stuff." What is the right stuff to become a professional pilot? I've spent 17 years heavily involved in the hiring process for a major airline. To me, what makes a professional pilot can be summed up in one word—attitude.

Before you launch your career as a professional pilot, I suggest that you assess your attitude toward work and life in general. Are you committed to excellence in everything you do? If you can honestly say you do strive to be the best—in everything from your academic preparation to your performance in the cockpit—and that you take every opportunity to improve and learn and perfect your skills, then, in my opinion, you're on the right track.

People often measure excellence in terms of flight hours. I don't believe that's an accurate gauge. I've hired pilots with 350 hours and pilots with 20,000 hours. I believe these pilots can perform equally well if they first have the proper attitude.

After 35 years of professional flying, I still personally critique every flight I make, whether I'm flying a Boeing 747 or a single-engine aircraft. I write down everything I can think of to improve the flight next time, and I review those comments from time to time. I'm still waiting to see a perfect flight.

Always strive to be the best as a pilot, and good luck. There's a great opportunity for those who are willing to make the commitment.

William Traub
Captain, B-727, 737, 747, DC-6, DC-7, DC-8

Introduction

"The flight was short, but it was nevertheless the first in the history of the world in which a machine carrying a man had raised itself by its own power into the air in full flight, had sailed forward without reduction of speed and had finally landed at a point as high as that from which it started."

Orville Wright in a statement to the press
December, 1903

WHEN I WAS A KID FINISHING HIGH SCHOOL, I wanted to fly more than anything else in the world. I spent much of my free time riding my motorcycle out to places like Chicago's O'Hare International Airport and Midway airport, as well as some of the general aviation fields around Chicagoland, just to spend hours parked outside the fence watching the aircraft come and go. This was the mid '60s, so there were still plenty of opportunities to see some of the famous propeller-driven airplanes like DC-3s and DC-7s, as well as the turbo-prop Lockheed Electras that have since marched into history. Then there were the jets, DC-8s, Boeing 707s, DC-9s, and the Convair 880s and 990s. Twin-engine corporate turboprops were just appearing at the general aviation fields. I knew all those names as well.

I spent hours thinking about how I'd feel behind the controls of some airliner or corporate jet. I took pictures, too . . . hundreds of them, most of which survive to this day in albums stashed in the closet. I think those pictures helped me stay motivated and focused on my goal. As I parked my old motorcycle by the airport fences, I knew that I wanted in, somehow, anyway I could manage it. I was 17 years old.

I wish I had known someone involved in the aviation industry then—a mentor, someone who could have shown me the ropes, who could have helped me avoid many of the pitfalls. If I'd had someone like that to teach me, I never would have spent so much time moving in so many different directions over the years, some directions that actually seemed to lead me further away from my goal rather than closer to it. I didn't wear my first airline uniform until I was in my 30s.

The '60s was a time, too, when airline pilots were hard to find. Believe it or not, I once saw a newspaper ad for airline pilots for a major carrier. The only major requirement was a private pilot's license. The airline paid for the rest of your training if only you'd be good enough to come and work for them. Many pilots did.

But this is the '90s, the time of belt tightening in all industries. Many of the airlines that took to the air before and since airline deregulation began in 1979 are now history, victims of fierce competition from both the economy and other, stronger airlines. As the number of major airlines shrinks, so too will the need for thousands and thousands of pilots at some of those carriers. The competition for jobs at the major airlines will be stiff, as will the competition for corporate flying jobs. The military also will use fewer pilots. The fall of the Communist Empire has brought with it a decline in the numbers of American military aircraft needed to cope with a threat against the United States.

Does this mean then that your dreams of flying are swiftly disintegrating? Absolutely not. As the old saying goes, "When the going gets tough, the tough get going." Searching for a professional flying job in the '90s is going to be work, but looking for work in any profession during the '90s is tougher than it used to be. You might find that the path toward that coveted flying job—be it airline, corporate, or military—might not be quite as direct as it was for new applicants even five years ago. You need to be prepared for some challenges along the way, perhaps spending time in one kind of flying job that you didn't expect—towing banners or even instructing. You might even realize that your eventual goals need modifying as time goes by. If you keep your goals well within sight and you're willing to be realistic about the competition as well as your own skill level, a career as a professional pilot is certainly available to you.

These days, the world and some of your friends might try to tell you to give up. Don't! Just because there are fewer jobs in some segments of flying doesn't mean that you can't be one of the people who lands one of those jobs. During the course of this book, I won't pull any punches with you. I wrote the text primarily as a consumer's guide on how to reach the goal of becoming a professional pilot, so you'll learn some practical tips on training as well as some potential traps to avoid as you make that trek toward the left seat. With this book, you'll discover just what's really happening within the industry in 1993, as well as the current forecasts for the future.

I've also included some relevant articles of mine—as well as interviews and remembrances of pilots within the industry—to let you hear how their careers were formed and to help you put your best foot forward and find the flying job you want. I've chosen to use bits and pieces of information that I've picked up over the years about a variety of different aviation topics. I hope that some of the practical experience pieces will make you consider some ideas that you might not have thought about before. But a word of caution here. Please don't take any of my interviews as blanket approval of any of the organizations I mention. Only you can gather training, job, and consumer information to arrive at the best final decision about whether or not a particular company or publication will work for you.

1

Your career starts here

I CAN'T IMAGINE A BETTER PROFESSION THAN FLYING 30,000 feet above the earth and looking out from a vantage point that few others have, finding yourself in one of the greatest theaters in the world as you watch thousands of miles of wondrously changing clouds and landscape pass beneath. It's a treat that's tough to surpass. In addition to enjoying the beauty and majesty of this perspective on the world, I've spent a better part of my life making money at some form of flying . . . and so can you.

Flying airplanes for a living is a proud profession that dates back about 75 years to an era when flying meant a very serious risk to your life, not to mention the lives of any passengers you were carrying. (See Fig. 1-1.) In the days of the barnstormers, aircraft engines were simple but unreliable, so total engine failures

Fig. 1-1. Early days of commercial flying.

were commonplace. The fuselage and wings of the first commercial aircraft were nothing more than cut pieces of aircraft spruce that were nailed and glued together to form the frame. Then, the fuselage and wings were covered with fabric and painted with many coats of aircraft dope for strength. A wood and fabric airplane is a concept that probably sounds a bit scary to people watching shiny aluminum 747s, 757s, and MD-11s fly overhead. But, for the record, that doped fabric and wood airframe was incredibly strong, much stronger than the engines.

The first commercial aircraft carried names like Ryan, Douglas, Curtiss, and Boeing (Fig. 1-2). They ranged from simple, single-engine aircraft capable of carrying just one pilot and a few pouches of mail to more sophisticated types that could carry 6 to 8 passengers with a little room left over for baggage. As aircraft grew more sophisticated, the title of commercial pilot began to take on the meaning of someone with, if not yet a respectable job, at least a regular salary. Notice, though, that no one said anything about longevity because, in the '20s and '30s, it was still considered quite risky to be flying for a living. Although pilots were always viewed as somewhat crazy, they were also looked on as supermen and superwomen of sorts: brave individuals, adventurers who defied the odds and cheated death every time they took to the skies. It's because of these men and women that modern aviation evolved into what it is today.

Peter M. Bowers Collection

Fig. 1-2. Early United Airlines Boeing 247.

Over the years, aircraft reliability increased to where passengers were no longer considered completely crazy to fly. But pilots have still, to this day, been looked on by most people through somewhat heroic eyes (Fig. 1-3). Walk into a social situation and watch people's faces turn impressively toward the man or woman who tells the crowd they haul people around the sky in shiny silver airplanes. If you haven't seen that, there are only two reasons. One, you don't hang out with the right people yet. And two, you haven't been watching the faces of people at parties very well. You might think I'm bringing up some rather egocentric topics here, and I must admit that I am, but with good reason. Pilots tend to have rather outgoing, assertive personalities. This nature of theirs is a large part of what makes a pilot good at his or her job, but it's certainly not a requirement. A flying career will bring you years of pleasure, job satisfaction, and adventure, not to mention some rather superb financial rewards. So, if you're looking for a profession that will turn people's heads, as well as your own, I might add, there's nothing better than flying.

Fig. 1-3. Pilots have always seemed somewhat heroic to passengers.

WHAT IS A PROFESSIONAL PILOT?

Many people might initially identify a professional pilot as an airline pilot, but there are many more kinds of professional pilots around. There are corporate pilots shuttling the chief executive officers of some Fortune 500 companies. All over the world, there are pilots flying aircraft of all shapes and sizes, loaded to the gills with boxes and mail destined for just about every other point in the world . . . and someone needs to fly those airplanes. Freighters run the gamut from the sophisticated, new Boeing 747s (Fig. 1-4) that cargo carriers like Fed Ex and UPS fly, to older commercial jets like the DC-8s that you'll find flying their tails off for smaller freight carriers like Detroit-based American International Airways. Small freight operators like Chicago-based Viking Express operate a few of the famous old airliners, the Douglas DC-3, as well as old pewter-colored Beech 18s.

Robert Mark

Fig. 1-4. Northwest Airlines Boeing 747.

At the local general aviation airport, you'll see another group of professional pilots—the flight instructors. These men and women will turn the sometimes confusing chapters of your journey from private to professional pilot into knowledge designed to make you a better professional aviator. Teaching is a noble profession, not one to be taken lightly. Have you ever passed by a farmer's field and watched a small aircraft swoop low over a soybean field and spout a cloud of mist from behind? These crop dusters earn their living everyday saving fields of produce from the destruction of pests and disease. If you want to talk about thrills, imagine flying along at 20 feet off the ground at 100 mph and wild-looking gyrations at the opposite ends of the field to maneuver the airplane back for the next pass.

There are also air ambulance pilots. They're on call for a 24-hour period, just in case there's an emergency that requires them to transport a severely ill or injured patient from one place to another. In this kind of flying, the hours are never the same, and the destinations are seldom repeated.

And I'm not finished yet. There are banner tow pilots who fly low over a field to grab a long banner, trail it behind the airplane, and display an advertising message to thousands of people below. You don't cover much territory, usually, but the flying is a real challenge.

Still hungry for professional pilot jobs? How about a forest fire tanker pilot? Obviously, they don't operate in as many locations as other forms of flight operations, but tanker flying can be a real adventure. For Hollywood's look at this side of the profession, try renting the video "Always," starring Richard Dreyfuss.

Consider the heroes of the FAR Part 135 Air Taxi rules, known as on-demand charter pilots. They could be called out to fly a quick load of freight from a parts plant in central Illinois to an auto maker in Detroit to protect an assembly line from a needless shutdown. On-demand could involve last-minute plans by a dignitary or the local appearance of a rock-and-roll group. Not long ago, I saw a crew load up a Lear jet for a trip carrying only a single box the size of an egg crate. It contained a human heart headed for an anxious recipient 900 miles away. Don't forget the pilots who fly canceled checks or who report highway traffic from inside a cockpit each day.

Consider the helicopter pilots, too (Fig. 1-5). These often unsung heroes fly sleek rotorcraft not only from the local airports for corporate operators, but also from the tops of buildings where the headquarters of many businesses are located. Helicopters are special-use flying machines that can be stopped virtually on a dime and can vertically descend into a tight space to accomplish their mission. Be-

Helicopter Association International

Fig. 1-5. Commercial helicopter at work.

sides their use as a corporate shuttle vehicle, helicopters, by virtue of their agility, are one of the prime pieces of transportation used by Emergency Medical Services (EMS) for roadside evacuation of accident victims. In some locations, helicopters often compete with aircraft for aerial spraying and traffic reporting jobs.

But even after talking about some of the flying jobs available from time to time, I still haven't really put a finger on what makes a pilot a professional. Some people believe you're a professional only if you fly large aircraft. Some think that the moment you begin receiving your first paycheck, your status is transformed from trainee to pro.

Personally, I don't think any of these definitions is truly accurate. I think professionalism really begins with the person (Fig. 1-6), not the job. If you measure your self-worth and your position in the world by either the aircraft you fly or the numbers on your paycheck, you're involved in the wrong profession, whether it's flying or brain surgery. I've known flight instructors who flew around in four-place Cherokees in a shirt and tie who were more professional than some airline pilots I've known who had become truly jaded by their aircraft type and their six-figure income. Make no mistake about it, a six-figure income is a paycheck we'd all like to have. But if all you pick up from flying is a paycheck every two weeks, you're missing some of the best that this career and life itself have to offer. Fly because you love it. Fly because you can think of no greater job in the world. If you begin your career like this, then nothing that happens to you will dim that flame of enthusiasm.

Fig. 1-6. Professionalism really begins with the person.

But, like any profession with a good salary and benefits, these flying jobs will not just fall into your lap. Don't be surprised if, after your initial training is complete, airlines, corporations, or the military don't fall all over themselves lining up for your services. Finding a good flying job in any economy is tough, but as I write these words, we're only just now beginning to pull ourselves out of one of the worst tailslides the aviation industry has seen since I can remember. These downs are always followed by ups; this is part and parcel to the aviation business.

Whether you're a Republican or a Democrat, whether you believe the turmoil of this industry was brought on by deregulation or the new robber barons of the aviation management, the fact is that in the past three or four years, airlines have disappeared from the American landscape at an alarming rate, some by merger, some through bankruptcy. Great companies like Braniff, North Central, PSA, Eastern, Midway, and Pan American will never be seen again. And with these airlines went the jobs of pilots. Private corporations, also a good source of flying jobs for many years, began to lay pilots off in the late 1980s and close entire flight departments, some that had been around for 30 and 40 years. Even major airlines announced massive layoffs in 1993 or continued the cuts begun in 1992. As of mid 1993, estimates say close to 10,000 pilots are unemployed, depending on which source you believe. Why then, with the field in such obvious turmoil, would anyone want to even consider a career in flying? Simply because flying is the best job in the world.

If you've spent time reading the history of aviation since airline deregulation in the late 1970s, you'll see that what began as unbelievable expansion of flying activities turned quickly to not just a preoccupation with the companies' bottom line, but also a rather myopic concentration on the dollar as the only consideration in running a flight department. What that has left for you potential flyers today is a route that can easily be planned but not as easily executed. But no matter what, FAA forecasts of flying activities believe that there will be growth within the industry, and so do I. How much and where is another story, but, according to those 1993 FAA-released figures, the total population of pilots in the United States is expected to rise to approximately 795,000 by the year 2004. The FAA expects the total number of commercially licensed pilots to grow by almost 14 percent, while ATP-rated pilots (Fig. 1-7) will increase about 3 percent.

But a moment of skepticism is certainly required here. The government could be wrong, and the figures could be worse . . . or they could be better. Even if there's currently minimal hiring at the major airlines and corporate flight departments, there's growth at the regional airlines. Many forecasts expect more growth in the regional industry than in the majors, as the majors relieve themselves of unprofitable short routes and pass them out to their affiliated regional carriers.

Pilot hiring is cyclical, as are so many other industries in the United States. You'll have to face the fact that, if you're 25 right now, you might not be able to quickly and easily jump into an airline or corporate cockpit for awhile. But how important is that, really? Don't let your solid career plan be tarnished by the '80s desire to "have it all . . . right now." (Fig. 1-8.) If you need a bit of consolation as you accept your first flying job, consider those pilots over the age of say 45 or 50. While a young pilot can wait around for a few years for the industry to turn

Fig. 1-7. The captain on this A340 would hold an ATP certificate.

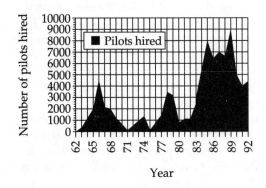

Fig. 1-8. Pilot hiring is cyclical.
FAPA

around, those older pilots will be well into their 50s, which makes employment for them very difficult. So, if you're 25, just beginning your flying career, or employed in a flying job that you don't want to make a career out of, stay calm. Look at the job as a means to get to your career goal of becoming a professional pilot. The industry will get better. Pilots will grow older, and they'll retire, making way for more people to move up the ladder.

ATTITUDE: HOW'S YOURS?

Your job is to become a professional pilot. If you're to be successful, you must adopt a professionally correct attitude. For without the right attitude, attaining your goal of becoming a professional pilot could just be the toughest plateau you've ever set up for yourself. You must mentally prepare yourself for the challenge of not just learning to fly, but also for the even greater challenge of finding the right job after you've learned to fly and gained the experience necessary for attaining your goal.

But please don't confuse my dose of aviation reality with the thought that the career is not worth pursuing. Quite the contrary. Flying professionally is worth the work it takes to get there, but finding the right job in aviation is going to be work. Just like a doctor or a carpenter, though, owning the basic skills doesn't guarantee an instant job.

What's the attitude, the right stuff, so to speak, for getting ahead in aviation? Rest assured it's not just maintaining a positive mental attitude. A positive attitude is only a part of becoming successful. Think about it; don't you know some people who are very bright, people who know just what they should do to become successful, and yet they never really succeed? No matter how bright they seem to be on the outside, they just never seem to get the right break or be in the right place at the right time or sell themselves in the best way possible when the time is right. So, just positive thinking isn't going to make you a professional pilot. I believe the reason most people don't succeed at the flying game is not because they don't want to succeed, but because they're afraid of failure.

Fear of failure probably squelches more careers than just about anything else. You must believe you can accomplish your goal, but even more than that, your plan must include a highway towards that goal, a path that's designed to help you leap past those points where the rejections arrive. Your plan must include a method for you to take action on that plan.

One young lady I interviewed for a story a few months back told me she had been asked to interview three different times by United Airlines before she was finally hired in 1992. Most people either give up after being rejected once or don't bother to interview at all because they're afraid of not being accepted. I'm no psychologist, so I'm only going to give you my feelings on this—what I've heard pilots tell me over the years. You can't fail if you don't apply . . . some say. Others believe they were rejected because the people at the airline or company specifically didn't like them. Don't give up; keep trying, no matter what. This is the only attitude for success.

Sure, there'll be times when you might not give a good interview, but ask yourself, and answer yourself truthfully: Were you really prepared? Did you possibly set yourself up a bit for failure? So what about the woman hired at United that I mentioned a moment ago. How did she cope with so much rejection from such a large organization? She knew her goal was to fly for United, and she wouldn't let anything turn her from that path . . . nothing. If they rejected her, she didn't take it personally. She took a deep breath and asked herself which way to turn around this obstacle in her path.

Do you believe that most medical residents enjoy working 36-hour shifts at hospitals that often take them away from their family and friends as well as away from much-needed rest? I doubt it. But what these people do realize is that it's useless to have a plan that only talks about goals, with no way of dealing with the hurdles life is going to toss at you along the way. The people who make it are the ones who understand that, while they can't control life, while they're unable to predict what kinds of roadblocks will be tossed in their paths, they can control the way they react to events. You're in control of your own life. If there's such a thing as a positive attitude, I believe you must be positive about just what you can really control.

THE PLAN

There's no such thing as the perfect plan to take you from the ranks of private pilot to that of a professional aviator, but let's consider the following as a possibility . . . an option. It might sound a bit simplistic, but I begin every plan with a fresh felt-tip pen and a legal pad. First, define your goal . . . to find a flying job; more specifically, what kind of flying job? Here's where the brainstorming comes in; before you set your initial goal, be sure that you haven't left something out, that you haven't set your sites too narrowly—like finding a flying job only with the airlines.

Too often, pilots—young and old—believe that you aren't a pilot unless you're an airline pilot because that's where all the status is and all the money is. Personally, I don't agree. If you really believe that all there is to aviation is sitting in the cockpit of a 747 on a long international route watching the islands and ice packs flow by beneath you, then I think you're headed into the wrong field. I really believe what an old aviator friend who now happens to pilot a Lockheed L-1011 said, "Do what you like, and the money will follow." In other words, if you chase only the money, you're setting yourself up for unhappiness in the long run. Avoid the plague of the '80s, the "I want top dollar and I want it right now" disease.

The first words at the top of your list should be your goal. The gurus who research employment as well as personal goals tell us that the most important item you can accomplish in your plan to become a pilot is to write that goal down on a piece of paper. Writing the goal down in some concrete fashion makes the goal take on a life of its own. This is the first step toward making your goal become reality.

Your plan is only a road map (Fig. 1-9), a route for you to take to eventually arrive at your goal of becoming a professional pilot. But, like any route taken on the ground, your career plan shouldn't be so rigid that it's incapable of allowing you to take a detour where necessary. There might be situations that force you to change your plan slightly, such as an unplanned opportunity to fly an aircraft in a state 1,000 miles away on a short-term contract for six months. Do you ignore the chance just because you didn't have it written down in a plan you produced a year ago? I certainly hope not. Certainly, too, a time might come when a roadblock to your career will appear. Consider all your alternatives before you make any decisions. If part of your plan was to spend the summer months dusting crops or towing banners and the job you'd hoped for disappears because the company went out of business or perhaps hired someone else, what are you going to do? You must have some alternative course to steer your plan out of the muck and onto high ground.

Jetstream Aircraft Inc.

Fig. 1-9. A pilot's position on a regional Jetstream 41 requires a plan to achieve.

The best method for keeping your career aloft rather than waiting at the terminal is to keep your education dynamic. Currently, I read seven aviation magazines each month. One of these is published on a weekly basis, so that's like reading eleven. Very often, though, you'll notice the same story more than once and consider reading it a waste. For example, Beech Aircraft recently managed to place the story of its updated Beech Starship 2000A in about three different magazines I read in a single month. Great public relations! The point, however, is that if you're constantly in touch with your industry, always aware of what companies are producing what products, what aircraft are the newest off the line with what sorts of systems, you have a great chance of knowing just what to talk about during an interview. The other advantage of staying in touch through many magazines is the variety of perspectives you'll receive.

Another benefit, too, is the awareness of the job situation you'll gain. I recently read a story in one of the trade magazines about a company producing new aircraft in Wisconsin, and I wondered whether or not there might be a place for me, even in a small operation such as that. I had extensive experience with the aircraft they were producing, and I thought it was worth a chance to make contact with the firm and offer my services as a pilot. Unfortunately, this particular opportunity didn't turn out favorably. But it might have. My motto is that I have absolutely nothing to lose by asking; the worst that could occur is the company would say no, and no one ever died from being told no. Whatever your methods, maintain contact with the industry.

The plan you produce for yourself should be realistic. If you expect to fly right-seat on a 757 after college, your chances are slim—not impossible now, but slim. Flying jobs are more work to locate today, so make the plan flexible. When will you pick up your commercial license? How will you pay for it? What methods will you use to increase your flying time? What jobs are you willing to perform to reach each step of your goal? What will you not do? Would you take a short-term job? When will you complete your instrument rating? What's your organizational plan for sending out resumes? How will you locate the addresses of companies that hire pilots? Would you consider giving up a few years of your freedom to join the U.S. Air Force or Navy to learn to fly there? The list will grow as you spend more time on your plan, but very much like a business plan, a career plan is most likely never finished. Things will change, but the real trick is to know when to stick resolutely to your plan and when to take that detour. If there's any advice I can provide on this front, it's not to jump too quickly at anything, no matter how good it looks. Think how this decision will affect the rest of your plan. If you're not sure, ask a close friend to sit down and talk with you about an opportunity when it presents itself. Brainstorming can reap some incredible benefits.

Where do you see yourself in one year, five years, ten years? Don't hold back here. Let your mind run free. Do you see yourself in the left seat of a corporate G-V (Fig. 1-10) flying Trans-Atlantic? Maybe it's the left seat of a 757 for American or Delta Airlines. Perhaps you enjoy flying but really enjoy being home more often. A regional airline or local charter job or possibly even some kind of utility flying is what might be best suited for you.

If you're a woman or a member of a minority group, there's good news for you, too. Besides the federal legislation that mandates that a company not discriminate against you because of your sex or race, most of the major airlines and corporations actively seek candidates from these groups. Unfortunately, as one Vice President of Flight Operations at a major airlines noted, "We don't even receive enough applications from either of these two groups to hire very many as

Fig. 1-10. Corporate G-V.

pilots." If you're a woman, a place you can certainly begin your search for information about a career in flying could be ISA + 21, the International Society of Women Airline Pilots mentioned later in this chapter. For the members of other minority groups, all you need to know is that once you've completed your flight training, many of these companies will be waiting to interview you. Keep in mind that no one is promising anyone a job. Personally, I don't usually believe promises of work "someday when you have a little more experience," as one chief pilot told me once. Most of these promises never seem to pan out.

The Bureau of Labor Statistics Forecast for piloting careers says total pilot jobs by the year 2005 should increase to approximately 111,000 if there's relatively low economic growth, or as high as 126,000 if the economy really shifts into high gear. (See Table 1-1.)

Table 1-1. Bureau of Labor statistics forecast for pilot hiring

Year	Hiring	Women	Black	Hispanic
1983	69,000	2.1	n/a	1.6
1984	75,000	2.1	.2	n/a
1985	77,000	2.6	1.0	.1
1986	79,000	1.5	.9	.1
1987	78,000	2.2	2.8	.9
1988	88,000	3.1	1.4	1.5
1989	109,000	3.8	.2	2.7
1990	114,000	5.1	.6	3.3
1991	101,000	3.4	1.5	2.9
1992	97,000	2.3	2.2	2.5

The FAA published some predictions recently that give an overall picture of where they think some of the flying jobs will be, but more importantly, in what segment of the industry these jobs will appear. The numbers show how many will be major airline jobs and how many will appear in the regional (formerly called the commuter) airlines. (See Table 1-2.)

Table 1-2. FAA estimates of flying jobs until the year 2003

Year	Major	Regional
1993	1,588	2,866
1994	2,880	2,844
1995	2,561	2,910
1996	2,452	2,850
1997	3,127	2,718
1998	3,686	2,775
1999	3,252	2,874
2000	2,974	2,890
2001	4,073	2,941
2002	3,354	3,013
2003	3,396	3,052

THE FIRST STEPS TOWARD A CAREER AS A PROFESSIONAL PILOT

Before you even have a prayer of trying to become a professional pilot, you'll need the ratings. While there are numerous ratings available to you, depending on the type of aircraft you fly, there are only a few ratings that you really need on your certificate in order to get rolling. You certainly need a private pilot's license to begin. Follow that up with a commercial license. Your instrument rating will normally be a part of the commercial license. A multiengine rating will also be necessary in most cases. The flight instructor rating, while not required, certainly opens up a wide range of extra employment opportunities (Fig. 1-11).

THE MEDICAL CERTIFICATE

Before you can qualify for any of the certificates, you must also possess the appropriate class of FAA medical certificate for the license you're working on. In general, the medicals are categorized this way. The least stringent medical is the third class, valid for 24 months after it's issued and necessary to qualify for a private pilot certificate. Next comes the second-class medical, valid for 12 months and necessary for a commercial certificate, which is normally needed for the flight instructor rating. The granddaddy of medicals is the first class. Necessary for the issuance of an ATP certificate, the first-class medical is only valid for six months. Because an ATP certificate is necessary in most cases to be captain on just about anything these days, I'd find out very early on in my training where I stood in meeting the first-class medical requirements. One of the nice things about the FAA medicals is that they often serve more than one function. If, for instance, you were

Fig. 1-11. A pilot position on a Falcon 2000 is possible with the proper training.

to obtain a first-class medical certificate and you were not exercising the privileges of your ATP certificate, that medical could be good for 12 months from the date it was issued and also be perfectly acceptable as a second-class medical. Hold on to your first-class medical for two years, and you'll still be able to enjoy the privileges of a private pilot.

THE ACTUAL LICENSE REQUIREMENTS
Private pilot eligibility requirements

- At least 17 years of age.
- Must read, speak, and understand the English language. (If you can't, operating restrictions will be added to your license).
- Hold a third-class medical certificate. (This becomes your student pilot certificate too.)
- Pass a written, an oral, and a practical flight test on the subject matter for this certificate (listed in the appendix).

Private pilot, airplane—aeronautical experience. An applicant for a private pilot's certificate with an airplane rating must have had at least a total of 40 hours of flight instruction and solo time, which must include the following:

- 20 hours of instruction, including at least:
  - ~ 3 hours of cross country.
  - ~ 3 hours of night, including 10 takeoffs and landings (without this training, you'll have another restriction placed on your license).
  - ~ 3 hours of preparation for the flight test.
- 20 hours solo, at least 10 hours in an airplane.
  - ~ 10 hours of cross country.
  - ~ 3 takeoffs and landings.

Private pilot, helicopter—aeronautical experience. An applicant for a private certificate, rotorcraft, must have the following aeronautical experience for a helicopter class rating:

- A total of 40 hours of flight instruction and solo flight time in an aircraft, including at least:
  - ~ 3 hours of cross country flying in a helicopter.
  - ~ 3 hours night flying in helicopters, including 10 takeoffs and landings.
  - ~ 3 hours in helicopters in preparation for the flight test.
  - ~ A flight in a helicopter with a landing at some point other than an airport.
  - ~ 20 hours of solo flight time, 15 hours of which must be in a helicopter, including at least:
    - o 3 hours of cross country flying in helicopters.
    - o 3 takeoffs and landings in helicopters at an airport with an operating control tower.

Commercial pilot eligibility requirements

- At least 18 years of age.
- Read, speak, and understand English.
- Hold a second-class medical certificate.
- Pass the commercial pilot written exam.
- Pass a commercial license oral and a practical exam.

Commercial pilot, airplane—aeronautical experience. An applicant for a commercial airplane pilot certificate must hold a private pilot license. If you don't, you must at least meet the flight experience requirements and pass the private pilot written exam. The applicant must also hold an instrument rating. (Without this rating to your commercial certificate, you'll be restricted to only exercising the privileges of your commercial license on daytime trips of less than 50 miles. This restriction would make your certificate pretty useless, except for local flights like banner or glider tows.)

To apply for the commercial certificate, the applicant must hold 250 hours of total flight time as a pilot, of which not more than 50 hours may be in a ground trainer (simulator). The total flight time must include:

- 100 hours in powered aircraft.
- 50 hours in airplanes.
- 10 hours of flight instruction in an airplane with retractable landing gear, flaps, and controllable pitch propeller.
- 50 hours of flight instruction, including 10 hours of instrument instruction, at least 5 in an airplane.
- 10 hours of instruction in preparation for the flight test.
- 100 hours pilot in command (PIC) time, including at least:
  ~ 50 hours in an airplane.
  ~ 50 hours of cross country flights.
  ~ 5 hours of night, with 10 takeoffs and landings.

Commercial pilot, rotorcraft—aeronautical experience. An applicant for a commercial pilot certificate with a rotorcraft rating must have at least the following aeronautical experience as a pilot:

- Helicopter class rating. A total of 150 hours of flight time, including at least 100 hours in powered aircraft, 50 of which must be in a helicopter, including at least:
  ~ 40 hours of flight instruction from an authorized flight instructor, 15 hours of which must be in a helicopter, including:
    o 3 hours of cross country flying in helicopters.
    o 3 hours of night flying in helicopters, including 10 takeoffs and landings.
    o 3 hours in helicopters preparing for the commercial flight test within 60 days of the test.
    o Takeoffs and landings at 3 points other than airports.
  ~ 100 hours of pilot in command flight time, 35 hours of which must be in a helicopter, including at least:
    o 10 hours of cross-country flying in helicopters.
    o 3 takeoffs and landings at an airport with an operating control tower.

The instrument rating

To be eligible for an airplane instrument rating, an applicant must:

- Hold at least a private pilot certificate with an airplane rating.
- Be able to speak, read, and understand English.
- Comply with the applicable requirements of FAR Part 61.65.

Instrument rating—flight experience. An applicant for an instrument rating must have at least the following flight time as a pilot:

- A total of 125 hours of pilot flight time, of which 50 hours are as pilot in command in cross-country flight in a powered airplane with other than a student pilot certificate. (Your student pilot cross-country time will not count here.)
- 40 hours of simulated or actual instrument time, of which no more than 20 hours may be in an instrument ground trainer.
- 15 hours of instrument flight instruction, including at least 5 hours in an airplane.

Airline transport pilot (ATP)

To be eligible for an airline transport pilot certificate, an applicant must be:

- At least 23 years of age.
- Of good moral character.
- Able to speak, read, and understand English. Also able to speak the language without an accent or impediment that would interfere with two-way radio communication.
- A high-school graduate or its equivalent.
- Hold a first-class medical certificate.

Airline transport pilot, airplane—flight time. An applicant for an airline transport pilot certificate for airplanes must hold a commercial pilot certificate or be a pilot in the U.S. armed services.

An applicant must have had:

- At least 250 hours of flight time as a pilot in command of an airplane, or as copilot of an airplane performing the duties and functions of a pilot in command under the supervision of a pilot in command, at least 100 hours of which were cross-country time and 25 hours of which were night flight time.
- At least 1500 hours of flight time as pilot, including:
  ~ 500 hours cross-country flight time.
  ~ 100 hours night flight time.
  ~ 75 hours of actual or simulated instrument time, at least 50 hours of which were in actual flight.

Airline transport pilot, rotorcraft—ATP. An applicant for an airline transport pilot certificate with a rotorcraft category (Fig. 1-12) and helicopter class rating must hold a commercial pilot certificate or be a pilot in an armed force of the United States whose military experience qualifies for the issuance of a commercial pilot certificate under FAR 61.73.

Fig. 1-12. Commercial helicopters come in all sizes.

An applicant must have had at least 1,200 hours of flight time as a pilot, including at least:

- 500 hours of cross-country flight time.
- 100 hours of night flight time, of which at least 15 hours were in helicopters.

- 200 hours in helicopters, including at least 75 hours as pilot in command, or as second in command performing the duties and functions of pilot in command under the supervision of a pilot in command.
- 75 hours of instrument time under actual or simulated conditions, of which at least 50 hours were completed in flight, at least 25 hours in helicopters as pilot in command.

The flight instructor certificate

To be eligible for a flight instructor certificate, you must:

- Be at least 18 years of age.
- Read, write, and converse fluently in English.
- Hold a commercial or ATP certificate, with the appropriate aircraft rating.
- Hold an instrument rating, if applying for an instrument instructor rating.

There's no specific number of hours required for the issuance of a flight instructor certificate beyond what's required for the issuance of the commercial, ATP or particular aircraft rating. This means your instructor might not be terribly experienced, so be certain you discuss the instructor's experience before you begin.

Aircraft type ratings

To have an aircraft type rating added to a pilot certificate, an applicant must meet the following requirements:

- Hold, or concurrently obtain, an instrument rating appropriate to the aircraft for which the type rating is sought.
- Pass a flight test demonstrating competence in pilot operations appropriate to his or her pilot certificate and the type rating sought.
- Pass a flight test showing competence in pilot operations under instrument flight conditions.

Note: The preceding pilot certificate and rating requirements are only excerpts from the Federal Aviation Regulations (FARs). For the remaining flight time, ground, and flight instruction requirements, see the appendix.

LOGBOOKS

In chapter 8, I'll show you a few of the new and really fun flight simulator programs available for use on a personal computer. Also new is an electronic logbook program that takes most of the work as well as the whiteout from your mistakes out of the process. But, before we get there, I want to mention the importance of logbooks. Your logbooks should be guarded like precious gems. These books are the only record of the flight time and hard work you've put in toward your goal of becoming a professional pilot. A few years ago, I went to an electronic logbook because it reduced my workload considerably with the amount of flying I was doing. It's strictly your decision whether you keep a paper logbook or work with both paper and electronic media. Currently, there's nothing in FAR Part 61.51 that says your logbook must be paper. All this regulation states is that you must log aeronautical training and experience used to meet the requirements for a certificate, rating, or recent flight experience. That's it. You don't need to log anything else. That's the regulation. In reality, however, you'll be playing a pretty tough game trying to land a flying job if you don't have all your time logged. Let me give you a few tips about how to log your flight time.

- Solo—The only time you'll most likely log solo flight time is when you're a student pilot, but the regulation says you may log solo flight time any time you're the sole occupant of the aircraft.
- Pilot in command (PIC)—You can log PIC when you're the sole manipulator of the controls for an aircraft for which you're rated or when acting as a pilot on an aircraft for which more than one pilot is required under the type certification of the aircraft or the regulations under which the flight is being conducted. An example could be when acting as a safety pilot for someone wearing a hood during instrument practice.
- Instrument time—You may only log as actual instrument time that flight time during which you control the aircraft by total reference to the flight instruments under actual weather conditions. Simulated instrument flight, or hooded time, under simulated weather conditions must be logged separately.
- Flight instructor—A certified flight instructor may log all time during which they act as a flight instructor as PIC. If you fly with an instrument student in actual instrument weather, the CFI may log the time as actual instrument time.
- Second in command (SIC)—Pilots may log time as second in command when they act as SIC of an aircraft for which more than one pilot is required under the type certification of the aircraft or the regulations under which the flight is conducted.

Now you've seen the worst of it, the full set of requirements that will take you from rank beginner to airline transport pilot. This quest of yours will require time, money, and effort on your part if you're to be successful. In upcoming chapters, I'll be discussing all of these items to make certain you reach the rank of professional aviator with minimal fuss and maximum fun, because if you aren't having some fun along the way toward becoming a professional pilot, you probably should consider another line of work.

In every group there will always be naysayers, people who believe that you'll never be able to achieve your goal. "There are too many pilots now," they say. "The economy is too tough." "You're a woman" or "No one will hire a minority," they say. I happened across a story that I wish I had written. It's the story of a pilot who had a dream she never lost.

The following was printed with permission from UND Aerospace, Grand Forks, N.D., and Christy DeJoy, J. Patrick Moore, LaMaster, Farmer, Minneapolis, Minn.

Nine-year-old Jean Haley was to write an essay explaining what she wanted to be when she grew up. The assignment was simple; Jean knew she would be an airline pilot. But those dreams were nearly shattered when she saw the "F" at the top of her essay. Her third-grade teacher reasoned, "This is a fairy tale, not an essay."

The year was 1959, and the reality was that there was no such thing as a female airline pilot.

Fast forward to the year 1993, and Jean (Haley) Harper is a United Airlines captain.

The 34 years in-between have been filled with hard work, bravery, and commitment. Harper credits much of her success to her father. When young Jean brought her F-graded essay home, Frank Haley, a crop duster, said, "You can do anything you want."

She wanted to fly, so seven years later she began flying lessons. "I wanted to prove to myself I could do it. I figured I could prove the nay-sayers wrong by doing the things they said I couldn't do."

Harper determined that she needed to meet three criteria to become an airline pilot. First, she needed the appropriate licenses. So, at 20 years old, Harper took out a bank loan and spent six months getting her private, commercial, and instrument ratings. Second, she needed flying time—at least 1,500 hours. She started logging hours hauling skydivers and studied to become a flight instructor. And third, she needed a four-year degree. She enrolled in the aviation program at the University of North Dakota in Grand Forks on the advice of Mike Sacrey, a UND Aerospace graduate and the FAA pilot who checked her out as a flight instructor.

When Harper enrolled at UND in 1971, there were still no women airline pilots. "It was a scary feeling thinking I could spend the years and the money trying to attain it and still not be taken seriously. But not taking the chance of becoming an airline pilot was more scary," she said.

While female pilots were still a novelty at UND, she nonetheless became the school's first female flight instructor. "It was a first, but John Odegard was enthusiastic that I was there and was happy to offer me the position," she said.

During the next four years, Harper juggled her studies and a variety of jobs, including flight instructor, charter pilot, cloud seeder, crop duster, glider tower, and night airmail pilot. "I was spread thin," she admits, but was doing well enough to earn several scholarships and awards.

The best gift she received was from a UND student pilot named Tracy Van Den Berg, who told her in 1973 that Frontier Airlines had hired pilot Emily Howell. "I thought, 'Oh, my God. It happened. The last obstacle has fallen.' I finally had an honest-to-goodness role model." A few months later American Airlines hired Bonnie Tiburzi.

After graduation in 1975, Harper began writing to airlines asking for pilot application forms. She was getting little response until she started signing her name "J.E. Haley" instead of "Jean Haley."

Due to an industry down cycle, the airlines were hiring few pilots during this time. For nearly three years, Harper flew however she could—moonlighting as a flight instructor and flying with small cargo and commuter carriers.

At Meridian Air Cargo, Harper met a handsome pilot named Vic Harper. She used to switch shifts with his copilot so she could fly with him. Three years later they were to become matrimonial copilots.

In the meantime, airline pilot hiring increased. Harper interviewed with Delta, Allegheny, and United Airlines, and landed a job in Denver with United as a 727 flight engineer. She became United's third woman pilot, hired just weeks after the first two women. During that same time, Vic accepted a job with Frontier, also in Denver.

The person who most strongly supported Harper's dream of becoming an airline pilot never saw her in her United uniform. Harper's father died in an airplane accident not long after she graduated from UND.

In her 15 years with United, Harper has flown Boeing 727s, 737s, 757s (Fig. 1-13), and 767s. In November 1992, Harper, 43, flew her first line trip as a 737 captain—with her favorite first officer, Vic Harper, who has since joined United.

Fig. 1-13. New-generation United Boeing 757.

"Becoming captain was such an accomplishment for me. I'm so proud." She said her pride in her qualifications rubs off on other people, easing the minds of the few who might not be completely comfortable with a woman captain.

"The vast majority of comments I've received about being a captain have been very positive. Among the most enthusiastic congratulations I have received have come from the 'old timers'—the senior captains at United," she said. "I think my attitude has a lot to do with it."

In addition to her career achievements, Harper said she's also met her goals of a rewarding personal life. The Harpers juggle two airline careers and two children—Annie, 7, and Sam, 3½. In 1985, Harper became United's first pregnant pilot. United didn't even have a maternity leave policy for several years after that.

"I remember having serious concerns whether I could have this career and have a family, too. It bothered me that I might have to choose. No one would ever tell a man he couldn't be married, have children, and have a career," she said.

Harper has been able to have both career and family. "This is it. I have no more unfulfilled wants."

Perhaps Harper's third-grade teacher was right. She is living a fairy-tale life.

A final note of special interest to women pilots is ISA + 21, the International Society of Women Airline Pilots. ISA + 21 is an association of women airline pilots who have joined together to exchange ideas and information regarding the profession. One unique way ISA members assist each other is through the ISA Information Bank. Here, women airline pilots help other women pilots overcome the unique obstacles they might encounter in pursuing an airline career. Each member who wants information is paired up with another pilot who lives in their area and offers suggestions and advice. ISA also offers its members a scholarship program. Contact their Membership Chairman at ISA + 21, P.O. Box 66268, Chicago, IL 60666-0268.

2

Flight training

BEFORE YOU CAN EVEN THINK ABOUT the lofty goal of flying for the airlines, a corporation, or the U.S. military, there's a more simple goal to accomplish . . . learning to fly. Now, simple is a relative term here, and I'm really not trying to treat learning to fly in a matter-of-fact way. Learning to fly right is not only important to your goal of flying professionally, but it's also crucial to your long-term goal of keeping whatever flying job you eventually land. Without the right flying education and the right attitudes, skills, and habits, your career could take a very early nosedive.

Learning to fly is a much more involved process than just running out to the airport for a few lessons once a week, taking a test, and picking up your license. During the months or years that it might take you to gain the experience necessary to leap to the next stage of training for that commercial, instrument, or multi-engine rating, you'll be working on a regular basis with a number of different instructors. You might believe that the best way to progress through flight training is to find a "good instructor" and stay with that person all the way through to your first flying job. While that certainly is an option, it's one I would avoid.

That first instructor will seem like quite an authority to you in those early months of learning to fly. It's this first instructor who will, hopefully, sit patiently with you as you learn how the various parts are put together to form a real flying airplane. It's this instructor who will teach you first about lift and weather and federal regulations. But, along with those first bits and pieces of practical knowledge will come bits and pieces of an attitude. Student pilots tend to emulate what they see. If their first instructor is extremely careful about preflighting the aircraft before they fly or is constantly picking up the microphone while in flight to either use the air traffic control system or to check on a possibly threatening weather situation, the student will learn, too, that this is the way a well-managed cockpit is operated (Fig. 2-1). If, on the other hand, that first instructor is someone who flies somewhat carelessly, a person to whom just getting the job done is sufficient, an instructor who explains once and says, "Go back and read the rest on your own," and never spends the time to really find out what the student understands, the instructor is doing you a great disservice. If that same instructor chooses not to use a

Fig. 2-1. A professional pilot's career begins with a good instructor.

checklist, if that instructor has little regard for precise airspeed control in his or her flying, you'll come to believe this is the correct method for piloting an aircraft. Whatever the instructor does, you'll eventually find yourself mimicking.

And too, it's not just what the instructor teaches you that's important (Fig. 2-2); what that instructor leaves out of your training could be vital to your career and safety. One of the strengths of flying with more than a single instructor is the exposure that a student receives to another pilot's scrutiny. When the major aircraft manufacturers were designing their own learn-to-fly curriculums in the 1960s, they included a number of phase checks or minireviews. As a flight instructor in a Part 141 school, I was required to fly many of these phase checks. They were designed to give me, the assistant chief flight instructor, a look at not just how well the students were learning, but how well the instructors were teaching.

I remember a young female commercial student who arrived for a phase check one sunny Saturday afternoon. After a satisfactory chat about flying and regulations before the flight, I felt the woman seemed well versed in the subjects she needed to understand for the commercial flight test. After we departed the airport for the practice area, I quickly noticed her inability to hold an airspeed or a specified rate of climb. Initially, I put some of this off to nerves and flying with a new instructor, but within about 20 minutes or so, I realized this was a real problem. I

Fig. 2-2. Today's cockpits are more automated than ever before.

asked her to fly some more maneuvers for me, and I eventually realized she was not using a very basic tool, the trim wheel. The trim wheel in an airplane is designed to relieve pressure from the control wheel so an aircraft can be flown basically hands off for a good portion of the time, if this operation is performed correctly. Performed incorrectly, a lack of proper trim in an airplane forces the pilot to work much harder than necessary. The result of this distraction in the cockpit forces even more work on the pilot when there are other operations to cope with.

I was amazed that somehow this student had almost reached her commercial flight test and had somehow managed to skip this very basic concept. After I spent a few minutes showing the student the trim wheel and what it could do for her, she was surprised. I saw her a month or so later after she had successfully passed her commercial checkride, and she told me that learning about trim was one of the things that really made life easier for her during the checkride. Without the opportunity for another instructor to check her progress, this woman would have missed some very important training. If you were a history major in college, you'd never think of taking every single course with the same teacher, so why give your flying career such a handicap? Good or bad, the best, well-rounded flying education is with more than one teacher.

CHOOSING A FLIGHT INSTRUCTOR AND FLIGHT SCHOOL

If receiving a well-rounded, professional flying education is truly your goal, another important concern is "who" will teach you. Good pilots always use a checklist, a list that prompts them to be certain that they've not forgotten some important item like the hydraulic pumps or the landing gear. Good consumers use checklists of sorts, too, as they search for the best deal on a washer and dryer, an automobile, or a flight school. Let's take a look at some of the items you'll want to consider as you make the decision about which flight school will receive your training dollars.

First of all, begin with a legal pad and pencil close by to record your notes. Don't trust all these facts to your memory. First, you must decide whether or not you want to remain in the city where you live now and take your chances with the flight schools available there or whether you're willing to move to a new location for the training you might really want. We're talking about an investment that will pay you back over the rest of your life, so decide carefully.

If you intend to remain in your local area, the best place to begin is with your local telephone yellow pages. Look under the aviation listings. The local flight school could also be listed under the airport section. No matter how you find the listings, begin at the top and start calling. Ask for the chief flight instructor. Tell him or her of your plans and make an appointment to visit the school. If the school tries to steer you away from the chief or give you any difficulty, consider that school highly suspect as a place to spend your money. Most reputable schools will be happy to pass your name on to the boss, who should be able to spend a few minutes on the telephone with you. Rather than just telling the flight instructor you're intent on becoming a professional pilot and asking for his or her opinions, be certain to have a list of basic questions ready to ask. You'll probably find that the very best way to evaluate the entire range of flight instruction possibilities at a school is only with an in-person visit.

Some of the more important items to consider when choosing your first flight school and instructor are the age and general condition of the fleet the school operates. It's not necessary to be a mechanic to decide whether or not the school takes good care of its aircraft. Ask for a tour of the flight line where the school parks its airplanes. If you tour a line that's made up of dirty airplanes, I would suspect that poor care had been given to the insides of the aircraft, too. Tour the ground school classroom and take a closer look at the visual aids used in the facility. Look for a recent set of video training tapes on a wide range of subjects for students to watch during the training process. Ask for a meeting with a few of the flight instructors. Do they seem interested in you or only in how often you might be scheduling your flying lessons?

Ask what provision the school has for a change of instructors during your training. Keep in mind that you'll be spending a great deal of time with this instructor in a rather confined space inside a small training aircraft. You had better make sure the two of you like each other. Perhaps you don't feel comfortable with a male instructor or someone who is younger than you. Now is the time to discuss these ideas with the chief flight instructor and learn if the school's method of operation is compatible with yours. One very important point for you to realize as a student is that you're now basically in charge of your own destiny. What you do or say, or don't do or say, might have dramatic influences on your career or your life in general. The new student pilot must learn to be assertive. You're the consumer, and you're ultimately responsible for where your training ends up.

Next, check the flying schedule of the school in question. How often are the airplanes booked? Will it be tough to fly during the week? What about on Saturday afternoon? Does the school have a cancellation policy you should be aware of? Many flight schools have one large schedule sheet that combines the schedules of both the aircraft and the instructors. Are certain instructors booked more than others? Some might be booked more often because they've just been employed by the school for a longer period of time. However, they could be busier because they're better instructors. Sometimes, though, the newer instructor could be the better instructor because they're a bit more enthusiastic than some old-timers. Don't consider any instructor based only on the schedule, but do allow the schedule to point out certain trends to you. You must still be the final judge. Base your decision on how the two of you get along when you meet and talk.

Does your instructor use visual aids, or does he or she communicate concepts only with words? A good visual aid could be something as simple as a plastic model airplane to demonstrate relative wind and lift, or it could be a full simulator to show what the instruments really look like during an IFR approach. It makes no difference how many visual aids your instructor has; just be sure you know what they are and how they'll work into the curriculum.

PART 61 OR PART 141?

Two sets of regulations apply to flight school programs: FAR Part 61 and Part 141. The first, Part 61 (whose basic pilot experience requirements were discussed in chapter 1) outlines the actual certification process for you to become a pilot. Part 141 is the regulation that tells a formal flight school how it must operate, such as the requirements necessary for a chief flight instructor, how the school may advertise, and in what form the student records should be kept. Another advantage of the Part 141 school (besides the fact that it will be more formally organized) is that total times required before the flight test are less than if you were to pick up your license from a Part 61 operator. For instance, under Part 61, a private pilot must have a total of at least 40 hours of flight time before the flight test. Under Part 141, the requirement is only 35. For the combined commercial instrument rating program, Part 61 requires a total of 250 hours of flight time. Under Part 141 (Fig. 2-3), that requirement drops to 190.

So, then, is a Part 141 flight school better than the freelance flight instructor whose ad you might see in the local paper on the weekend? In all fairness to the Part 61 freelance flight instructor, and the Part 141 instructor, it can be pretty tough to say one is definitely better than the other. While the curriculum of the Part 141 school is certainly organized, it doesn't mean that a Part 61 operator is disorga-

Fig. 2-3. Part 141 flight schools offer formal classroom training.

nized. While being able to pick up a private pilot license in 35 hours instead of 40 is a benefit at the Part 141 school, the statistics say no one does it anyway. The average private pilot picks up their license in about 66 hours total time. At the commercial, instrument-rating end of things, it might make a bit more sense, depending on how immersed in the training you really become. Realize, too, that while total times will be less, the price per hour at the Part 141 school will usually be higher.

If you're searching for flight schools that have been in business for a long time, you'll find that, for the most part, they'll be Part 141 schools. At a Part 141 school, you'll find yourself engaged in regular phase checks with other school instructors as a system of checks and balances on your education. You'll also have some assurances that the chief flight instructor needed a set amount of flight time under his or her belt before being put in charge of the school. A Part 141 flight school must even meet certain requirements for its pilot briefing rooms, as well as the ground-training rooms in which you'll be spending a lot of time. At a Part 141 school, the FAA pops in on a regular basis to be certain that the quality of the students is up to par, too. If you were engaged in any training to be paid for by the new Veterans G.I. Bill, the Veterans Administration would require that your training be conducted at a Part 141 school, also called an approved school.

Why would anyone not want to attend an approved school, then? One of the first reasons could be that, in your location of the country, a formal Part 141 school doesn't exist. Another consideration is price, and that's often the most compelling reason people will choose a free-lance instructor. The reason the free-lance price is usually less is simple business economics. A free-lance instructor might only own one aircraft and possibly even rent an office for ground training. Of course, while there might not be all the amenities of the Part 141 school, the benefit comes at the end of the lesson with the lower overall bill. Recently, I happened across an ad for a free-lance instructor while I was traveling in a major East Coast city, so I called up the teacher. She used an older model Cessna 172 that she didn't own. Another friend owned the aircraft and leased it to the instructor with the insurance. The instructor charged $60 per hour for the airplane and $20 per hour for her time. At the same time, a nationally known flight school charged $78 for a C-172, plus $25 an hour for the instructor. The bottom line is that the facilities are nice and the Part 141 schools are more regulated, but you certainly will pay for those items.

Free-lance flight instructors might also be a little tougher to locate than a Part 141 school. Try searching the classified ads in your local newspaper, and you'll probably see, "Private flight instruction. Your airplane or mine, $20 per hour, call John . . ." Make the phone call, just like you did at the Part 141 school; make the appointment to visit the aircraft and make your decision. In both cases, I'd ask for the names and phone numbers of a few recent graduates to speak to as references. While the privacy laws in some cases could make the operator a bit wary of giving out these items, any legitimate school shouldn't have any trouble putting you in touch with people who have used their services. If they refuse, I'd walk out.

While prices could be considerably cheaper for the freelance instructor, there are some potential problems you should consider. If the instructor is only equipped with one aircraft, it might be pretty tough to book that airplane for some of the long cross country flights you'll need to complete your license. What if the aircraft has a mechanical breakdown somewhere along the way? A large school will simply switch you to another airplane while the freelancer might need to switch you to another day entirely while the machine is repaired.

Consider the difference. I've taken instruction in both kinds of operations, and I've also worked in both as a flight instructor. I once found that a simple cup of coffee drunk standing near the wing of a Cessna 150, listening to a free-lance instructor tell me some of his adventures and discussing what I wanted out of my private license was enough to make me work with him. Later on, for me at least, when I started working on my instructor ratings, I found working at a formal Part 141 school fulfilled my needs better.

Finally, reserve the right before you even walk through the door of the flight school, that if things just don't either look, feel, or sound right, you'll leave. There's usually going to be more than one flight school near your home, so make sure you like the one where you'll possibly be spending thousands of dollars.

HOW MUCH IS THIS GOING TO COST?

Asking how much it will cost to become a professional pilot is a bit like asking how much it's going to cost to purchase your first home; it depends on how many extras you'd like. If you were to work with a free-lance flight instructor in a Cessna 152 from zero time to your commercial, the 1993 figures in a major city might look like this.

250 total flight hours required, of which at least 100 must be pilot in command and at least 50 hours of dual. Keep in mind, too, that this price is based on FAA minimums with all training performed in an aircraft.

240 hours Cessna 152 @ $50 per hour = $12,000
50 hours dual flight instruction @ $20 per hour = $1,000
10 hours Cessna 172 RG @ $78 per hour = $780
50 hours ground instruction @ $20 per hour = $1,000
FAA checkride, approximately $200
Commercial pilot airplane total cost = $14,985

If you're considering an instrument rating to add to your commercial, the price from a free-lance instructor would look something like this. I'm assuming the pilot in question already holds a private pilot license and currently has about 75 hours total time logged. The applicant for the instrument rating, again, must have at least 125 hours logged (40 of which were simulated or actual instrument time) before the application is written. I'm also assuming that the entire rating is conducted in the airplane, with no simulator work of any kind. This would be a pretty realistic scenario from a free-lancer because they seldom have access to a simulator. The price of the written exam is also not included in this total because the methods of obtaining the written vary considerably. We'll talk about the writtens later on.

Note: The ground instruction mentioned in both the commercial and instrument rating costs aren't required, but were added to realistically reflect the cost of obtaining the rating.

10 hours in Cessna 152 @ $50 per hour to meet total time requirements = $500
40 hours in Cessna 172 @ $65 per hour for remainder of dual instruction = $2,600
25 hours of ground instruction @ $20 per hour = $500
Flight test = $200
Instrument rating total = $3,800

From the Part 61 operator, you could also begin your instrument with the same 75 hours total time, and all of the hours logged could count toward your commercial requirement of 250 hours total time. While the total for the commercial under Part 61 requires 250 hours, it doesn't necessarily mean it will take you 250 total hours to learn all the maneuvers proficiently enough to pass the exam, so why not take the instrument rating first? If you look at the total Part 61 price of $18,505, it seems like a great deal of money, and it is. Another benefit, though, in working with a Part 61 flight school is that the owner might be willing to bargain the rate down for you from the $18,505 total, if they know you'll give them this much business. This would not normally be something you could plan on accomplishing with the larger Part 141 operators. However, some of the large Part 141 schools might offer advantages that a smaller Part 61 operator might be incapable of.

THE WRITTEN EXAMS

All the pilot certificates and ratings I've talked about also require you to pass an FAA written exam prior to the day you take your final flight test for each rating.

The only rating I spoke about that doesn't include a written is the multiengine rating. These writtens have always been a requirement, but I personally question their value in deciding what kind of a pilot you'll become. I know of some pretty spectacular pilots who freeze up in a written test situation.

The writtens can be passed in a number of ways. You could buy any of a number of excellent books on each rating and study them on your own. You could sit down with an instructor for enough ground instruction to pass the test. You could also take a weekend ground school and spend 10 hours on Saturday and Sunday having the needed material crammed into your brain so you'll be ready for a Monday morning written exam. Another method, becoming more and more common today, is to buy a set of ground school video tapes from any of a number of companies that sell them, like King or ATC. The ads for their tapes can be found in many of the aviation magazines. The major benefits to this system are that you not only work on the ground school at your own pace, but you can also spend as much time on a subject as you need to make it sink in.

A final new method is to purchase one of the new software packages that includes hundreds of review questions and answers to the FAA exams for you to load into a personal computer. These systems offer you the chance to review at your own pace and study only the material you're having difficulty with; the programs will also ask you questions and record your progress. A new version of this ground school software is available from companies like Comair Aviation Academy, which produces the "Hangar Talk" series for the personal computer.

COMMERCIAL FLIGHT SCHOOLS

Today, large commercial flight schools can provide many more different types of services than they could just a few years ago. Sanford, Florida-based Comair Aviation Academy is just one of a number of large schools that specializes in just about everything a new pilot could need to point them in the right direction toward that eventual cockpit job. Comair Aviation Academy, a Part 141 school, provides, first of all, an accelerated professional pilot training program from absolutely zero time through the certified flight instructors ratings. The training is airline standards based, which is reflected in academics, simulator, and flight instruction programs.

Next up is Comair's Air Carrier Training Programs, marketed as Airline Qualification Courses (AQC) providing initial first officer training to client airlines and type rating programs in the EMB-120 Brasilia, the Saab 340, and Metro aircraft. Finally, there's the Academy's Flying Service Division. This organization offers self-paced, Jeppesen-Sanderson-based ground and flight instruction, accelerated weekend ground schools, written flight tests, and recurrent and refresher training. Located in Sanford, Florida (where good weather abounds most of the year), the academy operates 45 aircraft at their Central Florida Regional Airport facility. The flight department flies 20 Cessna 152s, 13 C-172s, 3 C-172RGs, and 9 Piper Seminoles. The school also operates 3 Frasca 141 single-engine simulators as well as 2 Frasca 142 multiengine units. The school flies about 5,000 hours of instructional time each month through the help of its 130 personnel. In the 1992-93 period, Comair Academy invested nearly $2 million in new facilities, courseware, simulators, and automation.

The standard of training at all schools might obviously vary some around the Part 141 regulations, but how those variances take their form is the crucial point. The Comair Aviation Academy, owned by Comair Airlines, a Delta Connection carrier, has chosen to market itself as an airline training school. Right from the start, academy students are taught with manuals written just like those provided at Comair, the airline. The Academy's Training Doctrine and Training Course Outline are based on the central concept of standardization, as the term is understood and applied in commercial airline operations. This concept is reflected in training aircraft standards manuals and checklists, in construction and content of all courseware, and in the selection, initial training, and transition training of flight instructors and the details of operations. Even the most basic aircraft in the Comair training fleet, the Cessna 152, comes equipped with a Cessna 152 Flight Standards Manual, just as a first officer in a Brasilia would receive.

Just what's the point of all this airline consistency? Why should a prospective professional even consider a place like Comair Academy for his or her training? Most people need only to look at the chance provided to some of Comair's graduates of the school's Airline Qualification Course for their answer. The course, built around the Embraer EMB-120 Brasilia, is primarily designed for pilots with some experience who are looking for that first step up into the right seat of an airliner. Currently, minimum qualifications are set at a commercial certificate with multi-engine land and instrument ratings, 1,200 hours total time, and 200 hours multi-engine time. The course will either qualify pilots as first officers in the Brasilia or (with added class and flight training) reward pilots with an EMB-120 type rating to attach to their license. Here's an opportunity to qualify for and get hired into the right seat of an airliner. Don't expect this to be a Boeing 727, however. It will be a turboprop regional airliner operated by one of the airlines that have contracted with a school such as Comair Aviation Academy for their services, like Comair Airlines itself. While Comair Aviation Academy is not the only flight school around that will train you and later assist you with the interview and hiring process at a regional, they're unique because they're owned by one of the hiring airlines themselves.

In the early 1990s, as hiring at major airlines began to slow due to the economy, the Gulf War, and intense competition, fewer pilots found work. With plenty of pilots to choose from bankrupt carriers like Midway, Pan Am, and Eastern, the simple business climate of supply and demand took over. The airlines could be much more selective about the people they did hire to fly their airplanes. While little changed at the major airlines in terms of how they trained their pilots, significant changes appeared at the regional carriers.

Regional carriers started demanding that pilots sign training agreements that basically held the pilot responsible for his or her training costs should that pilot not choose to remain with the carrier. The training contracts were an attempt to stem the tide of runaway pilots from the regionals. Unfortunately for the regional airlines, the contracts, for the most part, proved unenforceable when the pilots lived outside the state where the airline was headquartered. Undaunted, a marketing scheme was devised to charge pilots for their training before they were ever hired by the airline.

More and more of the regional carriers are now charging for airline training. In fact, in some cases, a third-party training organization like LaGuardia-based Flight Safety has actually assumed responsibility for an entire airline training department. This has resulted in lower costs for the individual airlines because they no longer concern themselves with the difficulties of organizing and maintaining a training program. The resulting cost savings to the airlines have made this approach quite appealing. However, the drawback for pilots is that they must have a way to finance their training before they can be hired. It also makes no difference whether the pilot is experienced or not. If you want to be hired at some regional carriers, you must pay first.

The process begins with an evaluation that might take the better part of a day to accomplish. At their own cost, the applicant flies to the training center and pays a fee of between $250 and $300 to fly a simulator, take some exams, and have a personnel interview. If the pilot is found competent, and if one of the training organization's contracting airlines indicates a need for new pilots, the applicant might be offered a conditional position with the airline, valid if the pilot completes the training program successfully. The applicant would then pay for training in a specific turboprop aircraft, currently costing somewhere between $8,000 to $10,000 for the complete course. If successful, the pilot will most likely be hired by the airline they interviewed with. The majority of the risk, however, is the pilot's. If the pilot doesn't complete the training, the airline has lost nothing. At major airlines, however, the company is still paying for the training of its pilots. Whether or not this system is good or fair is really for the individual to decide. What the self-funded training has accomplished is the weeding out of financially disadvantaged pilots. If you can't pay, you can't have the job. Certainly there are training organizations that will finance the training, but your credit must be sufficient to carry the debt, often at a time when the school loans from the previous round of aviation training are yet to be paid off.

How well does it pay off? A recent Comair Aviation Academy press release says it all, while it also explains a few more details about the program . . .

Comair Aviation Academy's AQC Program Places 18 Pilots with Client Airline
October 14, 1992—Sanford, Florida
Eighteen members of Comair Aviation Academy's Airline Qualification Courses (AQC) recently interviewed and conditionally accepted positions as new-hire first officers by United Express d.b.a. Atlantic Coast Airlines.

All eighteen are graduates of the Academy's Professional Pilot Course and have served as instructors, as well.

Fifteen of the members were asked by Atlantic Coast to enroll in the Academy's EMB-120 first-officer training. The remaining members entered a Jetstream 31 program conducted by British Aerospace.

AQC was incorporated into the Academy's curriculum to support the EMB-120 Brasilia. The Academy's client airlines have now requested that the Saab 340 and the Metroliner also be included.

Comair Aviation Academy's first officer training program is airplane specific. The curriculum includes Crew Resource Management, Aircraft Systems, and Flight Training conducted in both an advanced flight simulator and the actual aircraft.

Each applicant's resumé is screened against program and client criteria. Applications are offered to qualified candidates. After additional review, invitations are extended to participate in a technical evaluation process conducted at the Academy. Successful completion of the evaluation qualifies applicants for membership in the AQC program, from which client airlines request pilots for interview . . .

Certainly, a school like Comair Aviation Academy is a means to accomplish your goal of becoming a professional pilot, but the price is significant. The AQC program we just discussed costs $9,995. The course also requires that you have some previous flight time before you may even apply for entry. Contact Comair Aviation Academy at 800-U-CAN-FLY.

AB INITIO TRAINING

Another program you might consider is the ab initio system. Basically, the ab initio system takes a pilot from absolutely zero flight time up through the right-seat job in a regional airliner or, at the very least, all the professional pilot certificates, including the various flight instructor ratings. (See Figs. 2-4 and 2-5.) Although the expense for a flight training program such as this is considerably higher, the benefits are usually a flat price for all the ratings as well as a specified time period for completion. In Europe, this concept of training someone from the beginning in one location with a specific curriculum is used by major airlines such as Lufthansa. What the airline eventually ends up with when a student pilot completes the training (which often takes years) is a pilot who is totally immersed in this particular airline's methods of operation. The program also provides the airline with a certain amount of employee loyalty.

One young Italian pilot I recently met came to the United States as a part of his country's ab initio training because the price to train a pilot in the United States is considerably less than comparable training would cost in Europe. At the completion of his training (with a total of about 700 hours, much of it logged here in the United States), this Italian pilot returned to his homeland, where, with a final few months of training, he picked up a type rating in a BH-125-800 and then began flying in the right seat of a DC-9.

While a great deal of controversy surrounds the ab initio training from an operational status, there's no doubt in my mind that being totally involved with your career, be it medicine or airplanes, is the way to go. From an operational standpoint, many pilots don't believe a relatively low-time pilot belongs in the right seat of a high-performance turbo prop or pure jet aircraft. They believe that only actual experience, total logged hours, can really indicate a pilot's ability to cope with a difficult situation aloft. We've only to look at the military operations of the United States for another view of this controversy. In the United States, pilots with only a few hundred hours of total logged time are out flying high-performance supersonic fighter aircraft by themselves. Obviously, then, low-time pilots can become productive members of a cockpit crew.

Fig. 2-4. The Beechcraft Bonanza and Baron are often used in some ab initio training.

Fig. 2-5. See Fig 2-4.

The only problem with ab initio training, even for wealthy Americans, is the price, but even that's relative. Let's take a look at two fine, well-known flight schools: American Flyers College and Comair Aviation Academy. At the American Flyers College, based in Fort Lauderdale, Florida, the ab initio training curriculum and price sheet looks like this . . .

Career Pilot Course—Multiengine (prices current on 7/93)
The hours of instruction listed below meet or exceed FAA regulations. It should be understood that all people don't learn at the same rate; therefore, it's possible that some students might exceed these hours in order to complete their objective.
Prerequisites. To maintain enrollment, you'll need to possess at least a class II medical (second class).
Registration Fee. $1,690.
Course Contents. Manuals—Private, Commercial, Instrument, IFR Guide Manual; Flight Instructor—Airplane; Flight Instructor—Instrument; Flight Instructor—Multiengine.
Classes. Private, Commercial, Instrument; Flight Instructor—Airplane, Instrument and Multiengine.
Supervised Solo/PIC. Simulator—20 hours; Cessna 172—110 hours.
Instruction. Simulator—30 hours; Cessna 172—70 hours; Cessna 172 RG—20 hours; Cessna 310—28 hours; Pre- and Post-flight—130 hours.

In the information packet provided by American Flyers, the total price for the ab initio course leading to the issuance of the above certificates was $33,190. However, all flight training conducted at all of American Flyers facilities is not quite the same. Spokesman John Perry said, "Training in Fort Lauderdale is conducted in an academy atmosphere which can help us keep the cost down slightly from the individual programs at other American Flyers locations." At Fort Lauderdale, the program would cost approximately $29,000. Room and board aren't included, but American Flyers offers a dormitory room for $395 per month for a single. Zero time to all the professional ratings is accomplished in about 6 months. Contact American Flyers at 800-327-0808.

Another program offered at American Flyers to allow students to build their multiengine time is In-House Airline Training. While the American Flyers airline doesn't actually carry passengers, the training will give potential professional pilots the chance to become familiar with Crew Coordination, Crew Resource Management, and scheduled carrier flight planning. American Flyers flight instructors fly along in the right seat of the school's Cessna 310s over fairly long cross-country routes like FLL-ATL and FLL-LGA to offer the student, who is flying as captain, some real-time, real-life experience flying a multiengine piston engine aircraft with the need to stay on schedule.

By comparison, the Professional Pilot Course at Comair Aviation Academy is shown in Table 2-1. Also included is the $2,160 cost for 8 written and 8 FAA Flight Tests.

Table 2-1. Professional pilot course at Comair Aviation Academy

Private pilot single and multiengine land
Instrument airplane
Commercial pilot single and multiengine land
Flight instructor: Airplane single and multiengine land & instrument
Ground instructor: Basic, advanced and instrument

Flight time	Hours	Rate per hour
Cessna 152	148	45
Cessna 172	35	70
Cessna 172RG	13	90
Piper Seminole	24.5	155
SE Simulator	28.5	55
ME Simulator	11	70

The complete package (as of July, 1993) comes to $25,600. After students complete their training at Comair Aviation Academy, the pipeline toward a bigger and better job runs a slightly different course than at American Flyers. At Comair Aviation Academy, 80 percent of the school's graduates are hired as flight instructors. Comair Aviation Academy guarantees each graduate an interview, and the only people who can be flight instructors at Comair Aviation Academy are graduates of the school. As they progress in responsibility, the Comair instructors build their flight time, both multiengine and single engine; they also build their bank accounts because they're now employed in aviation. The goal is to reach the magic numbers of 1,200 total time and 200 multiengine. When each student arrives at that point, they're guaranteed an interview as a potential first officer with Comair Airlines, definitely one of the benefits of attending a school owned by an airlines. Comair Academy Director of Admissions, Susan Burrell, reports, "Ninety-seven percent of the students we send for interviews at Comair are hired. We give the airline a proven product in our pilots. They know the standards we train them to."

This comparison shows that there are definite differences in the curriculum of any school, as well as differences in price. You'll have to be a good shopper and spend the time to check out everything one school offers in comparison to another. But remember, too, that price shouldn't be your only deciding factor. Location can be important, as will the kind of housing you'll have while you're there. When you've pared your decision down to just two or possibly three schools, I'd take the time to visit the campus and speak to some of the people who run the school as well as to some of the students. Price and paperwork are certainly going to give you some direction, but again, I believe that only an on-site visit can make the final decision for you (Figs. 2-6 and Fig. 2-7).

But FAA ratings aren't the only items necessary to become a professional pilot today. While a pilot's position used to be reachable without the benefit of a college degree, that sheepskin is effectively a requirement in most segments of flying. Today, many airlines still list a college degree as encouraged, while other airlines and

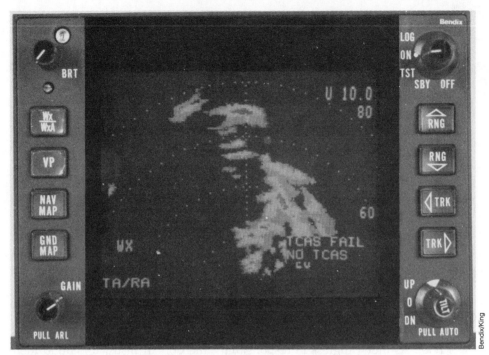

Fig. 2-6. Good training involves learning how everything in a modern cockpit works.

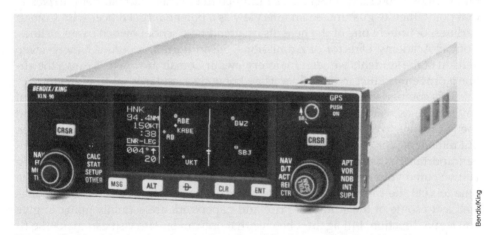

Fig. 2-7. Good training involves learning how everything in a modern cockpit works.

many corporate operators list the degree as a requirement. Either way, if you intend to compete with others in the aviation game, you're going to need a degree. There are many fine state universities such as Purdue, University of North Dakota, University of Illinois, Embry-Riddle University and others that combine a standard four-year degree with programs specifically designed to offer the student all the professional flight ratings they need to make their mark in the profession.

It's a tough call whether or not picking up your ratings on the side while you complete your college degree is less effective toward the goal of flying for a living than attending a four year university that also happens to run a flight program. Chief pilots I interviewed varied considerably from only caring whether or not the pilot held the ratings plus the degree to asking what the degree was in. Many corporations are currently asking about the degree itself, so a pilot can become a more useful member of the corporation during the time they aren't flying. Some chief pilots did seem to hold a soft spot for pilots who attended the same school as themselves, at least long enough for the new applicant to get his or her foot in the door. After that, the applicant needed to compete on the same footing as everyone else.

FINANCING

Most careers offer the student not only the chance at a lifelong job that they'll hopefully enjoy, but also a method of spending substantial amounts of cash in a relatively short period of time on the necessary training. Where do students look for the financing they need to cope with the big bills that accompany this kind of training? The best place to search for money initially is to talk to the school you intend to train with. If you're planning to work with a local free-lance instructor, the chances of picking up the financing you need are pretty slim. If, however, you approach the people at some of the larger flight schools or universities, they should be able to steer you in the right direction. While Comair Aviation Academy or American Flyers are certainly dedicated to the high-quality products and services they sell, they must stay in business to be able to offer those services, something that might be pretty tough if they had no way to help their customers pay their way. I doubt Sears or Wards would try to sell you a washer and dryer without offering you a way to finance the purchase.

Most local banks offer student loans normally backed by federal financing. Whether or not the rates are competitive will be a matter for you to decide. Because of the variables in financing (like interest rates and repayment plans) shopping for a loan can become just as big a project as finding the school in the first place. Depending on your individual financial state, be ready for the fact that many financial institutions might not be willing to make you a loan without a cosigner to guarantee repayment of the money. American Flyers, for instance, offers its students a plan called PLATO, their Student Assistant Program. The system allows students to apply for financing amounts up to $25,000 per year at reasonable rates, along with an extended payment plan. Comair Aviation Academy also offers a similar plan. The regular state universities will offer tuition financing through the financial aid office on campus, so the best advice on financing is to first locate the school you're interested in, and then talk to their financial aid counselor. Remember, too, that while the lowest monthly payments might at first look to be the best way to finance your education, a slightly higher payment or a slightly shorter repayment period could shave hundreds of dollars per year off the total amount of money to be repaid. Be sure to ask about these possibilities.

If you head to your local library's reference desk, you'll find a number of good books available to locate financing for your educational venture, so don't just depend on your local financial or educational institution for help. One school we interviewed was willing to finance a pilot's flying, but at annual rates near 14.5 percent, considerably higher than a regular student loan. People actually took them up on a regular basis because of one reason . . . the financing process was relatively quick and easy to complete. Many students, the financial adviser admitted, never even asked about the interest rate, being more concerned about how long the repayment period would be and just when the payments would actually begin.

Another possibility could be scholarships, but they're tough to find. Luckily, a nice bunch of people at the University Aviation Association put together a 52-page directory of all the information you'll need about scholarships for college. The price of the "Collegiate Aviation Scholarship Listing" is currently $9.95. Write the University Aviation Association, 3410 Skyway Drive, Opelika, Alabama or call 205-844-2434.

THE NEW G.I. BILL

If you're a veteran, you might be eligible for government assistance that could pay as much as 60 percent of the cost of adding additional flight ratings. As with any government program, there are requirements and possible red-tape delays, so if you think you might qualify, contact your local Veteran's Administration office as soon as possible. The Montgomery G.I. Bill is considered the new G.I. Bill because it's only available to veterans who served on active duty in an armed force of the United States after June 30, 1985. You must also have made deposits to the G.I. Bill program at the rate of $100 per month for the first 12 months of that active duty. To begin G.I.-Bill-qualified training, you must hold a private pilot certificate and meet the physical requirements for a commercial certificate. In addition to the school you select being FAA approved, that school must also meet the VA school requirements. Just being FAA approved doesn't necessarily mean the school is VA approved, either. The current Montgomery G.I. Bill expires in September, 1994. Whether or not a new bill will be submitted to replace the expiring Montgomery Bill is not yet known.

INTERNSHIPS

Internships are a career path that's open to you, but there aren't a great many of them, nor are they easy to win. Internships in most careers have been around for years as a method to expose young people to a possible career track while at the same time giving a potential employer a chance to see how the young person performs in the real world.

Most internships are arranged during the third or fourth year of college, as is the one we'll take a look at here: the pilot internship jointly arranged with United Airlines (Fig. 2-8) and participating colleges (see the following list). At United, this program, officially called the Flight Officer College Relations Program, has been running since 1983. A student enrolled at one of the participating universities fills out an application. If, after interviews, the applicant is accepted, he or she takes a full semester off from school to work at one of United's facilities. One student I interviewed did his internship at Washington, Dulles International Airport (IAD).

Fig. 2-8. The United internship program could lead you right to the cockpit.

Intern and now Boeing 737 first officer Arnie Quast began working in flight operations at IAD. "I had a chance to work closely with the pilots and get a good idea of what it was like to be a commercial airline pilot," Quast said. But what made Quast's internship truly valuable was that, "I had the chance to jump seat on all the United aircraft that flew from Dulles and observe firsthand what crew coordination was all about. I also had the opportunity to fly many of the 27 United simulators in Denver," he said.

After graduation, Quast continued to build his flight time as a flight instructor while he waited for the call from United. With just over 1,000 hours total time and just 25 hours multiengine experience, Quast received a United class date for the Boeing 727. He attended the United Training Center in Denver and found the training to be top-notch.

While the number of internships awarded recently by United has dropped, much of that might be due to the economy and the financial state of United, which has been relatively poor, as have the other major carriers. Before you sign up for a particular university program, check for information on these intern programs. A phone call to some of the other airlines will reveal whether or not they're involved in some type of internship program too.

United flight operations college relations (intern) program

Arizona State University
Tempe, AZ 85287-6406

Delaware State College
Dover, DE 19901

Embry-Riddle Aeronautical University
Daytona Beach, FL 32104

Embry-Riddle Aeronautical University
Prescott, AZ 86301

Florida Institute of Technology
Melbourne, FL 32901-6983

Kent State University
Kent, OH 44242-0001

Louisiana Tech University
Ruston, LA 72172

Metropolitan State College
Denver, CO 80204

Ohio State University
Columbus, OH 43210-0022

Ohio University
Athens, OH 45701

Parks College of St. Louis University
Cahokia, IL 62206

Purdue University
West Lafayette, IN 47906

San Jose State University
San Jose, CA 95192-0081

Southern Illinois University
Carbondale, IL 62901-6621

University of Illinois
Champaign-Urbana, IL 61801

University of North Dakota
Grand Forks, ND 58202

Central Missouri State
Warrenberg, MO 64903-5027

Daniel Webster College
Nashua, NH 03063

ALPHA ETA RHO,
A PROFESSIONAL AVIATION SOCIETY

Alpha Eta Rho is a collegiate fraternity founded to bring together those students having a common interest in the field of aviation. Started in 1929 at the University of Southern California, the fraternity has grown to more than 70 chapters nationwide, pledging nearly 1,000 new members each year.

The fraternity serves as a contact between the aviation industry and educational institutions. It bands outstanding students, interested faculty, and industrial leaders into one organization for the purpose of studying the problems of everyday life as influenced by this modern industry—aviation.

Alpha Eta Rho serves to actively associate interested students of aviation with leaders and executives in the industry. This close association, strengthened through the bonds of an international aviation fraternity, establishes opportunities for all members to inspire interest and cooperation among those in the profession who are also members of Alpha Eta Rho (Fig. 2-9). Alpha Eta Rho continues to grow, and it serves as a lasting tribute to the farsighted understanding and vision of its founder, Professor Earl W. Hill.

Fig. 2-9. Alpha Eta Rho members can be found in many different kinds of aircraft.

Philosophy and goals of Alpha Eta Rho

- To further the cause of aviation in all its branches.
- To instill in the public mind a confidence in aviation.
- To promote contacts between the students of aviation and those engaged in the profession.

- To promote a closer affiliation between the students of aviation for the purpose of education and research.

The constitution of Alpha Eta Rho declares that the success of aeronautics depends on its unified development in all the countries of the world and on the cooperation of different phases of aviation with each other. Alpha Eta Rho affirms its character to be international and declares that eligibility for membership is not dependent on race, religion, nationality, or gender.

The address for the Alpha Eta Rho national office is:

Palomar College
1140 W. Mission Rd.
San Marcos, CA 92069-1487
attn. Kent Backart

IS THE MILITARY A POSSIBILITY?

Since the winding down of the Cold War in Europe, the United States military has also entered what some experts call a slow-growth mode. This actually has become the same kind of downsizing that corporate America began experiencing in the early 1990s, with thousands less personnel being kept on active duty and many military bases around the world being shut down or reduced in size. What this change to the military means to you, if you're considering the military as a possible place to pick up your flight training, is best outlined in a story from the May 13, 1992 issue of *Aviation Daily*.

Military pilot pool will shrink under DOT cuts, industry told

The nation's airlines, which traditionally recruited 65 percent or more of their pilots from the military services, will face a shrinking supply later in the decade due to Defense Department budget and manpower cuts and as the services entice more of their pilots to remain on active duty, Senator John McCain (R-AZ), ranking member of the aviation subcommittee, warned yesterday. In the near term, however, airlines will reap a bonanza as the military downsizes in the wake of the breakup of the Soviet Union, McCain yesterday told a committee looking into possible future shortages of pilots and maintenance technicians.

James Busey, DOT deputy secretary, told the panel, which is expected to issue a report in about a year on what measures can be taken to ameliorate possible shortages, that a shortfall in either category could have a profound impact not only on the industry, but on the nation as a whole as far as its ability to compete on a global scale. "We're about to lose an important source of trained pilots from the military. The balance has now shifted and the supply will not be there," Busey said.

Due to the slowdown in the air transportation industry, it's now getting only about 45 percent of its pilots from the military, a figure that could get lower as the military pilot supply dwindles, said John Sheehan of Phaneuf Associates, the consultants to the panel that's chaired by Kenneth Tallman, President Emeritus of Embry-Riddle. He said air carriers will need about 2,400 pilots per year for the next ten years and that regional airlines will need about

28,000 pilots over that period. . . . The panel was originally to be a joint military-civil effort, but the downsizing military services aren't as concerned as they previously were. This will prove ominous for the industry later in the decade as a prime source of pilots disappears, both Sheehan and McCain said.

If you plan to try to enter the U.S. military at some time in the future, then you need to know that there will be fewer flying jobs and tougher competition then for those remaining cockpit positions. Certainly you'll need to talk to your Armed Forces recruiter when you're seriously ready to make this decision about your career because the volatile situation of the American military community could change at any time.

Let's look at the United States Air Force, for example. Because all Air Force pilots are officers, you'll need to apply and be accepted at Air Force Officer Training School (OTS) before anything else can happen. The U.S. Air Force Officer Training School is small and highly specialized. Candidates selected to attend OTS are college graduates and already have an academic foundation. OTS prepares them for positions of responsibility so they can lead the Air Force of tomorrow. The school's motto, "Always with Honor," reflects the ethical and professional standards expected of Air Force officers.

OTS is a fast-paced, three-month course. You complete it on-campus at Lackland Air Force Base in San Antonio, Texas. You study communication skills, leadership, management, military history, Air Force customs and courtesies, world affairs, and more. You take part in organized sports and physical conditioning to develop your confidence and teamwork abilities. The course is designed to aid your transition into the Air Force way of life.

To be eligible for OTS, you must be a United States citizen, 18–29 years of age, in good health, and able to pass a physical exam. You must be a graduate of an accredited college or university and have excellent moral character. You must also score well on the Air Force Officer Qualifying Test. To enter a technical or non-technical career, you must be commissioned before age 30. Pilot or navigator training applicants must pass a flight physical and enter training before age 27½.

Pilot training selectees without a private pilot's license attend the Flight Screening Program before going to OTS. This four-week course identifies your potential to complete undergraduate pilot training. Training time includes cockpit time in a single-engine Cessna 172, called a T-41 (Fig. 2-10) by the Air Force. You'll need a solo flight to complete the Flight Screening Program. If you already have a private pilot license, Flight Screening Program is waived.

After OTS, you'll begin an intensive flight training program (Fig. 2-11), which lasts about one year. (See chapter 7 for more details on Air Force training.)

Once accepted for OTS, you'll enlist in the Air Force in the rank of Staff Sergeant. The Air Force pays your way to OTS as well as your flight training costs. While in training, you'll be paid nearly $500 every two weeks. You live on base and eat in the OTS dining hall. You pay only for personal items such as laundry, postage, and telephone calls. A clothing allowance helps you defray the cost of uniforms. Upon graduation, you're commissioned a second lieutenant. OTS graduates who attend undergraduate pilot training incur an additional Air Force commitment of 8 years after training is complete.

Fig. 2-10. USAF flight screening candidates fly a T-41.

To learn whether you might be eligible to compete for a military flight training program, contact the information service of the branch of your choice at the numbers listed in Table 2-2.

Table 2-2. Information service numbers

Air Force	800-423-8723
Navy	800-327-6289
Army	800-872-2769
Marines	800-627-4637
Coast Guard	800-424-8883

No matter what route you use to gain your ratings, realize that everyone else started out pretty much the same way toward their goal of becoming a professional pilot: sweating it out on long cross-country trips building the flight time for a commercial certificate, or under the hood with a view-limiting device over their heads as they worked towards that instrument rating. There's no easy, quick way to a job in this industry. But all the work is worth it. You might not really believe that during all the tough months of training, but the first time you step into the cockpit of an airplane as a required crew member, you'll know that all the work was worth it.

Fig. 2-11. Successful USAF pilot training progresses to the T-38.

USAF

3

Ratings
What's really involved?

IN THE PAST FEW CHAPTERS, I SPOKE ABOUT THE REQUIREMENTS for ratings and licenses: the commercial, the instrument, the flight instructor, and the ATP. I also discussed where you might go to find some of the best training facilities to make your dream a reality; you could attend an organized flight school whose goal is also to make a profit, or you could go to a state university whose goals are usually a bit more academically lofty. I even spoke of using a free-lance instructor to help you move up from the ranks of a private pilot to the stature of a professional pilot.

Knowing what you need to earn your ratings, knowing how to pay for them, and actually picking up those ratings might seem like a simple matter. But the process is time-consuming and can at times be overwhelming to people who are unaware of just what they're getting themselves into. Certainly, choosing the right flight instructor is crucial here, for without a strong one-on-one relationship that allows the student to question or ask for and receive regular guidance, all the hard work necessary for these ratings could be wasted. Let's take a look at the ratings, then, piece by piece, and give you an insider's look at what really makes the ratings tick.

THE COMMERCIAL RATING:
WHEN TO BEGIN

In their quest toward a professional pilot career, most people begin with the commercial pilot certificate. Perhaps they begin here because this rating holds the first glimpse of things to come; it's usually the most time-consuming of the ratings, and some pilots want to tackle the toughest first. Personally, I enjoyed the commercial training more than just about any other. It seemed more like play to me than work, but then many professional pilots look at flying, any kind of flying, as anything but work. The commercial pilot certificate training takes you from the rank of novice, the private pilot, to the rank of someone who is really beginning to understand what makes an airplane fly in many different kinds of situations. The commercial pilot training could begin right after you receive your private license, but I encourage you not to go that route.

Training for the private pilot certificate takes a great deal of time and energy. By the time most pilots receive their certificate, they've logged an average of 65 to 70 hours total time, with considerably more on the ground. This is when you should take a training break. Go fly for 25 or 35 hours around the local area and on a few cross-country trips. Before you bog yourself down with more flight training, classroom instruction, and written exams, have some fun learning to use the skills you've spent many hard months learning. You need to experience the joy, the fun of flying before you become embroiled in too much work. Total cost is another advantage of putting some time in after you've received your private license. If you're working in a nonapproved school again, you'll need 250 total flight hours before you can be recommended for the commercial exam. With a special exemption, an approved, Part 141 school will only require 190 hours. If you pick up your private at 65 hours and start right in on the commercial package, you'll end up spending dual instruction prices for time leading to the requirements that you could have logged solo. If you start the commercial a bit later and have logged 25 hours on your own, that's 25 × $23 per hour (the instructor's fee), or nearly $600 you could save. That's a pretty hefty savings in anyone's book. After you have about 90 to 100 hours or so, sign up for the commercial course with the school of your choice (Fig. 3-1).

Fig. 3-1. Much of the flying for a commercial license can be in a Cessna 172.

THE PTS

Before you're through with aviation, hopefully many years down the road, I'm sure you'll have run up against more acronyms than you care to even think about. Here's one you're going to become very familiar with on the road to becoming a professional pilot. PTS, or Practical Test Standards, is the label given to a small book, one for each and every certificate and rating the FAA offers. These books will quite succinctly describe for you exactly what subjects you'll need to know to pass the flight test for the particular certificate or rating you seek, in this case the commercial. You must be able to perform and will be asked to perform each and every task set forth in the PTS. That might sound pretty straightforward right now, but when people were picking up ratings a few years back, the booklet in use was the FAA's flight test guide.

The problem with that publication was that the examiners could pick and choose which items they wanted to test you on. They were required to choose some, but not all. Unfortunately, as happens with human nature, some examiners picked the same maneuvers each time they gave an exam, and the word eventually got out. If you were weak on NDB approaches, find Fred; he never asks you to fly one anyway. Herb never cared about Chandelles on a commercial, so if you had trouble with those, you'd do your darndest to locate Herb to give you the test. To say the least, this made the entire test procedure rather unfair and at times much too easy to predict, which meant that sometimes people of various degrees of skill were awarded the certificate.

With the establishment of the PTS, much of the ambiguity of the testing procedure was eliminated because each applicant was told, long before the test, that they would be tested on everything in the book. This actually made things a great deal easier, even if somewhat more complex, because if the students could perform all the maneuvers to the required standards, they were prepared for the flight test . . . period. The FAA says this about the PTS concept . . .

"FARs specify the areas in which knowledge and skill must be demonstrated by the applicant before the issuance of a rating. The FARs provide the flexibility to permit the FAA to publish practical test standards containing specific tasks in which pilot competency must be demonstrated. The FAA will add, delete, or revise tasks whenever it's determined that changes are needed in the interest of safety. Adherence to provisions of the regulations and the practical test standards is mandatory for the evaluation of pilot applicants.

An appropriately rated flight instructor is responsible for training the student to the acceptable standards as outlined in the objective of each task within the appropriate practical test standard. The flight instructor must certify that the applicant is able to perform safely as a pilot and is competent to pass the required practical test for the rating sought.

The examiner who conducts the practical test is responsible for determining that the applicant meets the acceptable standards as outlined in the objective of each task within the appropriate practical test standard. This determination requires evaluation of both knowledge and skill because there's no formal division between the "oral" and "skill" portions of the practical test. It's intended that oral questioning be used at any time during the practical test to determine that the applicant shows adequate knowledge of the tasks and their related safety factors."

Additionally, people complained a number of years ago about some of the methods examiners used to determine just how qualified an applicant was. The main complaint was the examiner's use of distractions during a flight test. Some applicants believed it was unfair to toss in little questions or problems during a time when the applicant needed to concentrate on more important things. In the new PTS, the FAA addressed this issue . . .

Numerous studies indicate that many accidents have occurred when the pilot's attention has been distracted during various phases of flight. Many accidents have resulted from engine failure during takeoffs and landings where safe flight was possible if the pilot had used correct control technique and divided attention properly.

Distractions that have been found to cause problems are: preoccupation with situations inside or outside the cockpit, maneuvering to avoid other traffic or maneuvering to clear obstacles during takeoffs, climbs, approaches or landings.

To strengthen this area of pilot training and evaluation, the examiner will provide realistic distractions throughout the flight portion of the practical test. Many distractions may be used to evaluate the applicant's ability to divide attention while maintaining safe flight. Some examples of distractions are:

- Simulating engine failure.
- Simulating radio tuning and communications.
- Identifying a field suitable for emergency landings.
- Identifying features or objects on the ground.
- Reading the outside air temperature gauge.
- Removing objects from the glove compartment or map case.
- Questioning by the examiner.

This is what the examiner will be looking for when he or she gives you the flight test for the various ratings. Let's take a look at the commercial PTS and what's required to be successful at the test. As you can well imagine, a commercial pilot certificate allows you to carry passengers or cargo for compensation or hire. Another way of looking at the commercial is a rating that allows you to make money for flying. But, besides the ability to make money at flying, the capture of a commercial certificate for your wallet means you've begun to look at aviation in a whole new way—professionally. The maneuvers you'll be asked to perform as well as the subjects you'll learn are designed to offer you a significantly higher level of knowledge of flying, which you're required to demonstrate on the flight test. You'll find too that even though some of the maneuvers might appear similar to those you learned for your private ticket, the tolerances you'll be expected to fly to are much tighter (Fig. 3-2).

COMMERCIAL SUBJECTS

I'm not going to cover every single subject on the Commercial Flight Test; I'll cover just those that I think I can offer some particular insight into. As in the private pilot test, the commercial pilot will be asked to prove that the aircraft is airworthy by

Fig. 3-2. There's a PTS for helicopter flight tests too.

displaying and being able to discuss the various sorts of paperwork involved in making the aircraft legal to fly. This includes a possible discussion of the Minimum Equipment List (or MEL) for your aircraft, not to be confused with the FAA-required minimum equipment for day and night VFR and IFR flight. You'll also be expected to be able to prove that you're legal to conduct the flight test, right down to being certain that the information on the FAA Form 8710-1, the Application for

Airman's Certificate, is correct. One problem that almost caught one of my students recently was the location of the ELT in his new Bonanza. During basic questioning at the preflight, I asked the student where the ELT was located. When we looked in the small door in the rear, where the switch to arm or turn off the ELT was located, the student found nothing. He couldn't prove that the ELT was there. It took a mechanic with a flashlight to finally locate the device for us. Better for me to ask than to have been caught on a flight test with this question, so be certain you don't just listen to your instructor; take an active part and make certain you really understand what's being taught. Learning to fly is no place to be passive.

In every aircraft I've ever checked out in, I've always found the systems test to be the most difficult part of the new exam or, in this case, the commercial flight test. When it comes to a systems test, the key to passing this section is to not just understand that the landing gear, for instance, is hydraulically actuated, but also to understand the troubleshooting aspects of the system. What happens when the system falters? How do you lower the gear when the hydraulic pump fails? What's the backup if the alternate system fails? If you can't lock the left main, but the right and nose are down, should you land on two or bring them all up? If your landing gear is electric, take the time to learn more than simply the emergency gear extension. If the discussion turns to electrical, know what a voltage regulator is and where it's located on the alternator assembly. Realizing what kinds of electrical problems you can cope with is important for the oral, but so is being able to tell the examiner when your system has run out of options.

When it comes to weather, the examiner will be looking for an ability to read prognostic and radar charts as well as sequence reports and forecasts. The key here is being able to tell the examiner the trends from what you read. I don't mean forecast the weather for the next 12 hours, but be able to relate what you're reading with how that weather will affect the flight you're planning, in terms of routing, winds aloft, altitude selection, fuel required, and icing considerations. Sure, you might be able to tell the examiner that rotation about a low is counterclockwise, but on a cross-country trip, what does that mean regarding the weather and the changes to that weather that you'll encounter? When will you encounter a headwind or tailwind, when will the pressure change, and which way will the altimeter move? (Fig. 3-3.)

Another area that often causes a great deal of stress is emergencies. This shouldn't be such an unusual reaction because emergencies, by their very nature, are anxiety-producing situations. I've found that, for the commercial, the most common emergency is still total or partial engine failure. (Most will talk about an engine failure right after rotation in a single engine aircraft, but they shouldn't be even simulating this event below 500 AGL.) Know the memory items of your aircraft checklist and be able to recite them while you're being distracted with something else because that's most likely how the engine will die. It could quit in a steep spiral or during an eight around a pylon. Be able to tell the examiner what you'll do if the door pops right after rotation. I remember the time I learned how to show the examiner a simulated in-flight fire recovery in a BE-55. When he yelled fire, I chopped both throttles and almost rolled the airplane on its back as I headed down toward the ground. He quickly grasped my respect for the crisis.

Fig. 3-3. The use of automated weather reporting systems is becoming more common.

When it comes to cross-country planning, you actually get a break. Although you can expect to spend a portion of the oral explaining how you determine fuel burn and proper altitude and whether or not there are NOTAMs current for your route, the big factor here is how to plan for the unusual. You'll spend half an hour looking up data for Fred's Airpark and the examiner will look it over and say, "Yes, but now I want to go to He Haw International."

Find all the airport information and explain what you find. Before your flight test, be sure your instructor has quizzed you on every single symbol, color change, information box, and navaid symbol. It's not good enough to only point and say that's a VORTAC; you must understand what it means. So, here's the break. You don't actually have to fly a cross-country trip like you did for your private. You just have to be able to explain it.

During ground operation questions, be ready to tell the difference in colors between the fuel. Know that no color could be jet fuel in your tank instead of avgas. Be ready to explain just how frost might actually form and how you should remove it, as well as what you shouldn't try if the contaminate were ice (like beating it off with the handle of an ice scraper, which could dent the leading edge). Do you taxi and pay attention only to taxiing, or do you try to write ground control instructions or ATIS while you're moving? Both of these would show some serious judgment problems. Before you take off, how well do you organize the charts you use? Do you put them somewhere where you can easily reach them but they won't blow around on takeoff? Do you have a pen close by as you fly?

On your pre-takeoff check, you'll be expected to demonstrate a professional attitude toward the checklist. If there's any one thing I see students slip on, time and time again, it's checklists. Too often, students read the item and look, but they don't actually check to see if the proper operation was actually performed. For example, "altimeter. . .set." They look, but they don't actually change the setting in the Kolsman window.

When it comes to radio and ATC communications, you'll be expected to handle the radio like a pro. That doesn't mean you never miss a call or always understand what air traffic is trying to communicate, but it does mean that when you only catch part of the call, you take the proper action to repair the situation, like asking ATC to, "Say again!" That doesn't sound tough, but you'd be surprised how many pilots just sit there when they missed something on the radio or look over at the examiner and say, "Did you catch what they said?" Not a good idea. If you live near a TRSA or ARSA or TCA, be absolutely ready to explain when and how you'll request and enter the airspace. One student was recently caught when the examiner asked if the ATC facility repeating his call sign for entry into an ARSA meant he could keep going toward the airport. The answer is yes. When asked if it worked the same way in a TCA, the student said sure. Wrong! Without teaching you the new airspace designations, know that there's more to it than just saying a TCA becomes class B airspace. What happens if one type of airspace overlaps with another? (I already know. You look it up.)

When it comes to maneuvers, I think there are really only a few techniques to use to perform each maneuver. When you're performing eights around pylons, you either understand how to compensate for the wind or you don't. You either know where the reference point is supposed to be on eights on pylons or you don't. What's probably the most important part of the commercial preparation is that there's simply no substitute for plain old practice. Too many students want to rush it as soon as they meet the requirements. Whether it's crosswind takeoffs and landings or eights on pylons, you must get out and practice if you intend to display competence on the exam. Personally, I'd be out practicing a few hours, three times per week before the test, to become proficient enough to pass the flight test. Finally, in this discussion of the PTS there's one more simple concept, at least it seems simple to me. Know the tolerances of the maneuvers. For a lazy eight, know that when you're selecting your reference point, as the maneuver progresses you should never drop below 1,500 AGL, or that the altitude tolerance is plus or minus 100 feet at the 180-degree point, or that airspeed really must be within 10 knots at both the 90 and 180-degree point. The commercial license is the level where you're expected to fly professionally. Finally, If you don't understand what's expected of you at any point during the exam . . . please ask!

NOW THAT YOU HAVE THE RATINGS, WHAT'S NEXT?

This really seems like the grandest question of them all, but once you've picked up these various ratings, what do you do next? The most important answer is to keep flying. That might sound a bit simplistic, but do anything you can to keep logging and building your total time as well as the variety of your experience. One way to accomplish this is to stick close to an airplane any way you can, whether it's by buying an airplane of your own or renting. It all counts toward your total time.

Let's talk about that coveted logbook for a moment. Everywhere you go in this industry, you'll hear people asking how much time you've logged. It seems, however, that the problem of logged hours is not quite as significant for people who have surpassed the point of 3,000 to 5,000 hours or so. Less than 1,000 hours pretty much puts you in the range of unproven more than anything else. When you're working with total hours in the hundreds, then, total time to a potential employer is very significant, depending on the job you're trying to win. A pilot with 400 hours total time might find that the kind of jobs they'll be limited to will be sightseeing demo rides or perhaps glider-towing missions. Realize that a potential employer is limited, usually by insurance, as to what you can and can't fly, so be ready when this problem appears.

Another significant hurdle you'll run into during your career will be the amount of multiengine time you have under your belt. Multiengine time is much tougher to come by because it's not only expensive, but also difficult to obtain because, again, most insurance policies written on twin-engine aircraft pretty much prohibit low-time pilots from flying them solo. What you might be left with is trying to find a charter operator who will allow you to fly second in command (SIC) on one of their airplanes or perhaps a small company that will allow the same kind of SIC time in their twin. I won't pull any punches with you here. This isn't going to be easy. I remember the struggle: begging, borrowing, and running around the airport at all hours of the day and night to try to pick up that multiengine time.

I started out flying right seat on a light twin for a small Chicago manufacturing firm and eventually ended up in the left seat. The airplane was an early Piper Seneca 1, but it might as well have been a 747 to me. After a hundred or so hours in that aircraft, l found myself in the right place at the right time to be able to ferry some aircraft for an aircraft distributor, which eventually led me to a Piper Navajo job. As a ferry pilot, I would fly around the country with the power pulled back to economy cruise and everyone was happy. The aircraft burned less fuel on the trip and I logged more time. Even today, I still ferry aircraft just for the chance to fly someplace totally unscheduled.

Another option you might consider could be club operation with a twin. You might have to fly with an instructor for awhile before you can take the aircraft alone, but once you qualify, the rates will probably be relatively cheap. It will take some time and effort on your part to search out the bargains and opportunities, though.

Just when you find yourself with a few hundred hours of multiengine piston time under your belt and you start shopping for some of those flying jobs, you might run smack into another category of time someone will ask for: turbine time (Fig. 3-4). Turbine is basically a generic word for jet engine time. The time can be logged in two forms, however. The first is turbo prop time, where the aircraft is powered by a jet engine connected through gearing to a propeller. This could be a King Air or Cheyenne type of aircraft. The next is pure jet time. This would be Cessna Citation, Learjet, Boeing 737 time. After I had accumulated about 1,200

Fig. 3-4. Flight time spent piloting a turboprop counts as turbine time.

hours of turbine time in a turbo prop aircraft, I felt like pretty hot stuff. Then, when I went looking for a job, some of the ones I really wanted asked for jet time. It seems there's always going to be a carrot in front of you somewhere. As soon as you have jet time, someone will probably say they wished you had more time in that jet, or they'll tell you they wished you were type rated in some other kind of jet. That's just the way this industry works.

Now that you have the ratings, what's next?   **59**

AN INEXPENSIVE
METHOD OF BUILDING TIME

What about that pilot who has only a few hundred hours and is still seemingly too far away from twins and turbines and jets to even be concerned? What's the best way to build time, any kind of time, toward that first 1,000 or so? Looking back on what I know now, if I were a relatively low-time pilot, I would find a partner and purchase an airplane of my own and fly the pants off the thing. You might at first be aghast, considering how expensive you might believe airplanes to be, but I'm not talking about buying a twin Cessna or a Beech Bonanza for $100,000.

Recently, I saw an ad in a local Chicago newspaper for a Cessna 120. The aircraft, a taildragger and slightly slower version of the Cessna 152 (Fig. 3-5), was reportedly in good condition, and the asking price was $13,500. Let's assume there was no dealing at all and you actually paid the asking price. You'd be required to put down 20 percent of the purchase price as a down payment, or about $2,700. Your financed amount would come to $10,800.

Fig. 3-5. You could buy a single-engine aircraft to build time.

A recent chat with the folks at the AOPA sent me to the Maryland Bank, who quoted the following rates on this deal. Financing $10,800 at the current fixed rate of 10.9 percent would give you a payment of $184.98 per month. If you chose their variable rate of 8.75 percent, the payment dropped to $172.40 per month. The rate on the variable note changes quarterly with Maryland Bank and is always 2.75 percent above prime rate as seen in the *Wall Street Journal*. With a monthly payment of roughly $185 per month, I added another $75 per month for tiedown and about $40 per month for insurance. The aircraft burns about 4 gallons of fuel per hour, at about $2.00 per gallon. Oil is consumed at about a quart every 5 hours, so we'll add another 40 cents to the hourly cost. The Cessna 120 is a relatively simple aircraft to maintain, but we must put something on the side just in case, so we'll add another $4 per hour for possible maintenance costs. The grand total of how much it will cost you to fly this machine each hour depends greatly on how many hours each month you truly take to the air.

I'm going to assume, because you're trying to become a professional pilot, that you'll take advantage of having an airplane around to fly. For my calculations, I'll assume you fly the aircraft 30 hours per month, or about an hour a day.

Here's the cost breakdown:

$185 per-month mortgage
$ 75 per-month tiedown charges
$ 40 per-month insurance
———
$300 per-month fixed costs / 30 = $10 fixed costs per hour

$4.00 per-hour for fuel
$ .40 per-hour for oil
$4.00 per-hour for maintenance
———
$8.40 variable costs per hour

Total cost to you per hour would be $18.40 per hour.

One of the best parts about this is that you could take in a partner who also has the same goals and wants to fly as much as you do. With one partner, your down payment is half, about $1,350. All the fixed costs are halved too, although your hourly costs would remain constant. So with a partner, you pay just $150 per month in fixed costs, which works out this way.

$150 monthly / 30 = $5 per-hour fixed costs
$8.40 per-hour variable costs
———
$13.40 per-hour flying costs

Imagine, with a single partner in an airplane of this size, that you could be out building time at the rate of $13.40 per hour. I guarantee that you won't find a deal like that at any flight school anywhere. Keep in mind, too, that these aren't just pie-in-the-sky numbers. If you fly the airplane only one hour a day, you can certainly have time left over for your partner to fly one hour per day. Perhaps a better solution would be to alternate days. There are plenty of options, but remember, the pilot who succeeds is the one who's willing to take a chance on something a little bit different.

By the way, in case you think I skillfully skipped over the subject of down payment on that Cessna, I didn't. I just assumed that some of the money you saved on not spending $45 or $50 per hour to rent a time-building Cessna 152 could be used to pay back your parents or your brother or your savings account or whomever you used to help you get the plane in the first place. If you do buy a taildragger, have fun. Nothing makes a real pilot like a taildragger.

THE JOB HUNT

So, you've spent a ton of your hard-earned cash to pick up a commercial and instrument rating as well as a multiengine and perhaps even a flight instructor certificate. You've even managed to build some flight time, maybe even some multiengine time, and you think it's time to start looking for a way to bring in some money instead of just writing all the time. But where do you look, and furthermore, once you do find some job listings, what's the plan of attack to get the interview?

When it comes to finding a flying job, there seem to be two kinds of pilots; those who look for themselves and those who find someone to search for them. I've used both methods personally, and I think each has its benefits and drawbacks. If you search on your own, you'll be a busy person, indeed, at least if you work the way I do. I believe that a person who is not working really does have a full-time job. Their full-time job is looking for a job. Looking for a flying job (compared to talking about looking for a flying job) really requires not only hard work, but also a real plan of operation as to how you'll reach this new goal. There's that word goal again. Funny how it keeps creeping up, but I believe that, without clear-cut goals, a personal flight plan, if you will, you'll end up making emotional decisions that might not be in your best long-term interests.

Being involved with airplanes in general tends to be a rather emotional experience, so make sure you've some idea where you're headed before you go marching off toward a new job. What's your ultimate goal? If you're relatively low-time, almost any flying job will probably be beneficial, as long as you can afford the cost. And sometimes the cost can be dear, everything from asking you to move a few thousand miles away to starting wages that appear to rival poverty scale. Only you can decide.

If you're going to begin looking on your own, I suggest boring ahead with full steam because there are many places for you to look for that new flying job (Figs. 3-6 and 3-7). In this section, I'll tell you about some of the places you can locate information on companies who use pilots. Some will be publications, some will involve the use of a personal computer to access a database, while yet others will be full-fledged pilot recruitment services anxiously awaiting your sign up so they can give you their knowledge . . . for a fee. You can quickly accumulate a wealth of information about who owns aircraft and which companies are hiring.

Notice too, I don't mention "not hiring." If a company owns aircraft, they all must hire, eventually. It's a matter of finding out who they are, first of all, and then planning your appearance on their doorstep at the proper moment in time. Some of the magazine classified sections contain job ads, while some are ads for training schools. But, sometimes too, just talking to people at the training schools can generate some ideas to help your plan take shape. Many of the training schools also use 800 phone numbers, so call and ask questions. But your selection process shouldn't be just limited to the sources mentioned in this section. What follows are

Falcon Jet Corp.

Fig. 3-6. Is the corporate cockpit your goal?

Falcon Jet Corp.

Fig. 3-7. See Fig 3-6.

some of the sources. These sources are not organized by their importance. They are all important. But most important of all is what you do with the information you're provided, for no agency or publication in the world will be of any help if you don't act on the information you locate.

THE PUBLICATIONS

The first publication I would suggest you locate is *The World Aviation Directory*. Published by McGraw-Hill, the WAD, as it's affectionately known, is about ten pounds of more information on the aviation industry than you ever thought about or possibly even wanted to know. The WAD is a world-renowned directory to all things aviation, from airlines, to fixed-base operators to flight schools to parts suppliers to government aviation agencies. And best of all, the WAD covers the aviation industry worldwide. Let's take a look at some of the facts you can locate inside the WAD.

From the Industry Trends and Statistics section:

- Worldwide Carriers Systemwide Traffic
- U.S. Majors and National Carriers
  - ~ Domestic Financial and Traffic Summary
  - ~ Financial Indicators
  - ~ Expense Indicators
- Fleet Analysis
  - ~ U.S. Major Carriers
  - ~ U.S. National Carriers
  - ~ Worldwide Carriers
- U.S. Major Carriers Aircraft Operating Expenses
  - ~ Domestic
  - ~ Systemwide
  - ~ International

One section lists the name of every airline flying in the world, as well as their home base. These can then be easily cross-referenced to the air carrier list, which not only lists the correct address and phone and FAX number for an airline, but also the major executives of that carrier and the current fleet size, something that might come very much in handy during an interview. You'll be suitably impressed with the information that's also available on aircraft manufacturers and charter companies. Finally, if you know the name of a particular aviation person you're trying to track down, the alphabetical list could be just what you need. A current WAD (they're released twice a year) is not cheap, about $200 per year, but there probably is no better source of information in book form available. Most library reference sections will carry a *World Aviation Directory*, so you can go take a look before you shell out your hard-earned dollars.

Here's a glimpse of a few of the magazines in the aviation industry now. The best part about all of these is that they not only have classified sections that will steer you toward even more information for your job search, but they also contain stories about what's happening within the industry, such as a new airline start-up or a corporate flight department opening or closing. Such information might also influence your decisions. These magazines and information sources are listed without regard to price. Besides, the prices might change.

My advice on the use of any publication's information about flight schools is that I'd be very careful about schools promising work after training, unless you have some way to verify those claims. I can provide the information about sources, but you'll have to do the footwork to verify what you learn (Fig. 3-8).

Fig. 3-8. Some of the aviation publications available.

PROFESSIONAL PILOT magazine

Based in Washington, D.C., *PRO PILOT* calls itself the monthly journal of aviation professionals. The magazine contains spotlight articles on airline and corporate operators, as a well as technical articles on state-of-the-art electronics and flying techniques. The slant is definitely toward professional pilots, although newly rated pilots could benefit from the educational aspects of the publication. A recent issue contained these stories: a piece on aviation in Ohio, a story on the Canadair RJ jet, an avionics piece on Flight Management Systems, a profile on a hurricane-hunting NOAA pilot, a story on alcohol abuse, as well as a piece on Martin State Airport and a technique article on learning from experience. Regular features include an IFR chart refresher quiz and basic aviation news. The magazine's classified section recently listed various flight training schools that might or might not advertise in other publications, as well as a few listings for help under the jobs-available section. Contact *PROFESSIONAL PILOT* magazine at 3014 Colvin St., Alexandria, VA 22314 or 703-370-0606. This publication is not available on the newsstand.

FLYING

FLYING claims to be the world's most widely read aviation magazine. The emphasis is towards general aviation, although many articles highlight the newest aircraft and equipment in aviation, be it corporate, airline, or—occasionally—military. The magazine uses a number of regular, highly respected columnists, each with an interesting perspective on what's happening in the industry. The magazine's classified section has grown, and it now covers seven full pages. In a recent issue, no less than 46 flight schools were advertised. The classified section also included 13 ads for employment information, everything from an ad that asked for low-time pilots to one specifically aimed at corporate flying jobs. Recent articles in *FLYING* included a story on GPS, as well as other stories on the Bell LongRanger helicopter, the Falcon 2000 corporate jet, the Jetstream 41 regional airliner, Hypoxia, and how to update the IFR equipment on your instrument panel on a budget. Contact *FLYING* at 500 West Putnam Ave., Greenwich, CT 06830; call 303-447-9330 for subscription information. *FLYING* is available on the newsstand and at most libraries.

Business & Commercial Aviation

BUSINESS & COMMERCIAL AVIATION is definitely written for the crews of corporate aircraft, although many of the articles cover subjects of interest to all pilots. Recent stories included a piece on flying in the CIS, a discussion of the V1 flying speed controversy, and a pilot report on the TBM 700 turboprop. BCA has one of the better monthly aviation news sections too. The marketplace section is small, but many ads of various categories are scattered throughout the magazine. Contact BCA at 4 International Drive, Rye Brook, NY 10573 or 914-939-0300. BCA is not available on the newsstand.

Aviation Week & Space Technology

Av Week, as this magazine is known, is the weekly bible of what's happening in all facets of the aviation industry worldwide. With editors scattered in all parts of the globe, you can expect the most comprehensive description of aviation events that could affect your career. Coverage of the general aviation end of flying is a bit skimpy at times, but the magazine more than makes up for it with their coverage of airlines, military, and corporate aviation. If you follow aviation, this publication is something you must have. Their classified ads often hold some rather major flying jobs, along with employment services in the industry. Contact *Av Week* at PO Box 503, Hightstown, NJ 08520-9899 or 800-525-5003.

AIR LINE PILOT magazine

This publication is the voice of the Air Line Pilots Association (ALPA), so the stories tend to be oriented toward matters for airline pilots as well as the day-to-day politics of a union with more than 40,000 airline pilot members. The classified section is pretty short on anything of interest to aspiring pilots, except for a fair number of training schools. What makes this magazine particularly interesting is the insiders view—from a union perspective—of what's happening within the airline industry, such as how new FAA regulations could affect a pilot's job. Recent stories in *AIR LINE PILOT* included a look at the life of a regional pilot, a study on a recent EMB-120 Brasilia crash, an interview with the new Department of Transportation secretary, as well as regular comments by ALPA's President. *AIR LINE PILOT* is not sold on the newsstand. For subscription information, contact ALPA at 535 Herndon Pkwy, P.O. Box 1169, Herndon, VA 22070 or 703-689-4179.

AOPA PILOT

This is the publishing voice of the Aircraft Owners and Pilots Association. The magazine tends to be centered more on general aviation, but in the past year, it has added a very interesting and useful feature called turbine pilot to explain the intricacies of flying jets and turboprops to people used to piston engines. This feature alone could make the magazine worth the price to a relatively new, yet aspiring professional pilot. The magazine is offered as part of the annual membership dues from AOPA, currently $39. If there's anything to be said about AOPA, besides the fact that nearly 60 percent of all active U.S. pilots are members, it's that the $39 will bring so many extras that you'd be crazy to pass it up. Recent articles included flying with over-the-counter medicines, a report on the Beech Starship 2000A, what's doing at Lycoming and Continental Engines, and a new installment of airline pilot Barry Schiff's "Proficient Pilot." The classifieds tend to be rather lean here, but they would certainly be a good source for training school ideas. Contact AOPA at 800-USA-AOPA.

Career Pilot

CAREER PILOT is published each month by FAPA, in Atlanta. FAPA (which we'll talk about later in this chapter), is a company that's 100 percent devoted to bringing the latest information on pilot jobs to their members. The FAPA gurus sift through thousands of pieces of information and produce plenty of forecasts for the industry. Each month, *CAREER PILOT* highlights at least one airline, usually two, and tells all: history of the company, hiring requirements, fleet size, pay ranges, pilot comments, and tips on making it to the first interview. Recent articles include a cover story on Midwest Express Airlines, how to find international flying jobs, how pilots get conned in investment scams, and Trans World Express. Just to keep you up to date on who really is being hired each month, *CAREER PILOT* offers a new hire feedback section. Here, recent pilot hires are interviewed and relate their experience levels at the time they were hired. Here's a listing example from a recent issue, in which I switched my name with the real new hire. Rob Mark, 35:2, 20/100 vision, United. B-727 FE, 7,150 hours, 1,000 jet, 3,000 turboprop, ATP, FEw, CFII, MEI. A.B. degree. Cargo. LR-36, DA-20, BE-99, PA-31, Burbank, CA.

Broken down, this means this pilot was 35 years, two months old, with 20/100 vision. He was hired by United as a B-727 Flight Engineer with 7,150 total hours logged, of which 1,000 was in jets, 3,000 in turboprops. At the time of hire, this pilot held an ATP certificate and had passed the Flight Engineer written exam. He also held the instrument and multiengine instructor ratings as well as an associate degree. He flew mostly cargo in Learjets, Falcons, Beech 99s and Navajos. He lived in Burbank, California. *CAREER PILOT* is not available on the newsstand. Contact FAPA at 800-JET-JOBS.

Aviation International News

This is the big news magazine. It's not only big in the sense that's it's chock full of news about airline and general aviation, plus fixed-base operator topics, but it's also big physically. The *Aviation International News* format is glossy-magazine style, but twice the size of a regular magazine. While the content of the magazine is news, this publication allows for much longer articles than other magazines. Recent stories included a rather comprehensive job report about what the job market really looks like for pilots, as well as a pilot report about the new regional airliner, British Aerospace's Jetstream 41. The news stories make this magazine important, especially because there's no classified section. Not available on the newsstand, contact *Aviation International News* at 21 Cross Ave., Midland Park, NJ, 07432 or 201-444-5075.

General Aviation News and Flyer

This tabloid is normally devoted pretty much to general aviation. Upon reading a recent issue, I looked through their "Pink Sheet," which is GAN's classified pages, and I found some ads that could be of interest to a new pilot looking for methods to build time. Under the "Help Wanted" section, I saw, "Pilots fly 1,000+ hours per year with great pay. Alaska offers seasonal and full-time employment . . ." No promises here, but an opportunity in a place that a future professional pilot might not look. Also, GAN could be an excellent source of ads for the parts necessary to keep that airplane of yours in top shape. This tabloid is the sleeper of the publication list, so be sure to check into it. Contact *General Aviation News and Flyer* at 800-426-8538.

FLIGHT TRAINING magazine

This monthly magazine provides constant coverage of the flight training regime because the motto here is "back to basics." The issues are designed not only for the student of various ratings, but also for the instructor. The magazine produces an excellent national list of flight schools. Contact *FLIGHT TRAINING* at 405 Main Street, Parkville, MO 64152-3737 or call 713-455-5988.

Some other publications to check out are *Air Jobs Digest*, *Air Transport World*, *Commuter Air*, *Air Progress*, and *Flight International*. Again, I'd never pass by any aviation publication without investigating the classified ads. Keep in mind that names and addresses for most publications can also be found in the *World Aviation Directory*, which you might need because so many of these publications aren't available on the street. But don't think aviation publications are the only places jobs are advertised. I've certainly found them in the "Help Wanted" section of the *Chicago Tribune*, the *Denver Post* and even the *Wall Street Journal*.

ONLINE SERVICES

A final thought on sources of information would have to be online. In case you've been living in a black hole for the past ten years or so, online refers to information available to you through your personal computer and a modem that connects your PC through the standard telephone line to the outside world. Tell your PC to dial a number, and you'll be connected to a world of information that could easily dazzle you. If you do choose to look into an online service, be prepared to be astounded by the various services and the subjects they'll bring to light from the comfort of your home or office.

CompuServe

Based in Columbus, Ohio, CompuServe (CIS) members total more than 1,000,000 worldwide. You dial up the CIS computer through a local access phone number and you're instantly connected to another member in Garuda or Alaska or even Hong Kong, not to mention points a bit closer to home. You'll also find hundreds of services and sources of information on a wide range of subjects. But because I'm talking about aviation here, let's look at one of the oldest forums on the CIS, AVSIG or aviation special interest group. A forum is a place you can maneuver to with your computer to allow you direct access to other people with the same interests. You can talk one-on-one via your keyboard to ask questions of someone in Santa Fe or Los Angeles or Portland about the flying jobs available or operators who might look for pilots. You can download aviation weather or even programs of special interest to pilots. One program that we'll discuss a little later, AEROLOG, a computerized logbook program, was something I first ran into on CompuServe through a free demonstration program that the author offered. The list of possibilities is endless when you consider that you can converse easily with people halfway around the world who can give you up-to-date information on what's really happening in the job market in their state or country.

As I was writing this text, I put my word processing program on pause and went in to CompuServe and found another pilot's message about a question I had posed to any of the thousands of people who happened to check in on AVSIG. It's sure cheaper and quicker than the telephone. Here's a current list of the basic subjects available to pilots with personal computers on CompuServe's AVSIG library section.

- General Help.
- Weather/Weather Programs.
- Navigation.
- Air Traffic Control.
- Safety.
- Maintenance/Avionics.
- Instrument Flight.
- Training & Careers.
- Corporate/Business & Fixed-Base Operator.
- Sport Recreational.
- Medical and Human Factors.
- Fly-Ins.
- Places to Fly.
- Aviation Computer Programs.
- Aircraft Performance.
- FAA News.
- Want Ads.

This is just some of the overall topics that could be of interest to you on CompuServe. Contact CompuServe at 800-848-8990. But, while CompuServe might be the largest and best-known of the online services to pilots, there are definitely a few more services. Again, I won't list them all, but many hold little gems of information that would be of use to you as a professional pilot.

One of the newest services is the AOPA On-Line, offered through the Aircraft Owners & Pilots Association. The entire thrust of this online service is aviation oriented, and it's the only online service to my knowledge that covers just aviation. Although relatively new, AOPA On-Line plans to compete with the likes of CompuServe, at least as far as aviation is concerned. I wouldn't be surprised if some of the same people who work with CompuServe are also members of AOPA On-Line. The forums will be a bit different, and the slant is much more towards general aviation, but you never know when you'll pick up a lucky tip about a job or just a general piece of aviation information that could change your entire career game plan.

A major news service is Newsnet. While this service is considerably more expensive than either CompuServe or AOPA On-Line, this database offers you a path to locate the freshest news on aviation topics, often within hours of release because many publications are stored electronically, online, with Newsnet. Want to see the most up-to-date copy of *Aviation Daily* or *Business Aviation Weekly*? Log on to Newsnet and, within seconds, you'll find the information being downloaded to your PC through the modem.

Clipping services are another nice feature available to Newsnet as well as CompuServe. A clipping service allows you to locate information quickly, without even having to spend the time running the search yourself. Here's how it works. You initially set up a file with a few keywords that link the subject you're looking for. If you were trying to find data on a company you're trying to hire on with, you might use "Midwest Express Airlines" as the key phrase to begin with. Then, the database will search through the hundreds of publications it has stored online, many up-dated daily, for any story that contains those key words. When it locates one, the story is sent to your file for you to retrieve later when you log on again. You can also narrow the parameters of your search by adding other keywords such as "finan-cial" for only financial data on the airline or "aircraft" to locate a press release from Mid Ex about new aircraft and possibly new pilot positions. It's that simple. It will work for any company, any airline, any concept, as long as some kind of story or press release has been written and released about it. Contact NewsNet at 800-345-1301. Other online services include America On-Line and Genie.

PILOT JOB SEARCH FIRMS

But what if you don't want to do all the work? Two heads usually are better than one, so, if you can afford it, why not have someone help you locate job information while you continue to look on your own? There are a number of firms that will of-fer everything from career counseling to resumé preparation or even job offers themselves. Some specialize in just working in one segment of the industry, while others offer advice on many different facets of aviation.

One company—Detroit, Michigan-based Turner Group Services—serves as an aviation employment agency with even more specific parameters: They limit their service to assisting pilots looking for corporate flying work in the Great Lakes Re-gion (Fig. 3-9). The Turner Group gives you a personal information form to outline your experience. They also accept a copy of your resumé and any letters of recom-mendation you might have. The company collects a small registration fee, cur-rently about $150, before they begin work for you. The Turner Group uses their database and extensive client list to search, often on a personal basis; they claim a 30 to 60 percent success rate with the pilots who sign up.

How personal are they? If the Turner Group doesn't believe they can find you a job, they won't accept you as a client. The fee you pay to this organization is not an annual fee, either. One registration fee keeps you in the company's computer until they locate work for you. When a job offer is made and accepted, a placement fee of 10 percent of the first year's gross salary becomes due. The fee is sometimes paid by the pilot, sometimes by the employer, or sometimes split between the two. Unlike Turner, some other companies charge an annual fee to maintain you in their databank, whether they find you a job or not. Watch out for those organizations. If you choose, Turner will provide a list of corporations and contact names, by state, who employ pilots, and you can provide some of the footwork yourself. Contact the Turner Group at 313-726-6026.

If you consider hiring someone to help you with some of the work toward landing that corporate or airline flying job—nationwide or possibly even interna-tionally—consider a company like Atlanta, Georgia-based FAPA. While not the only aviation employment company, FAPA is certainly the most well-known to pi-lots. FAPA is an organization devoted to providing precise and timely information about employment opportunities for pilots. They use a number of products to per-form their service for pilots. The services are offered at various levels to allow the pilots to decide what their budget will allow.

Fig. 3-9. Some search firms only look for corporate flying jobs.

FAPA offers *CAREER PILOT* magazine (mentioned earlier) as well as a monthly *Pilot Job Report*. The monthly job report offers past, present, and possible future hiring data on all airlines in the United States, as well as some non-U.S. airlines and even helicopter operators. Corporate as well as airline employer names and addresses are included in the comprehensive *FAPA Directory of Employers*. The directory is supplemented by the annual *Pilot Salary Survey*, which informs a potential employee about starting and top-end pay, as well as all the rates in between for each airline.

Corporate pilot salaries are organized with a low to high range according to the type of aircraft. FAPA also offers the Aviation Job Bank for additional employment opportunities. To give you an idea of what to expect, the organization's Career Center will prep you, through their live telephone counseling, for an airline interview. They can offer sample interview questions about a specific carrier that could make the entire interview flow more smoothly. The reason FAPA has so much up-to-date information on hiring is the unique feedback system the company employs. They talk to their members after they've interviewed with a company as well as after they complete training, so FAPA often knows what's happening at a company before that company's line pilots do.

FAPA also provides a superb resumé service. Send them a copy of your current resumé and FAPA will help you put it into the best format possible for the job you seek. The cost of a FAPA membership is determined by the level of service you request. A subscription to *CAREER PILOT* costs $39 per year, while other levels, beginning with Bronze Service, begin at $108 per year and rise to the Platinum Service at $362. Bronze service includes the magazine and the *Pilot Job Report*. Platinum service includes all the FAPA services for one year. Contact FAPA at 800-JET-JOBS. FAPA can also be found in the Aviation Special Interest Group (AVSIG) on CompuServe. FAPA holds Career Day and Job Fair seminars in various locations around the country during the year, too.

4

Where are the jobs?

I'VE TALKED ABOUT PLACES TO TRAIN and some sources to help you find a job, but I believe a dash of realism is necessary. The number of jobs open to low-time pilots is somewhat restricted, but they do exist. However, I want you to be certain that you understand this logged-hour question because low-time is really a relative term. For this chapter, my definition of low time is a pilot with less than 1,000 hours, possibly less than 500.

Certainly a factor in looking for a flying job, any kind of flying job, is letting as many people as possible know that you're looking for work. I'd make sure to use the word-of-mouth method in addition to the other methods I speak of in this book. Many, many jobs are found by putting the word out to your friends. This can effectively multiply your own job search efforts many times. You just never know when a friend might run into someone else who has an opening.

THE RESUMÉ

But, before you begin looking for any of the flying jobs I talk about from this point on, you'll need something to announce yourself as a professional pilot in search of work. You'll need a resumé, in addition to a snappy cover letter that's specifically tailored to the company you're applying to. The thought of putting together a resumé makes some pilots cringe, but you might just as well become used to it if you intend to remain in the aviation profession, or just about any other.

I'm not going to sit here and give you all the resumé format details because they can be different, depending on who you're applying to, and there are people who can do a much better job at it than I can. While there are a number of excellent books on resumés currently available in your local bookstore, I would be careful of them. They aren't normally designed for pilots, who often have some unique talents that don't always fit into a standard resumé format. FAPA and a few other organizations run pretty nice resumé services. FAPA has already written an entire book on the subject, which includes samples of cover letters and resumés for you to use as guides.

At the very least, ask your other pilot friends for a copy of their resumés for you to study. Try to decide what you like best about their resumés as well as what you dislike about them. Remember, this is not just flying airplanes; this is business, so you must be ready to put on your business hat to win a job.

First, make certain your resumé is neat. If you don't own a computer/word processor yourself, find a word-processing or resumé service and have them type your resumé. Then, every time you need a few copies or need to make some changes to your resumé, the process is relatively simple. Your resumé is often the first glimpse of your personality displayed to a potential employer. Make sure they see a nice, fresh copy of a logically organized resumé. Every time you send an update letter about a job, I would include a fresh resumé too, unless the company has specifically asked you not to. United Airlines and American Airlines both use computerized forms for updates to your application, for instance. Changes to your flight time or qualifications must appear on their forms. If the changes are sent on a standard resumé, they'll see only the trash bin.

ROTARY WING FLYING

A source of jobs for pilots certainly is available in helicopter flying, but, although the requirements I spoke of in chapter 1 seem to indicate a similar kind of certificate, the difference between flying a helicopter and flying an airplane are rather substantial.

Here's a short and simple ground school in helicopters. Right from the beginning, as you look at the cockpit of a typical helicopter (Fig. 4-1) you'll notice that the pilot sits on the right rather than the left. Inside too, you'll notice a control stick (called a *cyclic*) instead of the control wheel found in most airplanes. Also, there's no conventional airplane-type throttle bulging out from the instrument panel. Engine power is varied through the use of the twist throttle (much like a motorcycle's) located on the collective bar. Pulling the bar is what changes the pitch of the rotor blade, the item on a helicopter that gives the machine its lift. Although the pedals on the floor look much like rudder controls, they actually vary the torque on the smaller tail rotor. Without this, the torque from the main rotor would spin the helicopter's fuselage like a top.

Like airplanes, rotorcraft pop up in many different kinds of flying work, such as commercial, military, and corporate. While certainly available to transport passengers like an airplane, a helicopter's unique ability to fly slowly and take off and land in a vertical manner, if necessary, opens a wide range of work that would be impossible in an airplane.

Helicopters are in constant use as aerial ambulances and flying paramedical units because they can fly right to the scene of an accident and treat as well as transport patients, if necessary. Copters are also used in pipeline and powerline patrol because of their ability to fly slowly, under complete control. Helicopters are also seen these days with flying traffic reporters and TV station camera platforms. Many scenes from hit movies and television series are shot out the door of a helicopter, too. Helicopters are also the vehicles that efficiently transfer personnel and

Fig. 4-1. Typical helicopter cockpit.

goods to and from offshore oil rigs. Fire fighting and wildlife management are two more areas where helicopters are often used.

If you decide that helicopters might be for you, many of the same techniques for finding a training school and a job (discussed in other parts of the book) pertain just as well to helicopters. But you must realize that the number of helicopter jobs is considerably less than in airplanes. The reason is simple. According to the AOPA's most recent "Aviation Statistics," of the approximately 205,000 aircraft flying the United States, only 6,300 are helicopters. The sale of new helicopters, however, does represent more than 26 percent of new aircraft sales in the United States. Of the total of 692,095 U.S. pilots, only 32,605 hold a rotorcraft-helicopter certificate. A fine source of companies that use helicopter pilots is the "Helicopter Annual" to members of the Helicopter Association International. Contact them at 1619 Duke St., Alexandria, VA 22314-3439 or 703-683-4646.

Many helicopter pilots are dual rated, with the ability to pilot both helicopters and airplanes, which, in today's tight job market, could only be an advantage. A helo pilot is also able to take advantage of some of the same types of realistic simulator training that's provided to fixed-wing counterparts.

Want to build your total helicopter time? Why not try the same method mentioned in chapter 3 for an airplane purchase, but buy a small, used helicopter or perhaps even build one of the kits currently on the market? The place to search would be in the want ads of *Trade-a-Plane* or *General Aviation News & Flyer*. If you try to build your total time simply by renting a helicopter, be prepared for a pretty stiff price tag. The average helicopter will rent for anywhere between two and three times per-hour what an airplane does. An ad I found while reading *General Aviation News & Flyer* mentioned a company called Caprock Helicopters, located in Lubbock, Texas. They advertise rates as low as $80 per hour, with Part 61 instructors available. Check them out at 806-789-8127.

CERTIFIED FLIGHT INSTRUCTOR (CFI)

If you considered the plan I offered earlier, you might already have your CFI rating. If you've not yet earned yours, you might want to give the idea some thought. With a CFI certificate, you'll be eligible to approach a flight school about a position. I would begin by calling the local flight schools in your area and simply asking for the chief flight instructor. Ask for a few minutes of their time or possibly set up an appointment to stop in and visit. It won't be a secret that you're a low-time pilot because the vast majority of new flight instructors are. Actually, many flight schools see this as a benefit. New flight instructors will not only have a great deal more enthusiasm for the job, but will also be much more familiar with the subject matter because they just completed the courses. Again, I would always try some local schools first. If the school is not interested in a new full-time instructor, ask if they'll consider you for a part-time teaching job. If you really want the job, I would try just about anything to reiterate your desire to work to the people who own the FBO. The worst they can say is no. And at that, the no means no just for right now. Try them again in a month.

If the local flight schools don't prove fruitful, you need to decide whether an out-of-town position is a consideration. In aviation, I've found that the best jobs always seem to be somewhere other than where I live. For awhile, I was lucky enough to work for an airline based where I lived. Unfortunately, the airline eventually went bankrupt and I was faced with a major decision . . . to move or not to move. I decided not to move and, a year later, I was forced to change my mind. Certainly you could sit around and wait for a position to open up at your local flight school, or you could just bite the bullet and start looking elsewhere (Fig. 4-2).

One method you could use would be to pick up a copy of *Flight Training* magazine's (see chapter 3) annual directory of flight schools. While the list is primarily designed as a guide for students seeking flight schools for their own training, it only makes sense that these schools need instructors. There always seems to be a turnover in flight schools as pilots move on to bigger and better things, so the job is to locate the school that needs another CFI. The school directory is broken down by states, so if your sights are set on Florida, there are 80 schools to try. If Colorado is more to your liking, the number is less, but still a hefty 25. The directory also includes full addresses and phone numbers to ease your job search, so tell the printer to run off a few dozen more resumés, put some money in the kitty to pay for the higher telephone bill this month, and get started.

Fig. 4-2. Sources of aviation work can be found in many locations.

A CFI'S JOB IS AN IMPORTANT ONE

On the first day of work as a CFI, you could easily be saddled with three new primary students and a commercial one as well. Obviously, the job is to prepare these students for their ratings, but there's certainly more to your job than that. No one should begin instructing without being aware of the awesome responsibility they hold. Because of you, or in spite of you, a student will eventually take to the skies alone, based on what you've taught them. Teach them well. Make certain your student's brain contains the knowledge they need to keep them out of trouble. Think about them before you send them up solo. Can this student handle an engine failure? How about 360s on downwind from the tower? A good crosswind that suddenly appeared from nowhere? You are your students' role model when it comes to airplanes. You can make or break a career with your attitude and your style.

I've never told this story to a soul because I was too embarrassed, but many years ago I wanted to be an airline pilot and attended a large state university with a flight school program to begin the work to make my dreams come true. I was 17 years old. Perhaps you'll keep this story in mind as you start off on your adventures as a flight instructor.

My flight instructor was a young man of only about 22, but he obviously knew a great deal more about flying than I did, so I settled myself down to learn. Dick was what they called a screamer in the military. (No, I didn't change his name. Perhaps he'll read this someday and realize what an idiot he was.) He didn't teach by presenting and reinforcing; he taught by yelling until students either really understood or were intimidated enough to say they understood. In the airplane, a 7FC Tri-Champ with one seat in front and one in back, Dick taught the practical portion of flying the same way. He yelled! Even worse, however, in the cockpit, Dick would hit me from behind if I didn't perform correctly. I still remember my first landing with him; it's like it was yesterday instead of 25 years ago. On final, I guided the aircraft fairly well, but he screamed at me the last few feet, "Flare . . . Flare . . . Flare!" Wham! We hit the runway. He just kept yelling flare on final, but he'd never bothered to tell me what a flare was. The man was a class A jerk. Unfortunately, at 17 years old, I could only cope with this for a short period of time. I finally left school, convinced that I was an idiot. I didn't fly again for five years.

You heard about the bad instructor. Here's how another instructor saved a career that had not yet begun. As a sergeant in the U.S. Air Force, I was assigned to a Texas air force base that just happened to have an aero club. At this point in time, I had not been inside a small aircraft for nearly five years. Looking back on this, it was pretty obvious to most everyone, except me, that I really did want to learn to fly . . . badly. I began hanging around the aero club but not going in. I just stood around outside, like some lonesome pup, looking at the three Piper Cherokees the club owned.

One day, an instructor happened to come out as I was walking around one of the planes. "You a pilot?" he said. "No," I said. "No, I'm not." "Sorry, you just sort of looked like a pilot." He smiled and walked away. About a week later I was back. Just snooping. The same instructor walked out of the hanger. "Boy. For a guy who isn't a pilot you sure hang around here a lot. Why don't you just join the club?" "No. I don't think I'm smart enough to do this," I said. He just stared at me for a minute. "Who told you that? Some really dumb instructor?" "Well, not exactly," I replied. "Hi," he said. "My name is Ray." I introduced myself and he told me he was about to fly the Cherokee out to check the VORs. "Want to go along?" I only waited half a second before I said yes. Ten minutes later we were climbing westward out of Austin, Texas. "Want to fly it awhile?" I took the controls and felt the airplane move to my inputs at the control wheel. I turned, I dove, I climbed and turned, and climbed again. When we landed, Ray asked me if I wanted to join the club now. I did, and I never stopped flying again. Thanks, Ray, wherever you are. You saved a flying soul that was almost lost.

Good teachers not only teach; they influence lives. Use your power wisely.

TIME BUILDERS

Once you have your certificates, don't be terribly surprised if some potential employer checks out your logbook and says, "Thanks. But call us when you have a little more time." For the most part, I can guarantee you that this is going to happen. Plan to grin and bear it, but take a look around for some of the flying jobs that perhaps aren't as glamorous as you might think at first. Let me share a bit of personal experience with you on a couple of the ways that I built quite a bit of my time over the years.

Ferrying aircraft

The first method is by ferrying aircraft, and the second is by towing banners. I still ferry airplanes around the United States. These very words are being written from a splendid Florida hotel where I've arrived after bringing one twin-engine aircraft down to trade it for another to take me back to Chicago.

Ferrying airplanes began for me about 15 years ago, just after I'd received my flight instructor rating. I didn't need the flight instructor certificate for this kind of flying, but the opportunity just happened around that time. I was instructing at an airport near Chicago, and after many months of hanging around everywhere on the airport, looking for a break, I got one. At the airport restaurant one afternoon, another pilot pal of mine introduced me to a young lady who just happened to run an aircraft rental firm (that, unfortunately, has long since gone out of business). During lunch, I mentioned that I had recently picked up my CFI and hoped for a professional pilot's job someday if I ever got lucky and could make the flight time requirements. She looked over at me very casually and said, "I need someone to ferry some airplanes around for our company. Would you be interested?" I almost choked on my lunch!

The first airplane I flew was a Piper Arrow. I think I must have had all of about 10 or 15 hours of retractable gear time, but they didn't seem to mind. I flew to St. Petersburg, Florida, on the airlines, got a checkout and made my plans for the trip back to Chicago. The experience was valuable. Not being too weather smart about Florida, I didn't know that leaving Florida in the middle of a hot summer afternoon was not the greatest of decisions, but I checked weather and left anyway . . . VFR, because the airplane had only one VHF radio and an ADF.

I spent the next three or four hours dodging showers, thunderstorms, and ever poorer visibility. By the time I reached the Atlanta area, the weather was terrible and I finally managed to land at Charlie Brown airport, thanks to a radar steer from a kind Atlanta Approach controller. I landed just in time to learn that the field had gone IFR in rain and approaching thunderstorms. The next morning the field was clear, with two miles visibility and fog, so I asked for and received a special VFR clearance from the tower and departed northwest bound. Once clear of the Atlanta TCA, I called Atlanta Center for VFR advisories. The rest of the trip offered me the chance to talk to more towers and centers on the rest of the trip back. All totalled, I put in about 8.5 flying hours. I gained experience as well as the time, which helped to make up for the fact that the pay was pretty poor. At the time, though, I felt that the low pay was more than worth what I received.

Before that month was out, a conversation with another man gained me another ferry trip. This time I was off to Miami to bring a Cessna 150 back to Chicago. From that trip, I gained 11.5 more hours in my logbook.

What made this whole venture really great was the way it sparked my enthusiasm to find more ferry work. Now, with two long trips out of the way, I was starting to feel more confident about my abilities. I began circulating to other operators at other airports. I had some business cards printed up with my phone number on them. I added an answering machine to my phone just to make sure I didn't miss any possible trips. Another month later, I made a trip to Colorado Springs in a single-engine airplane and came back in another. I ended up flying this trip twice. One trip, I logged nearly 20 hours round trip, the next about 16. It all counted toward increasing those total hours (Figs. 4-3 and 4-4).

Fig. 4-3. A ferry pilot could fly a single engine one day and . . . a turbine aircraft the next.

Just in case you think this is all glory and fun, though, let me give you a real-life example of just how a typical ferry trip ran just recently. It began with the phone call. "Hi, Rob. It's Jan. Are you free for a two-day trip tomorrow?" There's seldom a great deal of notice in this game. "Sure," I said. "What's the trip?" "First of all," Jan said, "You're going to catch a ride with Tim in the Mooney over to Du-Page to pick up a Cessna 421. You have 421 time don't you?" She was relieved when I said yes, because I possibly could have been one of a dozen pilots she called who were either busy or not interested in the trip. "We'll want you to leave as early in the morning as possible. Actually, you'll be taking the 421 to Naples, Florida to drop off Chris, who's going to look at a Mooney. Then you'll be flying the 421 back up to St. Pete." "Sure, no problem," I said. We hung up and I called my wife to tell her what was happening.

Before the phone call was complete, my call waiting beep told me something had changed. "Hi Rob, it's Jan. Change of plans. Why don't you get here around 10 A.M.?" "Fine," I said. The next morning, all packed and ready to go for a two-day trip, I checked my bag. All my IFR charts were current. I don't carry Jepps anymore because the NOS are easier. When they expire I just buy new ones like the VFR charts. If I don't fly IFR for a month, I don't end up spending money on charts I don't use. Next item is a book. Never take ferry flights without a book. You never

Fig. 4-4. A ferry pilot could fly a single engine one day and . . . a turbine aircraft the next.

know when you'll find time to read. Finally, clothes. It's a two-day trip, but I pack for three . . . just in case.

Before I get ready to leave the house for the airport, this morning I call in. "How's the trip coming? Everything okay?" "Hang on just a minute, Rob," Jan says. "Be here around 11 A.M."

"Elevvvven . . . Ah. We're going to have a tough time getting all the way to Naples and back up to St. Pete if we don't get going 'til almost noon. I have to be back here Friday morning." "Okay," she said. I show up and we head out for the ride to DuPage to pick up the 421. After my ferry pilot pays the bill, I do a thorough preflight; this is important! Never fly a ferry flight without a thorough preflight and answering many questions about the airplane because this is where ferrying airplanes becomes serious work. You must realize that today, most ferrying work is to transfer aircraft from one place to another so they can be sold. Sometimes the aircraft will be sold before you take off; sometimes you'll be the first contact a potential buyer has with the sales company and the aircraft. Always remember that it's very much like buying a used car. Some people take meticulous care of their machinery, while others are lucky they change the oil . . . ever.

With aircraft, you take a look at the logbooks to trace the history of the machine as well as whether or not the aircraft is legally capable of IFR flight. Your duties as a pilot involve your being sure of the aircraft you fly. Don't take someone else's word for it. Check the aircraft for oil or hydraulic leaks. What shape are the tires in? How close is the aircraft to its next annual? Most sales occur as the airplane approaches the annual. The current owner might just not want the expense, but there could be more problems.

When I preflighted the 421, it looked fine, as did the logbooks. I noticed, though, that the right engine was fairly high time. It had just about reached its TBO. That was definitely something I wanted to keep an eye on, but the aircraft had passed the last annual, so it was legal to fly. After I sat down in the cockpit I took a few minutes to refamiliarize myself with the 421 cockpit before I started running the before-start checklist. When I reached engine starts, I hit the button for primer and starter, and the left prop growled for about a half turn and stopped. The battery was dead. I called for a GPU. The first GPU didn't work, so a second was brought as a replacement. Once the aircraft was started, I taxied slowly, checking ground steering and making sure that all the electrical systems were up. Remember, I still didn't know what had flattened the battery.

After a VFR takeoff (I wouldn't have left IFR with an almost-flat battery), I watched the engine gauges closely. Things looked normal during the short 15-minute flight to the next airport at DeKalb, where I arrived at about 1:30 P.M. So much for a crack-of-dawn departure! At DeKalb I waited for the other pilot, who was supposed to be there when I arrived. He wasn't. I checked weather towards Florida while I waited, and I learned that thunderstorms were building near Chattanooga and Atlanta. There had already been a few funnel clouds at St. Petersburg, thanks to a stationary front about 40 miles from there. I just shook my head and sat down to wait. If my passenger didn't show up soon, the chances of making that kind of distance would be slim, not even counting the state of the weather, which was becoming more exciting by the hour.

The problem with just waiting while the destination weather gets worse is that your anxiety level tends to rise. My passenger didn't arrive until 4 P.M., 5 P.M. Florida time. We launched by 4:20 and made it as far as Birmingham, Alabama, where we stopped for fuel and a potty break. We would have been a bit closer to south Florida if the thunderstorms had not made us deviate west. Along about Chattanooga, where the cumulo bumpus really began, I realized that the aircraft's radar was out to lunch. As I did the walk around at BHM while the fuel was being added, I found an oil leak in the right engine. Not just streaks, but a fair amount dripping off the inboard side of the cowling. It was now 8:30 P.M. Florida time, and the flight was definitely ending right here, right now, until a mechanic could check out the leak, which would not be until the next morning. Don't fool around with this kind of thing. If you're going to ferry airplanes, you must know when to cry uncle. To tell you the truth, the fact that the radar had already rolled over and died had already made the decision for me that I definitely wasn't flying after dark. There would be no way to see what was ahead unless I only tried to avoid the areas of lightning, and I'm not that brave!

The next morning, the mechanics found a loose fitting; they tightened it up and replaced some of the oil we'd lost. By 10:30 A.M., I was on my way. Notice I said I; my passenger had left. He needed to be in south Florida earlier, and he caught an airliner out, so all I needed to do was fly to St. Petersburg. That took about 2 plus 20 right up to the hangar of the waiting buyer. Of course, by this time, I was almost a day later than I had planned. Good thing I had two day's worth of clothes. The mechanics would be inspecting the aircraft before the buyer decided to buy or not and said they might be finished by noon the next day. Other commitments were now conflicting with this late time frame, and I called the sales office to let them know it could be a problem. They weren't happy about it, but it happens. These days, there are a lot of freelance ferry pilots, with very few on salary to anyone. This is a benefit to the sales company because they only pay for you when they need you, but it does sometimes cause headaches.

By the next morning, I was starting to get concerned because of my commitments. If I brought the buyer's aircraft back (a Piper Seneca) it would take seven hours from St. Pete back to Chicago, but there were a ton of thunderstorms between Florida and Illinois. The two-day trip was now in its third day, looking at a possible fourth. Luckily, the salespeople realized the dilemma before I even mentioned it again. The 421 stayed in St. Petersburg, as did the Seneca for the next pilot. I took the airlines back to Chicago and made my meeting with an hour to spare. Of course, I did manage to add almost six hours of C-421 time to my logbook.

Is ferrying airplanes for you? Well, in this little scenario I've tried to give you a look at some of the bad along with the good. Ferrying aircraft can be a great adventure and a heck of a lot of fun. I've gotten to fly many different kinds of aircraft into places I'd often only heard of. Becoming involved in this kind of word tends to have a cumulative effect, too. Once people know you're around and available for a trip, they tend to use you. More than once, I've been called by more than one firm to fly trips on the same day. Then there might be times you might not fly any for a month, so while the work can certainly be interesting at times, it definitely is not steady. A friend of mine and I both ferry for the same company, but I seem to be called more often than him. This is where being assertive helps. I call the scheduler about once a week, just to say hi. I'm convinced that's why I'm called out more often.

The pay for ferrying aircraft is hardly union scale. The pay is based pretty much on a couple of things: how badly the company needs you or an airplane somewhere else, and how good a negotiator you really are. I remember ferrying airplanes years ago for $50 a day plus expenses. Today the rates are higher, but you'll have to stand up for what you think you're worth. Just be aware that some other people might not value your services as highly as you do.

The only regrets I have are having missed some of the really great trips. Last winter, I was set for a trip from Chicago to Tacoma, Washington, in a C-172. It probably would have been about 12 or 15 flying hours, but the scenery would have been great. I was weathered out. The other trip I really wanted was ferrying a couple of C-421s from London, England across the Atlantic back to the Midwest. Stops in Iceland and Greenland and Labrador would have made for quite an adventure.

I don't think I would ever call ferrying airplanes boring, as long as you realize your limits—just how far you're willing to go in what kind of an airplane and into what kind of weather. If you ever run into a ferry job where the contractor seems to care more about his machines than about your life, there's only one solution. Run—fast!

Banner towing

Banner towing actually turned out to be more interesting than I first expected. Let me tell you how I found the job. This might have been just luck; I don't know, but as I was wandering around a local airport, I happened along on an airplane of a slightly different model than one I had once owned, a 1968 7ECA Citabria that I logged some 600 or so hours in during the few years I owned it. As I was wandering around this airport, just being generally nosy, which means looking and talking to people, I happened to see another Citabria painted in the same scheme as my old one. Because taildragger aircraft are such a rarity these days, I walked over to look at it and found the aircraft to have an unusual array of what looked like chicken wire strung beneath the aircraft from wing to wing. The tail also had some sort of unusual hardware attached near the tailwheel. As I found myself wondering what it was all for, the owner walked up and we started talking. I mentioned I had owned a similar aircraft.

He told me the hardware on the back was for the tow hooks to grab aerial banners, while the chicken wire arrangement was a night sign that from the air would look much like the moving marquee at a bank that tells you the time and temperature. The contraption that ran the night sign was a big steel box that sat between the pilot's feet and in front of the control stick. I guess the owner figured out I was okay when he heard how much taildragger time I had logged. All totaled, I probably had about 1,000 hours at that point in time. He told me he'd be looking for a new tow pilot in a month or so and to give him a call if I was interested. I must say I made a regular weekly pest of myself. I called just often enough to let him know I was interested. He finally called back to say the training would be in a week, and he asked if I could make it. I was there in a flash.

Because I already had time in the airplane, the training process was greatly reduced. The ground school lasted an hour, I think, while Barry explained the main parts of both the underwing night sign and the tow system. Considering what the job was, aerial advertising, the equipment was really quite simple. For a banner tow, the pilot connected three long lines, each with a hook on one end, to the hardware at the back of the tailwheel. The hooks as well as the rest of the rope were pulled back inside the cockpit. As the pilot needed another hook and line for a new banner, he or she simply opened the door in flight (better be buckled in), and tossed the rope and hook clear of the aircraft. It then swung free about 15 feet below and behind the plane. Each time you were through with the banner, you'd pull a lever in the cockpit, and both the banner and the rope would drop free back to the ground. Sounds easy.

If there was a tough part, it was picking up the banner, which was nothing more than a large length of a fiberglass screening with the attached letters making up the message. While the sign itself is not terribly heavy, perhaps 25 pounds total, the problem comes from the amount of drag that the aerial sign adds to the aircraft. In effect, you've added the drag of a large sail to the aircraft at just the point when you need maximum climb performance—at takeoff.

It's impossible to take off with the banner already attached because the drag would make acceleration difficult, if not impossible. The second problem with attempting takeoff with the banner already connected is the possibility of the banner catching somewhere along the runway and flipping the aircraft over. Most banner towing is performed in aircraft the size of a Citabria or a Cessna 172. I even flew a super 150 for a towing season. The super Cessna 150 runs with a 150-hp engine under the cowling.

The only option is to grab the banner from the air. This is accomplished by a relatively simple system. Two 15-foot poles are held straight up from the ground with the banner's attachment rope strung between them. The banner pilot tosses a rope and hook out of the door of the aircraft, and (with the rope and hook flying behind the tow plane) makes the approach to the banner pickup site. The site need not be an airport, and usually it's not because it could present possible conflicts with other air traffic. I towed from an empty field near a monastery (Figs. 4-5, 4-6, and 4-7).

Fig. 4-5. A good banner tow is a three-step process.

Here's the action from the cockpit of a 7KCAB Citabria tow plane. Downwind to the banner site, I'd slow to around 70 knots and toss out the rope and hook, being careful to throw it down so it wouldn't tangle on the horizontal stabilizer or

Fig. 4-6. A good banner tow is a three-step process.

Fig. 4-7. A good banner tow is a three-step process.

elevator. With the hook fully extended, I flew the aircraft maintaining at least about 70 around my pattern to be sure to keep the rope and hook away from the aircraft. The idea is to descend on base and establish yourself in level flight on about a quarter-mile final approach to the two poles. A descent on final could be fatal because your final is flown at about 20 feet off the deck. At this altitude, you need to constantly be aware of items like trees and fences sticking up from the ground. If the hook should ever catch on one of those, you're towing days will end very quickly.

Once the aircraft is stable on the final approach, the pilot adds full throttle. The idea now is to fly the aircraft as fast as possible because, once you grab the banner, the drag will just about stop the aircraft in mid air if you aren't careful. Maintain 20 feet, full throttle, as you maneuver the aircraft between the poles. At the last minute, you add just a bit of forward pressure on the elevator to bring the aircraft down to just below the tops of the poles. If you don't, the hook and rope will never drop low enough to grab the rope between the poles. As you pass between the poles, haul back on the stick to make the aircraft climb and make sure the banner doesn't get caught on something sticking up from the ground. You'll know whether or not you caught the banner because, if you did, the aircraft will feel like someone just dropped all the flaps and landing gear simultaneously. You'll feel yourself pulled forward against your shoulder harness as the aircraft decelerates.

You must immediately lower the nose of the aircraft or the airplane will quickly stall. But, if you lower the nose too much, the aircraft will never climb. On a hot day, the right speed is the one with the stall warning blowing in your ear and a positive rate of climb. Sound scary? Sometimes it is. With this kind of performance, you'd better make certain there are no obstacles near the field you tow from. Once you've grabbed the banner, you proceed to the target area and hope you've gained enough altitude to proceed with the advertising when you arrive—usually about a thousand feet AGL. If you go much higher than that, the banner will be too far away for people to read. After you spend about 30 minutes circling over a baseball game, shopping center opening, or political convention, you head back to the pickup area and descend to a safe 100 feet or so. As you fly by the ground crew, the pilot pulls a handle in the aircraft, the hook on the tail lets go, and the banner falls safely to the ground.

In case you might be wondering about the safety aspects of banner towing, I can tell you there's obviously a certain amount of danger in this work, especially if the banner doesn't release from the tow plane when it should. But if you link up with the right company, the financial rewards can make it all worthwhile. The money I made in the mid '70s as a banner tow pilot was pretty good, even then. A one-hour banner tow put about $75 in my pocket. A good weekend was the fourth of July, when I could normally bring in $500. Check into the reputation of the operator before you hire on, though, because aircraft maintenance is crucial.

Pipeline patrol

Pipeline patrol jobs are tough to locate, but they certainly can help you build time—quickly! The days are long, and the airplanes or helicopters are sometimes small (Fig. 4-8). One company I know of employed a pilot in a Mooney to begin in Minnesota on Monday and follow a natural gas pipeline (visible from above by certain markings unique to pipelines) and follow it for almost 800 miles down through Louisiana. To avoid the risk of missing something on the ground, the flying couldn't be performed at high speed, nor at high altitude. I've seen pipeline patrols that finished five states away from where they began, only to take the pilot off on some tangential course in some other direction three more states eastward.

Fig. 4-8. Helicopter on pipeline patrol.

The flying speed in the Mooney for this work was around 80 knots, so the flight took a very long time. Altitudes were often at 500 feet or even less in uncongested areas. Realize too, that pipeline or powerline patrol is not always flown in good VFR weather. One powerline pilot told me that special VFR can be a way of life for this kind of flying. It can be dangerous, but you certainly will see a great deal of the country. When the pilot in this flight finished his patrol, he'd turn around and fly the reverse track along the route to his starting point again. One of my friends found his pipeline job by word of mouth, just hanging around the airport and telling everyone he met that he was looking. You might also try calling local utilities. Their public relations departments should be able to tell you if that company uses aircraft to patrol their lines. If not, they might be able to steer you in the right direction.

Freight flying

In case you're wondering why I'm bringing up freight flying as a somewhat alternative job when everyone knows the pilots at Federal Express or UPS are flying big aircraft, DC-10s, and Boeing 747s, let me say that those jet carriers represent only a small portion of the freight carried in this country. There are literally hundreds of small charter companies flying mail and small packages or even boxes of nuts and bolts to where they need to be—usually to small towns or medium-sized cities. Often these freight routes are flown in older aircraft specifically selected for their ability to haul large amounts of cargo, but not necessarily in conditions some pilots might find ideal.

A company here in Chicago flies night freight in Beech 18s and DC-3s, both old radial engine aircraft from the era of World War II. The reason they use these aircraft is they're like flying Mack trucks. They'll fly with just about anything that can fit into the fuselage cargo doors. I recently had an old freight pilot, Mark Goldfischer (now a DC-9 first officer for an airline), tell me what he recalled about his time flying cargo.

I was employed at Zantop International for almost four years (May, '85–March '89). Believe it or not, I first learned of Zantop from an old FAPA issue, while flying canceled checks in Florida and California. Through the article, I realized that they would consider me with my 2,000 hours total at that time; I was 25. I was also parking next to Zantop at the Atlanta freight ramp most nights. Using this opportunity, I spoke to a couple of pilots, and they said to get the Flight Engineer Turboprop written out of the way, then call Zantop. I did, and I landed an interview and the Flight Engineer job on the Electra (L-188).

I spent my first year and a half flying out of Willow Run Airport in Ypsilanti, Michigan. The operation involved transporting civilian freight to most of the major cities in the United States. This was Zantop's headquarters, although, at the time, they had three Logair bases under yearly contract to the U.S. Air Force.

Zantop had a fleet of 23 Electras at the time, the largest Electra operator in the world. The Electra is a wonderful airplane from a pilot's perspective. To this day she's my favorite. Lockheed made her as strong as a workhorse, with plenty of power. I've talked to many pilots throughout this industry who have flown the L-188, and I always see a twinkle in their eye and a warm smile on their face when they think of the days when they used to pilot her around the skies. Whether flying people or boxes, she's a real treat. Zantop also operated DC8s and Convair 640s.

Flying freight takes a toll on your body and health, though. Whether you make $25,000 or $125,000, it doesn't matter; your body doesn't know the difference. I can honestly say that 50 percent of the time in the saddle, I was fatigued, and 25 percent of the time I was too tired to be flying. That was the worst part of the job. Inevitably, when your body's clock struck bedtime, it was time to go to work. Of course, I've said nothing of all the time spent eating out of machines, trying to stay awake by gulping coffee in absurd quantities, and all the other wonderful luxuries that come with the freight industry. (See Fig. 4-9, " The Sign of the Freight Dog.")

On the other hand, directly clearance to your destination, less weather to worry about, and uncluttered radio frequencies and airways are part of the good side to hauling boxes when the rest of the world is sleeping. Hotel time? Yes, plenty of it. For the most part, package pilots spend all too much time in the "pilot prisons." One year, I spent 250 out of 365 days in hotels! Ouch! Lucky for me, I didn't have a family back home.

Fig. 4-9. Freight Dogs Anonymous. Order of the Sleepless Knights.
Mark Goldfischer

Yet, through all the sham and drudgery, somehow I still managed to have a lot of fun. What do I miss the most? The guys. My fellow freight dogs.

For some reason (and I'm sure I'm not being totally impartial) freight pilots seem to have more varied and vivid personalities than their people-pushing cronies do. Freight pilots are more humble and likable as people. For some reason, their egos don't get overinflated with huge salaries and flirting flight attendants. They do their job silently and safely and go home without much ado about anything. They don't get enough credit for a job that's done as well as any passenger pilot who works for some major airline. I miss their kind.

The schedules vary, depending on your company, base, and equipment. At Zantop in Ypsilanti, I worked three to four days a week. Weekends were mostly free because most freight companies didn't move freight the whole weekend. Zantop played the game a little differently, though, because, on Saturday, they'd spend the money to commercial flight you back and out to whatever city on Monday in time for the Monday night hub. Most companies don't foot this bill. A typical show time would be 4:00 P.M. If you had to come in and go out on the same hub, that would really take the wind out of your sails. The wait time was about three hours. You could either go to the Lazy-boy lounge for sleep or to Denny's for eats. Needless to say, you get to know Denny's menu real well. And sleep was always that kind of unsatisfying, dirty sleep.

Logair was different. I spent my last year as FE in Warner Robbins, GA, flying freight for the Air Force. Schedules were a week on, and a week off. Actually, Logair was where you wanted to be. You were home almost every night.

I left for two reasons. One was, of course, to further my career at Pan Am, and two was because I had simply had enough of freight flying. It was starting to affect my health, which I couldn't accept. I would definitely recommend a freight job to build time; it's a neat side of the industry to experience and learn about. As a career? Well, for some, maybe. It's up to the person. I can only speak for myself in that it wasn't meant to be. For some, it could be very rewarding. Incidentally, my qualifications at time of hire were CFII, MEL, A&P, turboprop FE written, and a four-year B.S., Aviation Technology, from Embry Riddle.

5

The regional airlines

Regional airline aircraft

by Robert Mark
Reprinted by permission, *AIR LINE PILOT*

Now is the time to set the record straight. "Commuter" pilot is out, and "regional airline" pilot or simply "airline" pilot is definitely in. If you're flying a B-737 or an Airbus, you might wonder why anyone cares, but to a regional pilot, "commuter" pilot just doesn't tell the right story anymore (Fig. 5-1).

Fig. 5-1. New-generation regional airliner.

In years past, a commuter pilot was someone who drove little airplanes—Aztecs, Navajos, King Airs, and the like. Those eventually evolved into Metros, Dorniers, Shorts, and Beech 99s, hardly little airplanes, but still the name "commuter" pilot stuck. With that name came an impression of the pilot—someone young and inexperienced and flying little scooter airplanes. Certainly not something to encourage much respect in the major airline circles. But, as Bob Dylan once said, "The times they are a'changin'."

At the time, the norm for regionals was a loud, cramped, 19-seat turboprop. Today, only a few companies produce 19-seat airplanes. New regional aircraft appear today with glass cockpits and sophisticated flight management systems to squeeze out every ounce of bang for the buck. Even the level of regional airline cabin service is improving: On some flights, instead of packs of peanuts, meals are served. Because the vast majority of regional airlines now code-share with a major airline, the overall trend of the '90s is to provide a class of service that closely resembles that of the regional airline's major partner.

A current market forecast says, "Regional airlines are already a key element in the strategy of majors and flag carriers, and will continue to demonstrate strong growth in the long term." The forecast, recently released by Bombardier/de Havilland, also states that, "The number of seats offered by regional carriers is expected to grow at an annual average rate of 3.7 percent . . . with delivery of 7,420 aircraft in the 15- to 90-seat range . . . over the next 20 years."

Collins Avionics' Manager of Economic and Market Analysis Karl Zaeske said in the Regional Airline Association's 1991 annual report that, "Seat size, seat cost/yield economics, and better-managed airline services are creating a changing fleet structure." Zaeske believes that the most dramatic growth in new regional airline aircraft will be in the 20- to 39-seat category, with these aircraft capturing about "44 percent of the new fleet by 2001." ALPA-represented regional airlines maintain a fleet of 782 aircraft.

Along with increased seating capacity comes increased range as regionals opt for small, pure jet aircraft. Certainly a less well-publicized aspect of pure jet aircraft is curb appeal. Some passengers think a jet is safer, more comfortable, and overall, a better machine to fly on. A recent Bombardier study says that as many as 100 new city pairs might materialize from agreements between the United States and Canada, routes that would be perfectly suited for the regional jets soon to hit the market.

Business Express, a Delta Connection and an ALPA carrier, has ordered 20 BAe RJ70s, while Comair, another Delta Connection company and ALPA carrier, expects to take delivery of the first of 20 Canadair RJs in late 1992. But the new turboprop regionals soon to be showing at major airports everywhere will give the jets, and even the majors, a run for their money when it comes to treating passengers in style and safety.

Some of the new regional aircraft are brand new, while some evolved from earlier models. And some fall somewhere in between. The Saab 2000 looks like a superstretched version of the Saab 340. The Fokker 50 looks like an F-27. The Canadair RJ looks just like a stretched Challenger business jet. Yet, while these aircraft resemble earlier models, their performance places them in quite another category. The RJ seats 56. The Saab 2000's 360-knot cruise is almost 80 knots faster than the smaller Saab 340 and the fastest of the regional turboprops. The Fokker 50 slices through the sky nearly 40 knots faster than the F-27. The Dornier 328, the ATR, and the Embraer Brasilia are all new designs, while the Beech 1900D is a new version of the 1900 first introduced in 1984.

If you've flown a Boeing 737-300, a B-757, or even an Airbus, you'd feel right at home in a new-generation regional airplane. Almost every regional airliner leaving the factory these days incorporates a glass-cockpit design that brings to these aircrafts the efficiencies of advanced flight management and engine and avionics control systems, which until recently were the domain of only large air carrier aircraft.

Regional carriers operating the de Havilland of Canada Dash 8, for instance, expect to begin certification of crews to Category II standards in the near future, too. The new 35-seat Dornier 328 will use a sophisticated Honeywell SPZ-8800 integrated avionics system to give the crew a simple, yet precise, answer to whether climbing to FL 250 even with a headwind or staying low is more efficient for the best fuel burn.

This all means that much of the back-breaking work involved in regional operations, like eight or more instrument approaches a day, will be reduced. At some regional carriers today, large aircraft—like the Shorts 360, which weighs in at 26,000 pounds, or like the 46,000-pound F-27—are being hand flown on 12- to 14-hour duty days because the aircraft have no autopilot. Many of the 19-seat aircraft, such as the BAe Jetstream 31 and the Dornier 228, have the more common two VORs, an ADF, and a transponder for continuous operation. When was the last time you flew a 12-hour day by hand in a B-737?

As cruise speeds for turboprops continue to rise and as more and more jet aircraft join regional airline fleets, the typical trips that regionals fly are changing dramatically. No longer will all regional airline pilots be found banging around in the bumps and weather at 6,000 feet and 200 knots. Many regional pilots are moving into the big leagues with the aircraft they fly. But these new airplanes are going to force changes in the way people—such as airline managers, FAA officials, and fellow pilots—view regional operations.

BAe Jetstream 41

(See Fig. 5-2.) The British Aerospace Jetstream 41 that rolled out of the Prestwick, Scotland, facility in March 1991 might look very much like just a stretched version of the Jetstream 31, but it's not. One of the most obvious differences between the 31 and 41 is the two-piece windshield of the 41 and the wide scan visibility it now provides. A four- or five-tube Honeywell electronic flight instrument system (EFIS) dominates the instrument panel of the 41, while a Honeywell Primus II system controls the radios. Although the aircraft will also carry a flight data and cockpit voice recorder, the autopilot is again an option. Most North American operators are expected to order the aircraft with this option, however.

Although the cabin of the Jetstream 41 will seat as many as 30, most airlines are expected to fly the aircraft with just 29 passengers. This will allow operations

Fig. 5-2. Two Jetstream 41s.

under the less stringent Federal Aviation Regulations Part 135 (see "President's Forum," April). British Aerospace will continue producing the 19-seat Jetstream 31 even after the company begins deliveries of the first of the 114 Jetstream 41s already ordered. The aircraft should pass its FAA certification tests by fall, 1992, with deliveries to begin in mid-1993. (See Table 5-1.)

Table 5-1. Jetstream 41 specs

Max. takeoff weight	22,370 lbs
Payload	5,298 lbs
Range	600 nm
Engines	Garrett TPE-3341s @ 1,500 shp
Max. passenger load	30
Vmo	250 kts
Cost	$7.1 million

British Aerospace RJ70

(See Fig. 5-3.) A derivative of the successful BAe 146, the RJ70 is poised for a head-to-head fight with the smaller Canadair RJ. To expand service as well as gain operating experience with a jet in the regional airline marketplace, Business Ex-

Fig. 5-3. British Aerospace RJ70.

press began operating five leased BAe 146-200s while the carrier waits for its RJ70s to arrive. Air Wisconsin, WestAir, and other ALPA regional airlines have been operating BAe 146s for many years.

The RJ70 is expected to operate with essentially the same reliability as the proven BAe 146, which currently shows approximately 99 percent dispatch reliability. With five-abreast seating, the RJ70's cabin, which will seat 70 passengers, is only four inches narrower than a B-737. The RJ70 is also compatible with most airport jetways. While the early BAe 146s were equipped with standard analog flight instruments, the RJ70 will incorporate a full four- or five-tube Honeywell EFIS system designed especially for this aircraft. Full major airline cabin service will also be available.

A new two-engine version of the RJ70 is on the drawing board, too, featuring seats for 136 passengers and a fly-by-wire control system. The RJ70 is one of the largest of the regional aircraft available. (See Table 5-2.)

Table 5-2. BAe RJ70 specs

Max. takeoff weight	84,000 lbs
Payload	19,000 lbs
Range	1,135 nm
Engines	Lycoming LF 507s @ 7,000 lb thrust
Max. passenger load	70
Mmo	0.73 Mach
Cost	$19.75 million

BAe ATP

(See Fig. 5-4.) While airlines operate fewer British Aerospace ATPs than either of BAe's two other regional aircraft, the BAe ATP (for advanced turboprop) is a massive aircraft when viewed from the traditional scope of 19- to 29-seat airplanes; the ATP seats as many as 72 passengers.

Fig. 5-4. BAe-ATP.

In the United States, Air Wisconsin is the only airline operating the ATP, with 10 currently in service. They're configured for 64 passengers.

The ATP also features a Smiths' glass cockpit for the primary flight instruments system and the navigation display. The ATP operates with two Pratt & Whitney PW 126As, which produce 2,653 shaft horsepower each. Hamilton Standard division of United Technologies has designed and is manufacturing a new-generation six-blade propeller for the ATP, which gives the aircraft an extremely low operational noise level. (See Table 5-3.)

Table 5-3. BAe ATP specs

Max. takeoff weight	55,550 lbs
Payload	15,200 lbs
Range	600 nm
Engines	P&W 126As @ 2,653 shp
Max. passenger load	64
Vmo	227 kts
Cost	$13.65 million

De Havilland Dash 8

(See Fig. 5-5.) The original de Havilland of Canada Dash 8-100 first flew in 1983. It's configured for 37 to 40 passengers, but a larger model 300, arranged for 50 to 56 passengers, will soon be available. In March, 1992, de Havilland announced the launch of the Dash 8-200 model, which essentially is the airframe of the –100 model with the engines and propellers of the –300 model, giving the aircraft a 30-knot increase in speed as well as improved single-engine capabilities. A glass cockpit is the standard in new models of the series.

Fig. 5-5. De Havilland Dash 8-100.

U.S. Air Express is the largest operator of Dash 8 aircraft in the world, currently flying 43. In all, de Havilland has delivered 304 Dash 8 aircraft and has an order backlog of 80. (See Table 5-4.)

Table 5-4. Dash 8-100, –300 specs

Max. takeoff weight	41,000 lbs
Payload	11,500 lbs
Range	840 nm
Engines	P&W 120As 2,150 shp
Max. passenger load	(–100)40
	(–300)56
Vmo	271 kts
Cost	(–100)$8.6 million
	(–300)$10.5 million

Saab 2000

(See Fig. 5-6.) People fly where they're going quickly. With a 360-knot top cruise speed and a service ceiling of 31,000 feet, the Saab 2000 will accomplish that goal easily. Designed to carry 50 to 58 passengers, the 2000 will complement the 34-seat Saab 340; the company also markets to the regionals. The 2000 is outfitted with a Collins Pro Line 4 avionics system, which includes a six-tube CRT display system as well as electronic engine indication and crew alerting system (EICAS). The Saab 2000 is expected to be one of the first turboprop regional airliners certified for landings down to Cat IIIa minimums.

J. Lindahl

Fig. 5-6. Saab 2000.

Saab has delivered 266 of the smaller Saab 340s and has a backlog of more than 100 aircraft. At present, the manufacturer has nearly 200 firm orders and options for the Saab 2000. (See Table 5-5.)

Table 5-5. Saab 2000 specs

Max. takeoff weight	48,500 lbs
Payload	13,000 lbs
Range	1,200 nm
Engines	Allison GMA 2100s @ 4,152 shp
Max. passenger load	58
Vmo	360 kts
Cost	$12.85 million

Beech 1900D

(See Fig. 5-7.) The Beech 1900D is one of the last remaining 19-seat aircraft in production. The D model features a stand-up cabin of 5 feet, 11 inches tall, an unheard of height in a 19-seat aircraft. The cockpit contains a four-tube EFIS with full flight director and autopilot systems. Three different airlines have 89 of the 1900D models. The original Beech 1900 was first introduced in 1984. (See Table 5-6.)

Table 5-6. Beech 1900D specs

Max. takeoff weight	16,950 lbs
Payload	6,510 lbs
Range	700 nm
Engines	PT6A-67Ds @ 1,279 shp
Max. passenger load	19
Vmo	289 kts
Cost	unavailable

Beech Aircraft

Fig. 5-7. Beech 1900 D.

Fokker 70

(See Fig. 5-8.) With an expected delivery date of 1994, the Fokker 70 will be a 70-seat version of the new Fokker 100 twin jet currently operated by major carriers

Fig. 5-8. The Fokker 70 looks just like its slightly larger brother, the 100.

such as American and USAir. The aircraft will slide right into the regional jet competition between the Canadair RJ and the BAe RJ70. The 84,000-pound Fokker 70 will have the same cockpit arrangement as the Fokker 100. This includes a six-tube EFIS arranged in the "dark cockpit" concept based on ARINC 700 digital avionics. The Fokker 70 will be certified to Cat IIIb autoland standards. The aircraft operates with a crew of four. (See Table 5-7.)

Table 5-7. Fokker 70 specs

Max. takeoff weight	84,000 lbs
Payload	20,187 lbs
Range	1,200 nm
Engines	Rolls-Royce Tays @ 13,850 lbs thrust
Max. passenger load	70
Mmo	0.77 mach
Cost	$21.2 million

Fokker 50

The only thing the two new models of the Fokker 50 have in common with the basic 1958 model F-27 is a similar airframe shape. Throughout the airframe, the Fokker 50 makes extensive use of new plastics that are reinforced with carbon, aramid, and glass fiber. Connected to the Pratt & Whitney engines are new, six-blade composite propellers that pull the Fokker 50 along at 282 knots. With a four-tube EFIS system, the Fokker 50 can be certified to Cat II standards.

The Fokker 50 uses a unique power lever system that has no standard prop control levers inside the cockpit. Instead, like a pure jet, the cockpit has only two power levers on the pedestal. Basic changes to the propeller are made at the touch of a computer control button on the instrument panel. (See Table 5-8.)

Table 5-8. Fokker 50 specs

Max. takeoff weight	43,980 lbs
Payload	13,404 lbs
Range	723 nm
High weight version	1,827 nm
Engines	P&W 125Bs @ 2,500 shp
Max. passenger load	50/58
Vmo	282 kts
Cost	$12.5 million

Dornier 328

Until the Saab 2000 was announced, the Dornier 328 hoped to be the fastest turboprop regional airliner around. Now it's the second fastest. But at 345 knots, it's still a quick way to shuttle 30 people around by most anyone's standards. The near supercritical wing is similar to that used on many large jet aircraft. The 328 is also made from a number of composite materials to save weight and speed the construction process.

The advanced avionics of the Dornier 328 cockpit equipped with a Honeywell SPZ-8800 are what will attract pilots, though. The initial aircraft, destined for Horizon Air, will be certified with a head-up display (HUD), like that on Alaska's B-727s. With the instrument panel in the Dornier dominated by as many as five 8-by-7-inch CRTs, the cockpit of the 328 looks much like a foreign car with a clean, smooth appearance. Operators have a full range of options for the 328, including full flight management systems (FMS) and a laser inertial reference system (LIRS). To date, 146 of the 328s are currently on order or optioned. Dornier still produces the unpressurized 19-seat model 228. (See Table 5-9.)

Table 5-9. Dornier 328 specs

Max. takeoff weight	27,558 lbs
Payload	7,606 lbs
Range	700 nm
Engines	P&W PW119s @ 1,815 shp
Max. passenger load	30
Vmo	345 kts
Cost	$7.85 million

Canadair RJ

(See Fig. 5-9.) Anyone who has ever flown the corporate Canadair Challenger jet will like the 50-passenger Canadair RJ. Those who have never flown the Chal-

Fig. 5-9. Canadair RJ.

lenger will certainly like the RJ anyway. Basically a stretched version of the Challenger, the RJ competes with the BAe RJ70 and the Fokker 70. Comair, based in Cincinnati, Ohio, enters the jet age of regionals as the launch customer with 20 RJs on order. (See Table 5-10.)

Table 5-10. Canadair RJ specs

Max. takeoff weight	47,450 lbs
Payload	13,878 lbs
Range	1,435 nm
Engines	GE 34 3A-1s
Max. passenger load	50
Mmo	0.80 Mach
Cost	$16 million

ATR 42 & ATR 72

(See Fig. 5-10.) Produced in Europe by the partnership of French Aerospatiale and Italian Alenia, ATR's two models—the 56-passenger ATR 42 and the 74-passenger ATR 72—offer something for each end of the regional spectrum. Currently in operation with American Eagle's Simmons Airlines, an ALPA regional carrier,

ATR

Fig. 5-10. ATR 72 & 42.

the ATR has a cockpit that was designed with the technology that Aerospatiale used in its partnership designs on the Airbus A310.

The ATR uses composite materials extensively in the wing and propeller structures. Up front, the ATR uses a four-tube EFIS connected with a King Gold Crown III avionics package. The ATRs can be certified to Cat II standards. (See Table 5-11.)

Table 5-11. ATR 72 specs

Max. takeoff weight	47,400 lbs
Payload	15,870 lbs
Range	1,220 nm
Engines	P&W PW 124s @ 2,160 shp
Max. passenger load	74
Vmo	284 kts
Cost	$13.35 million

Embraer Brasilia (EMB-120)

Until the Saab 2000 and the Dornier 328 actually come on line, the Embraer Brasilia (EMB-120) still reigns as the fastest of the turboprop regional airliners. Capable of 300-knot airspeeds, the EMB-120 carries 30 passengers at altitudes up to 32,000 feet. The large, roomy cockpit is dominated by a standard five-tube EFIS panel and a system layout that most Brasilia pilots agree is the best training around for anyone who is planning to move up to jet aircraft. But most of all, the

EMB-120 is fast. Even down low, Brasilia pilots are used to being asked to slow down for the B-737 ahead. (See Table 5-12.)

Table 5-12. Embraer Brasilia (EMB-120) specs

Max. takeoff weight	25,353 lbs
Payload	6,700 lbs
Range	550 nm
Engines	P&W PW 118s @ 1,800 shp
Max. passenger load	30
Vmo	300 kts
Cost	$8.5 million

CODE SHARING

So now you've had the opportunity to learn a bit more about what the regionals are all about and to take a look at some of the aircraft they fly. As I write this, the major airline industry is still attempting to pull itself out of one of the worst economic times in its history. They've lost about $10 billion to date, more than all the combined profits of all the airlines, since commercial flying first evolved from the old biplane mail-carrying days. There has been one bright spot in the airline industry, however, and that's at the regional level. If you were to take a look at the financial profitability of three of the most successful airlines, you'd find one of them to be Southwest Airlines, which flies Boeing 737s. The other two, Atlanta-based Atlantic Southeast Airlines (ASA) and Cincinnati-based Comair are regional carriers. And these two regional carriers aren't just meeting their payroll, they're making money hand over fist. Another carrier on the East Coast, Atlantic Coast Airlines, is also making a tidy little profit, too, although they've not been in business as long as these other airlines. Predictions are that more and more jobs for pilots will be appearing at the regional level as major airlines change the way they do business to try to make a profit.

One major change to the airline industry has been code-sharing. In the early days of regional airlines, back when these airlines really were flying fairly small, poorly equipped aircraft, the commuters, as they were called then, became involved in agreements with major airlines in a kind of "I'll scratch your back and you scratch mine," kind of deal. The major airlines, like American, for instance, contracted with a small carrier to provide a feed from the smaller cities to American's jets at a hub location like Chicago O'Hare. It was much cheaper to run a 19-seat turboprop from Peoria to Chicago than it would have been to fly that route with one of American's DC-9s.

To make sure that the turboprop aircraft were flying as full as possible, American allowed these turboprop airlines to use American Airlines flight codes in the massive SABRE reservation system. So a travel agent could book someone through from a large city to a smaller one and fly on American all the way, or at least what the passengers thought was American Airlines all the way (Fig. 5-11). Quite a few passengers were shocked to exit a large American Airlines jet to learn that the remainder of their trip would be aboard a turboprop that only looked similar to an American Airlines aircraft.

Fig. 5-11. The interior of a regional aircraft now looks like that of a major airline aircraft.

For the airlines, at least, it seemed a match made in heaven, for awhile. With the profit margins in the airline industry being as tight as they are, some of the commuter carriers were not able to survive, and carriers like American would often awaken one morning to find out that one of their code-sharing companies had closed up shop the night before, leaving hundreds of American Airlines passengers stranded. The airline knew this couldn't continue, so American began buying the code-sharing regionals themselves. At least by owning these carriers, the airline could be certain of controlling its partner airlines.

This all might sound pretty enlightening and, indeed, you might wonder, then, why they're so successful when the other airlines are losing their shirts. The reason that some of the regionals are so successful is that their cost structure is considerably less than the major airlines. As you saw earlier, while the price of regional airliners is certainly in the millions, that's a drop in the bucket compared to $125 million price tag on a Boeing 747-400. The other major factor, besides the relatively low cost of purchasing these regional aircraft, is that the salaries paid to regional pilots is much lower than at a major airline.

The recent edition of FAPA's *Career Pilot* salary survey tells the entire story, so hold on to your hat. Some representative salaries read like this. At American Eagle carrier Simmons Airlines, a first officer will begin at $1,044 per month, based on a guarantee of 72 flight hours. A captain on the 42-passenger ATRs that Simmons flies would begin at $2,419 per month. When maximum pay for a captain is reached, when there are no longer any annual longevity raises, the annual salary in the ATR is $43,000.

Continental Express, owned by Continental Airlines organizes their pay somewhat differently. All first officers are paid the same amount, no matter which aircraft they fly, as are the captains. Other carriers normally pay more money for larger aircraft. At Continental Express, a new first officer begins with the same $1,040 as the American Eagle Simmons pilot. By the second year, the pay has risen to just under $1,300 per month. A captain begins at $1,800 per month, rising to $2,040 the second year and a maximum cap of $56,640 after at least ten years on the job. Continental Express, however, expects its pilots to fly a minimum of 80 hours each month. If there's a secondary benefit to flying for Continental Express, it's a seniority number at Continental Airlines as soon as you hire on with the Express. The airline believes you'll stay with them longer if they offer you the incentive of being able to move up into the jets if you just hang around long enough. When Midway Airlines and Pan American were still in business, they too had a similar arrangement with their wholly owned regional carriers.

Finally, let's take a look at USAir Express, most of which, but not all, are wholly owned by USAir. At USAir Express Henson Airlines (recently renamed Piedmont), a first officer begins at $1,607 each month based on an even higher 85-hour guarantee. In year two, this rises to $1,831 monthly. A Dash 8 captain is being paid $3,885 per month in year ten, and the salary caps out at $50,102 after at least ten years service. While most of the regional carriers offer some type of pass benefits in addition to standard health insurance, the retirement programs at regionals leave a great deal to be desired. Most only offer pilots the chance to participate in a 401K program, and nothing more.

REGIONAL JOBS

Earlier, I mentioned that you might have better luck hiring on with a regional than a major carrier. This is not a suggestion of the only way to win an airline job, if that's your goal, but it's certainly a method toward reaching that goal. A presidential panel that met in 1992 believed that the demand for pilots at the regionals would be up just slightly over that at the majors, about a 28 percent increase at the regionals versus a 25 percent increase at the majors by the year 2003.

Is finding a job difficult at a regional airline? As with any other job, the path to the cockpit door is similar to other flying jobs. Through some of the sources I've already mentioned, find the list of who is hiring, then begin sending in your application and updates to that application on a regular basis. I can't emphasize this enough. Merely sending in your application and waiting for the phone to ring won't get you an interview. I currently have applications on file with two regionals and two major carriers, and I make certain I update them on a regular basis, unless, of course, the airline requests something different. The folks in personnel at United seem content with an annual update. One of the regionals wants to hear from me every six months. I'm not saying you need to make a pest of yourself, but you do need to let the airline know of your continued interest. If you have a friend already working for the carrier you'd like to become employed with, ask if they'll write a letter of recommendation. I've never heard of a company yet that didn't like to see a note from one of their own employees, a known entity, talking about a potential employee. It just makes good sense. If you don't have a friend at an airline, make one. But most importantly, let the airline know you're interested.

A new form of training, totally alien to the airline industry until recently, has begun making itself felt at the regionals . . . pilots paying for their own training. In addition to changing the ground rules, this new procedure has changed the participants, because soon, only pilots with enough money to pay for training will be able to accept these jobs. Let's take a look then at some of the ups and downs of training at the regionals so you'll have a better idea of what to expect.

REGIONAL AIRLINE TRAINING GROWS UP

by Robert Mark
Reprinted by permission from *AIR LINE PILOT*

Pilot training for regional airlines is becoming more sophisticated. That's the good news. . . .

The thunder's crash was not overpowering, but it was loud enough to be heard over the whine of the large turbines that hung on each wing. The flashes of lightning around the departure corridor prompted the captain: "Tell tower we want to line up on the active to check the radar before takeoff." The first officer complied. The captain knew well the telltale signs of a passing cold front but decided the risks were acceptable for the takeoff. The gusty wind outside varied the intensity of the rain against the cockpit glass.

The captain told the first officer he was ready, and after receiving clearance, he advanced the power levers. As the heavy aircraft picked up speed, the wind rocked the aircraft about. At the first officer's VR callout, the captain pulled back on the wheel and called for gear up just as the fire warning light and bell on the left engine sparked to life. Outside, the wind seemed to blow even harder as the crew struggled to put out the fire and keep the machine in the air using the drills they'd been taught over and over.

But the lack of full climb power and near max takeoff weight, combined with the high-density altitude this night, quickly showed their effects. As the airspeed began to decay, the captain instinctively lowered the nose of the aircraft, but in vain. The airplane's left wingtip was first to make contact with the ground, lurching the aircraft violently left so quickly that the two pilots saw only a blur of lights outside before the red explosions were added to the violent rocking. In the final seconds, the crew knew that nature had won. Then everything stopped.

What happened

"Let's talk about what just happened here," the instructor said as he turned up the lights in the cockpit. The crew was still recovering from the savage, though nonfatal, crash they had just experienced. Many of you might have realized this story began in a Level C simulator. But most of you didn't know that this night, the crew training here was from a regional airline, testing the crew's skills against one of Flight Safety's EMB-120 Brasilias.

In the past five years, the level of sophistication in regional airline training has changed drastically (Fig. 5-12). Checking out in a regional airliner used to include performing a stall series in the aircraft in the middle of the night, often in actual IFR conditions. Another favorite was pulling a power lever back with the gear still in transit to simulate a V1 power failure.

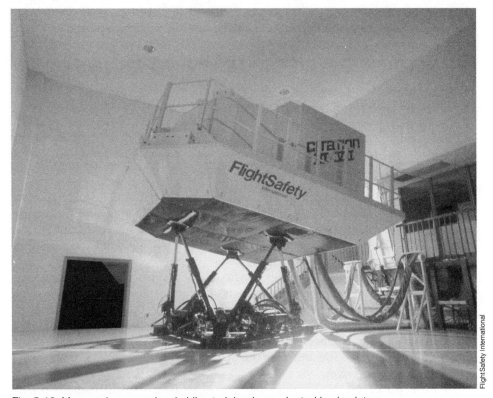

Fig. 5-12. More and more regional airline training is conducted in simulators.

For a number of reasons today, however, training at the regionals is catching up to the majors with state-of-the art full-motion simulators that allow an instructor to demonstrate a complete range of emergencies and unusual situations with no risk to the crew or aircraft. Just how dangerous training in the aircraft can be was demonstrated yet again in December, 1991, when a Business Express Beech 1900 crashed during a middle-of-the-night training flight, killing the three pilots on board. A BAe 3101 Jetstream belonging to CCAir also crashed during a training accident.

What made the Business Express crash doubly ironic, though, was that the carrier had just signed an agreement with Flight Safety International. The training organization, based at LaGuardia Airport in New York, will perform all of Business Express's turboprop crew training in simulators. Business Express recently began acquiring British Aerospace BAe-146s, training for which will be conducted at the British Aerospace Washington Dulles training center.

Another reason for a more rapid conversion to training programs like those of major airlines is a certain amount of what Flight Safety Manager of Product Marketing Bruce Landsberg calls "societal pressure." Airline passengers who fly a regional-size aircraft painted in a United, USAir, or American paint scheme usually believe that the training standards demanded of these crews are the same as those of the pilots flying the MD-80 or B-737 they just connected from. Until recently, nothing was further from the truth, because regional training standards were approached with a more hurried pace—"a rush-them-in and rush-them-out kind of training," as one pilot put it.

Previously, most regional carriers, often still called commuters, were operated under Federal Aviation Regulations (FAR) Part 135 rules that grew into "scheduled air carrier" regulations from the ranks of the on-demand charter services. As the size and capacity of aircraft grew, though, they often passed the 30-seat or 7,500-pound useful load cutoff that transformed those carriers into Part 121 operators.

Two training curriculums

This caused a great deal of turmoil because it required some airlines to provide training departments and records that could cope with the differences between the two training curriculums. Some that still flew both sizes of aircraft had to operate both programs simultaneously as a money-saving move. The FAA doesn't currently allow a Part 135 carrier to train to Part 121 credit standards because the agency believes this policy might be in conflict with the FARs themselves.

In December, 1991, the Regional Airline Association (RAA) petitioned the FAA, requesting an exemption to Part 135 to allow regional air carriers to substitute pertinent sections of Part 121 to improve quality control and cut down on duplication. In their exemption request, RAA cites the FAA's own words: "FAA recognizes that the airman and crew member training, checking, and qualification requirements of Part 121 will always meet or exceed the requirements of Part 135. This is consistent with the recognition that Part 121 affords the highest standards of safety in civil flight operations."

Elsewhere in the petition, RAA makes another significant point when it "recognizes the growth and maturing of the regional segment of the scheduled air carrier industry . . . because carriers operating under Part 135 are acquiring airplanes of increasing sophistication and are upgrading their training programs to take advantage of improvements in flight simulator capabilities and training techniques . . ." FAA is currently reviewing RAA's petition, which ALPA views as a major step forward for this segment of the industry.

Why have regional carriers waited so long to embrace simulators as the means of training their crews, even though majors have used simulators for decades? Most regional airline managers give the reason quite matter-of-factly . . . cost!

But training costs aren't always black-and-white issues. When Navajos, Metros, and Bandeirantes made up most fleets, taking the airplane off line at night and sending an instructor and a couple of trainee pilots out to fly when the airplane would otherwise have been sitting on the ground made good dollars and sense.

Training in aircraft

One of the problems inherent in late-night training is that the aircraft to be used for training would often end up at an outstation late at night, requiring the training crews to position themselves away from base awaiting the airplane's arrival, often a large time waster.

The training sessions were seldom good learning situations because they were conducted in the middle of the night, when most people's brains are in the sleep mode. If the training crews broke something on the airplane during the night, that aircraft would often be unavailable for the first flight in the morning from that station, causing untold conflicts back at the hub. Then, too, maintenance would sometimes take a back seat to the need to upgrade a first officer or two.

Consider the overall quality of training. Simulating a good engine failure is pretty tough when the student sees the instructor reaching up to pull a power lever back, even if the movement is covered up with a piece of cardboard. When the instructor, trying to simulate a fire about to eat a wing, reaches over to hit the fire warning test circuit, the student knows deep inside that it's only pretend.

In fact, most aviation training experts believe that only about 25 percent of the emergencies and unusual situations can be simulated in the aircraft itself. Before the simulator, many other kinds of aircraft problems were only talked about.

Finally, as if all these other items were not enough, the strength of the cost-effectiveness argument truly loses its impact in the safety aspect. How does an airline determine the cost of the lives of an instructor and two or three pilots, not to mention the loss of just one aircraft while training?

Some airlines saw simulator training as relatively inefficient, though. One carrier was giving its new first officers 10 hours in the simulator and another 5 to 10 hours in the aircraft before they took their Part 135 second-in-command (SIC) ride. The company subsequently learned it could train new first officers to take the ride in the same 5 to 10 hours in the aircraft and save the cost of the simulator entirely.

To bean counters, the elimination of the simulator would seem to be an easy place to cut costs, but doing so certainly raises the question of quality. A pilot simply will not emerge as proficient after 10 hours of training as he or she will after 20 hours. The question then becomes, "Are companies trying to install competent first officers in the right seat, or merely training pilots to pass a check ride?"

Today, more and more airlines are training their crews to proficiency—until their knowledge of the concept has set in—whatever reasonable amount of time that takes. Another problem with the old-style cram method is that even if you can force-feed the pilots' brains to pass the test, their grasp of the material two weeks after the ride is minimal. This is fine when you're a cook and can open a book if you need to, but deadly when the right prop overspeeds in an airplane.

Simulators' cost effectiveness

British Aerospace Manager of Marketing and Business Development William Grayson outlines one of the best economic as well as safety reasons for carriers to train in simulators. "When training in an aircraft, only one pilot at a time receives credit. In a simulator, both pilots train as an effective team and receive credit for the same flight. So really, the aircraft would have to be twice as cheap to operate as a simulator" to be truly cost effective.

Although some carriers are still sending first officers to one class and captains to another, the ability to train in a true crew concept is a benefit that shouldn't be minimized. With a simulator, regional crews can now learn flying and nonflying pilot duties the way they would actually happen in the aircraft on the line.

While the cost of a regional airline simulator is about $10 million, a few of the regional's major airline code-sharing partners view the cost as worthwhile. USAir purchased a Dash 8 simulator that's being installed at its Charlotte, N.C., training facility for use in USAir Express training. AMR Corporation operates an ATR-42 simulator for Simmons Airlines pilots at American's Dallas/Fort Worth training center.

In 1978, a United Airlines DC-8 with a landing gear problem ran out of fuel and crashed near Portland, Oregon. United management decided this would never happen again, "at any cost." The cockpit resource management (CRM) program was the result. While this program has been a part of major airline training for years, it's only just beginning to make its way into the regional airline system. Both Comair, a Delta Connection carrier, and Henson, a USAir Express carrier, use CRM as a part of their regular training program.

The regionals seem to be looking at CRM and installing the program on their own timetables instead of merely reacting to an FAA mandate. Because carriers with an active CRM program have lower overall accident rates, instituting such a program should reflect positively on a carrier's insurance rates, too.

For the pilots, CRM is a win/win situation because they get specific human-factors training to help them cope more efficiently with problems on the flight deck. ALPA's chief accident investigator at Comair, Captain Mitch Serber, says, "The airline's CRM program will soon be linked with a line-oriented flight training (LOFT) program to add additional feedback to the cockpit crew training loop."

One regional airline pilot, however, calls the CRM program in the regional system merely a buzzword to keep the FAA off the carrier's back. He says the reason his carrier instituted the program was because management believed "the system is safe and the equipment is reliable, so most accidents must be caused by pilots." Other pilots said their CRM programs were sometimes no more than a short video or an even shorter speech from the chief pilot.

Outside training

Tough economic times often bring innovative new programs to an industry. One controversial program that has gained momentum recently is the management of an entire regional airline's training program by a professional training organization and not by the airline itself. A case in point is the December, 1991, Business Express agreement with FlightSafety International. Any pilot now interested in employment with Business Express is automatically referred to FlightSafety, which conducts all the initial screening of new hires. FlightSafety then determines which applicants will be referred to Business Express.

FlightSafety conducts all new-hire aircraft-specific training for Business Express, too. But the real sting in this program comes from the $8,500 bill that the applicant receives for that training. Opinions differ as to how or why a young, low-time pilot applicant would want to pay for their own training, but a leading reason seems to be that with the current supply of pilots far exceeds the demand, so an airline can pretty much call the shots: Want to fly? Pay the bill!

The strongest motivator to the airlines, though, is the cost savings, because an airline no longer needs to fuss with the paperwork or cost of running a training department. This kind of "shoe-on-the-other-foot" program also allows the airlines to recoup some of the money they had been losing over the past five to seven years when pilot after pilot left the regionals for the majors, taking their valuable training with them after a year on the line.

Another thorn in the side of experienced pilots is that even those type rated in a particular airline's equipment are tossed into the same pool with the inexperienced pilots. Experienced pilots must pay to get hired. All the airline does is sit back and look at the fully trained applicants that FlightSafety sends them. (This training procedure is sufficiently unorthodox that ALPA's president, Captain Randolph Babitt, has instructed the Association's Collective Bargaining Committee to review the pros and cons of such training and to make suitable recommendations for dealing with the issue during work-agreement bargaining sessions.)

FlightSafety conducts full-service training for four other airlines in the United States and occasional initial screening service for Atlantic Southeast Airlines (ASA).

While this program might make company accountants smile each time they look at the money they save on a class of new hires, many of the pilots we interviewed believe that the airlines that use this pay-for-training system are courting disaster. While no instances have been recorded where the quality of pilots flying the line has significantly diminished because of this kind of program, some ALPA pilots believe that day might be just around the corner. Again, this speculation is just that—a prediction of what might come to be.

"I think (the Flight Safety Program) looks good on paper," one pilot said. "These crews coming from the FlightSafety Initial Training program might really know the checklist and what to do if the antiskid fails, but these new training programs don't historically address the weakness of an aircraft. It takes an airline ground school, run by airline people, to address these kinds of things, the day-to-day problems you run into on the line—that's situational awareness. An instructor who might have come from teaching the Mooney program last week is not going to be able to teach a new-hire how to cope with an aircraft's drawbacks and how to be an airline pilot."

While many international airlines do put low-time first officers into the right seat as the FlightSafety program is doing, "Those pilots sit in a classroom with, say,

Lufthansa for two years before they jump into the airplane," one pilot said. "Then they sit in the right seat for years before they can upgrade." He emphasizes what he thinks is a potential for tragedy: "Some of these new first officers could be moving over to the left seat with some very low total times as well as experience levels."

ASA and WestAir are two carriers that eventually decided against turning their entire training departments over to FlightSafety after initial discussions. We shouldn't let the opinions of some cast aspersions on all, but we should also not let these predictions pass unconsidered.

One regional pilot sees the following scenario possibly unfolding because of what he believes is a potential conflict of interest: "Imagine an airline telling a pilot that even though that pilot paid for and passed the training, performance was marginal, but that the airline is going to give him or her a chance anyway. If the airline tells the pilots it expects them to really stay in line, this could really set the tone for how those pilots will react to a great many things in his or her future flying."

"Some examples might be the inability to say, 'No, I won't go out and fly around those areas of thunderstorms,' or 'No, I won't fly an aircraft that has not had proper maintenance.' Some of these kinds of pilots just won't have the good sense and experience to make good, sound decisions even though they technically meet the requirements. The company owns their soul, but I think having pilots that won't give them any resistance is just what these airlines want."

Because the airlines can save vast amounts of money with this kind of program, pilots are likely to see more, rather than fewer, of them. Whether the preceding predictions come to pass, however, only time will tell.

THE SCHEDULES

Flying schedules at the regionals tend to be similar to the majors, yet different. At a regional airline (Fig. 5-13), you could find yourself with only ten days off per month if you're the low person on the seniority poll. That means you're flying basically five days a week. But, I know a new Boeing 737 captain at a major airline who is only receiving 12 days off per month. What you'll find, however, is that it's not how much time off you receive, necessarily, but rather how that time is organized. If you have split days off or your trip ends late one day and begins early on another, your time off can seem even less than it really is. Asking to see a copy of a monthly bid line would not be out of line during a final interview. Depending on the carrier, and the scheduler, I have also seen regional airline schedules with lots of flexibility, sometimes offering many lines of 14, 15, and 16 days off each month.

The rules of the game are different at different airlines too, depending on what set of FARs they operate under. Some regional airlines that fly aircraft with less than 30 seats are allowed to operate under FAR Part 135. More than 29 seats, and the airline becomes a Part 121 carrier, which is basically the same as the major airlines operate with. The training regulations are slightly different, as are the flight time and duty times between the two sets of regulations. Most regional carriers don't have duty or trip rigs. (We'll talk more about those in the next chapter.)

Robert Mark

Fig. 5-13. AMR Eagle ATR 42.

SENIORITY

A constant subject at any flight department, be it corporate or airline, is seniority. Basically, seniority is based on who showed up first at a corporation because the number of pilots they often hire are small at any one time. At an airline, your seniority is not just an important thing. As one pilot said recently, "Seniority is the only thing." Your seniority at a carrier will determine which aircraft you fly, what schedules you can obtain, when you can upgrade to captain, even when you can take your vacation.

Seniority numbers at an airline are usually established during initial training. The oldest member of the class is normally assigned the lowest seniority number. Some airlines today are choosing seniority numbers by a lottery system within the class, too. The seniority system is quite easy to understand. When two pilots bid the same schedule, the pilot with the lowest seniority number is the winner. If a new hire class is assigned different aircraft, the more sophisticated will usually be assigned to new hires with the lowest class seniority. If a pilot wants to live in a particular domicile city and he or she has a lower seniority number than you, you'll be stuck in a city that's not your first choice until your seniority number is low enough to be able to hold that city. Just in case you were wondering, your seniority number does change with your company longevity. Each time a senior pilot leaves the company, a new pilot beneath him on the seniority list moves ahead to take over the old number. If you're given the option in a hiring situation of a later class date, but the aircraft you want, I'd take the earlier class date. Remember, seniority is everything.

I spent three years of my flying life at a regional carrier (Fig. 5-14), and, for the most part, I enjoyed it. There's no doubt that the days are sometimes long and the pay could certainly be better, but the people were great. At an airline like United, where seniority numbers are currently near 10,000, knowing the people—other than the immediate ones you work with—is often impossible.

Al Statts

Fig. 5-14. Saab 340B Business Express.

6

The majors

IT SEEMS THAT, IN THE WORLD OF AVIATION, if you tell people you fly for a living, they always assume that you fly for a major airline. Let's take a look at this segment of the flying world and see just what it contains that seems to make so many people want to work there. First of all, realize that no matter what other pilots might say, the size of the aircraft they fly is important to them. All of us pilots have big egos. It just seems to come with the territory. But, what you'll find is that flying the biggest aircraft might not always be the best for you.

Earlier, I spoke of the currently sad, but slowly improving, state of the airline industry in this country. While airline bankruptcies seem to have stopped, for awhile at least, we've lost some major players like Midway, Pan Am, Braniff, Eastern, and others. Besides those that have disappeared, others have cut back. As I write this in mid-1993, Northwest, TWA, America West and USAir have pilots on furlough. Delta and American plan to lay off pilots this summer. Northwest Airlines is on the verge of bankruptcy, while America West and TWA are already in bankruptcy. Continental Airlines just recently emerged from chapter 11.

So why all the blue news? Not to make you decide not to fly for the majors, but to make you aware that flying for the airlines, any airlines, is a game whose rules have changed over the years, as have the rules of corporate America in general. Or have they really? Twenty years ago, you considered yourself fairly safe if you managed employment with a United, an American, or a Delta Airlines, but, actually, there were layoffs years ago. A friend who is now a captain for one of the top three major carriers was furloughed two different times in his first eight years with the airline; the first happened the day he left B-727 class.

Take a look at the historical hiring chart (Fig. 6-1A). The airline business is full of ups and downs. The pilot who is successful will be the one who learns how to roll with the punches. Sure, hiring is tough right now. It will get better, but you might have to wait awhile. Look at the next chart of retirements (Fig 6-1B). Where do you think the new pilots are going to come from? So be patient in your job search. Don't become frustrated if the best airline job in the world doesn't hit you right away, because I'm telling you right now it most likely will not.

Jet airplane pilot hiring by year
1975-1992

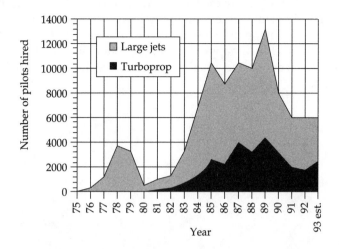

Major airline pilot retirements
(Age 60)
1990-2010

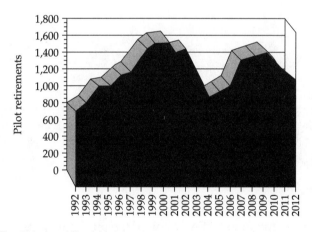

Fig. 6-1. Jet airline hiring by year.

FAPA

GETTING ORGANIZED

Back to some of the same methods we used earlier for locating the airlines that are hiring. An important point is to be certain that you meet the minimum requirements for the airline you approach. It's a waste of everyone's time to shuffle the paperwork off to Southwest Airlines if you don't hold a type rating in the Boeing

737 (Fig. 6-2) because, no matter how great a pilot you are, you aren't going to get the interview. Southwest also requires at least 1,000 hours TURBINE PIC time. If you don't have that, don't chase them. Try something else. At United, for instance, the total time requirements are considerably less, about 350 hours total time. At United, they just don't happen to believe in the total-time god that so many other airlines have faith in. United happens to believe that there are other means available for the airline to determine whether or not you're the best possible candidate for their cockpit.

Fig. 6-2. Boeing 737.

While a subscription to FAPA or any of the other publications can be a valuable asset, these services aren't necessary to learn the basic information about an airline, although they can provide that to you at a cost we've already discussed. If you decide to research this information on your own, you'll need to write letters, but that can save you quite a few dollars. I would suggest that, before you even begin looking for that major airline job, you spend a little time getting your paperwork in order.

A few simple steps could save you a great deal of work and frustration later. First decide, by whatever means you choose, which airlines you intend to concentrate on. You might be tempted to say "any" at this point, but I caution you against that. Take the time to read about the different airlines before you apply. I've already pointed out that the financial state of some of the three majors is not too good right now. Perhaps you should set your sights somewhere else, or perhaps on some airline in addition to the big three. But without some organized plan to approach these carriers, or any other flying job, the work will become three times as tough.

First, pick up a box of manila pocket folders, the ones that are open at the top, with closed sides. Label one folder for each of the airlines where you intend to apply. Find a location in your home where the dog won't chew on them or the kids won't try to use them for coloring books. From this moment on, every piece of information you collect about this airline should be stored in this folder. If it fills up, that's a good sign. Start another folder, a part two to continue the process. Record the date of every letter or update you send out, as well as the response, or lack of it. Look through all the folders at least once a month to make sure you haven't missed an update that was required or to learn whether or not a follow-up letter was ever answered. Then, if you're offered an interview, you'll have a veritable wealth of information on the airline to look over before you go in. Regularly scanning your files is going to be work, but the organization will give you a monthly update on just where some of the opportunities might be appearing.

THE PSYCHOLOGICAL EXAMS

If you haven't heard of the MMPI, the Minnesota Multiphasic Personality Inventory, hold on to your hats. This is one of the more common evaluations given to pilot applicants during some airline interviews. I took one at a major carrier a few years back. This test contains about 500 multiple-choice and true-false questions. It's designed to tap into many different aspects of your personality as well as determine how truthful a person is. With this exam, there are so many questions that it's virtually impossible to beat it. Most people try to outsmart the exam and make themselves look worse in the end. The exam also revisits the same question more than once to learn whether you're consistent with your answers. An example of a question is "I never lie." True or False. If you answer true, most people would find that pretty hard to believe. If that's true, then say true, but realize that the question will appear again worded slightly differently. Conflicts in these answers help give an overall picture of your personality to the airline to assist them in their evaluation of you as a pilot candidate. Seldom would any airline make a hire or not-to-hire decision based solely on the MMPI profile results. This section is designed only to tell you that tests like the MMPI exist, and you can't study for them. But the good news is you can't fail the computer-scored test either. More good news is that not every airline requires these exams.

THE INTERVIEW

I'm going to make this section short because I think there are so many variables in the interview process, depending on which airline you interview with, that trying to handle each on a case-by-case basis would be inefficient as well as possibly old news by the time you read this. One of the generalities that applies to most all the carriers, however, is that virtually none of them will hire you with simply one interview. One midwestern airline brings you back for as many as four interviews, while United, for instance, now believes that they have candidates pretty much figured out in two interviews. There's just no hard-and-fast rule here. Some airlines treat you as total professionals and won't even ask you to take a written exam, while some others, I've learned, practically make you crawl on your belly like a snake from one phase to the next. One airline is known for asking extremely personal questions about you and your wife or girlfriend. These questions are designed not just to gain information about you, but also to see how you react in stressful situations. One comrade of mine was asked about how long he thought it might be before his wife became pregnant, as well as whether or not they were trying to have children in earnest or not. He told me it took every ounce of his strength not to get up and walk out of the interview. The point here is be ready for anything, but try to find someone who has been through the interview process. Personally, if I didn't know anyone, I'd hang out at the terminal and ask questions of the pilots I met who worked for the carrier I was interviewing with. FAPA's preinterview counseling could also help (Fig. 6-3).

Number of airline pilots hired - 1992
total hired = 4,238

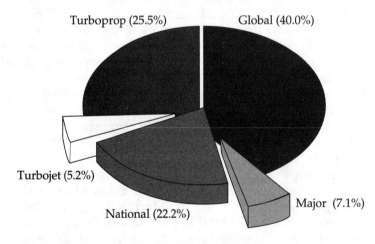

Fig. 6-3. Number of airline pilots hired in 1992. FAPA

Let's get to the main point of any airline interview. I tell you this based on the ones I've been involved with as well as those that pilots I've interviewed have related. The most important part of the interview is your attitude. One midwest carrier says there's not much an applicant can do to study for the interviews, so, "We just tell the applicants to be themselves." The most important part (other than doing some homework on the airline itself, either through recent research or by using the information you've gained and stored in your folder on the carrier) is to convey the idea that you're committed to working at that airline. No one is telling you to bounce off the walls when you arrive for the interview, but you must convince the airline that you want the job.

SIMULATOR CHECKS

When you arrive for the interview at some airlines, you'll be expected to fly a simulator and demonstrate your skills as a pilot. All airlines, however, don't require a simulator check, although many regional carriers will. Corporations will not normally have a simulator on premises to be able to test your skills. Never arrive at a simulator check cold, with no recent IFR training. Unless you're a real ace, the chances of getting through the test are slim. Here are some other facts to consider because good instrument skills are what produce a good simulator session (Fig. 6-4).

Fig. 6-4. FlightSafety F-100 simulator cockpit.

The simulator check: It's not such a monster

by Robert Mark
reprinted by permission, FAPA

I arrived for my airline prehire sim check with the idea it would be flown in a Cessna Citation. I'd been flying a Piper Navajo and had never flown a pure jet, so the Citation seemed task enough. When I learned that the Citation simulator was down and I'd be flying the Boeing 707, I almost hyperventilated.

The Frasca trainer I flew before the checkride made me IFR current, but the thought of flying a 300,000-pound airplane scared me to death, especially in light of all the guys I was lined up with that were flying C-141s and C-5s. I listened carefully to the preflight briefing but couldn't think of a thing to ask before I sat down in the left seat. The instructor sat in the right seat, set the power, and raised the gear and flaps. I flew the maneuvers as best I could, but it took half the ride before I even felt a bit comfortable in the big Boeing. I practically crashed on breaking out of the 200 and a ½ weather when I overcontrolled for the centerline. At the end of the ride, the instructor said I did just fine. I departed feeling good about the ride, even though I was never hired. It wasn't until a year later that I learned that the standard exit phrase at the training center is "you did just fine."

In retrospect, I realize how ill-prepared I was for that ride. Today, I'd want as many cards stacked in my favor as possible. A copy of FAPA's *Airline Simulator Training Manual* would have helped. Besides describing the various types of maneuvers used by each airline, the manual describes flight instruments that might be unfamiliar to a pilot who's not now flying large aircraft or others like an RMI with needles, which some pilots of larger aircraft might not have used. The manual also includes pull-out picture panels of every simulator in use by the airlines today.

Next would be a phone call to FAPA's counseling center for the most up-to-date information available on what type of simulator each airline is using and, sometimes, even the simulator profile being used. Also, I might want to review the *Instrument Scan Technique and Flight Management Workbook* and the book *Maintaining Control*, both of which present time-honored techniques for successful instrument procedures. (Both books are available through STI Press, 19011 16th Ave. S., Seattle, Wash. 98198, (206) 241-1854.)

To pass a simulator ride, you should know the reason for giving you the ride in the first place. At Federal Express, Bruce Casper said, "We're trying to verify two things with the simulator ride. One is that the guy's alleged flying time is accurate. If you only look at the logbooks, they can sometimes be inaccurate or misinterpreted. The second thing we want to verify is that the pilot does have the instrument skills that should go along with that flight time." Bob Carollo, president of North American Airline Training Group, a California company that teaches prehire simulator training, expanded on that idea. "The major airlines just don't trust what they see in a logbook. They bring a guy in with all kinds of time and sometimes they just can't fly. What the airline is saying in these rides is, 'You have all this experience. Show me what you can do.'"

Brian Golden, FAPA's pilot services manager, said the airlines are looking for instrument scan, instrument knowledge and interpretation, the ability to hold altitude, airspeed and heading, and holding entry knowledge. Jim Neubauer, a B-727 check airman at UPS said, "We're trying to evaluate the applicant's . . . thinking skills too. Basic flying and thinking skills as well as situational awareness are our real clues about whether or not a pilot knows what he is doing."

Ray Brendle of Crew Pilot Training said, "The airlines are looking for instrument techniques, the rules and regulations. They really put very little emphasis on whether or not you know when to bring up the gear and flaps." Thomas Cufley,

Alaska Airlines' vice-president of flight operations, also stressed this in an article on Alaska Airlines in the February issue of *Career Pilot*. "It helps . . . to have a significant amount of current instrument time," he said. Describing a new-hire applicant he encountered from a military precision flight team, he said the pilot "wiped out" in the simulator. He pointed out that the aerobatics learned on the flight team are all done under visual flight rules. "The applicant's instrument flying skills were terrible," Cufley said.

If the airlines are evaluating your flying skills and trying to be certain you don't have any counterfeit time in your logbooks, a question arises about just how well a pilot must fly the simulator to get through the ride. Today, some airlines like America West use B-737 and even B-757 simulators for their prehire simulator rides, while United uses a generic Frasca trainer and UPS uses an AST-300 with no motion and no visual presentation at all. A pilot from the general aviation ranks might have an easy time with an AST-300, while an F-16 pilot might be snowed on that same ride. If America West's B-737 is busy, a general aviation pilot could enter into a potential nightmare in the company's glass cockpit B-757 simulator.

Bruce Casper said that Federal Express does the simulator rides in a B-727, but they've "not been made so complicated or difficult that we can't identify the skill level of the pilot. I think the Navajo pilot has just as good a chance as the guy who has been flying C-141s. I just don't see any discrimination at all because of the way that we've structured the check." Ralph Pedigo, flight manager at America West, feels the same. "They (new-hire applicants) all fly to the same standards. If the pilot has been flying 727s, he will know how to set the power. If he hasn't, we pick up on that pretty fast and our pilot in the right seat will set the power for the applicant. The guys that fly light aircraft actually do quite well, because we're looking for IFR technique and procedures. They either know it or they don't."

Carollo agrees that "they're looking for airline standards on the simulator ride. But it's the applicant's responsibility to get up to that standard. There just aren't any points for second best. Why should the airlines put passengers into an airplane with pilots they can't expect the most out of? This isn't mister-nice-guy stuff."

How valuable, then, is some simulator time before the checkride? If the applicant is not IFR current, some type of simulator training is mandatory. Brendle of Crew Pilot Training said, "Pilots coming out of small aircraft get tossed into these large simulators with all the gadgets and buttons and horns and it's dark and they're under the gun and they get pretty nervous. I've had many of them come back after the sim check and say, 'Thank God I had enough brains to get some simulator time before the checkride or I would never have gotten through.'"

Kerry Moser, a recent new hire at Federal Express and a C-141 pilot for the Air Force Reserves said, "I know a number of fighter pilots that knew enough to get some simulator training before they took their checkrides. I'd recommend it. I don't think anyone I knew went in there stone cold." Carollo said he's had students tell him they thought "it was cheating to take some simulator training before the ride. I tell them not to throw themselves into a sim ride unprepared because they're going to eat you alive. It's a common problem, though."

Of course, a pilot who's had a job flying in a lot of weather conditions or flying bank checks or cargo at night will have a lot of experience in instrument flying.

If you're one of those pilots, you might not need additional simulator training, particularly if you're interviewing at one of the airlines using the more basic trainers. But, if you know you're going into a large full-motion jet simulator and you need a little extra confidence, buying sim time might be exactly what you need. It also can help if: you're used to a full-motion simulator and you're getting checked in a nonmotion simulator (or vice versa), your instrument proficiency and/or instrument time is low, you're going to receive an unusual procedure, or you just need some extra assurance.

If you do decide to attend a simulator training course, be sure it includes a few hours with an instrument instructor reviewing the IFR system. Be certain you understand holding pattern entries and the associated airspeeds, as well as the basics of the ILS approach. And don't forget some nondirectional beacon (NDB) work too. Each applicant should have a working knowledge of the air traffic control system. No one will explain the 200-knot speed limit in an airport traffic area or beneath the floor of a terminal control area (TCA). You're expected to know. If you don't know, the ride will continue and no one will mention the violation. You'll just lose points.

Even a generic simulator like a Frasca or desktop could be a place to start brushing up on procedures. As Delta's manager of public relations, Jackie Pate said, "The simulator is only used to verify qualifications as stated on the application. We're not looking for any knowledge of a particular aircraft type." Consider too the shock of walking into the cockpit of a B-737 after just leaving a desktop simulator. Carollo summed it up best: "The airlines have really failed to address this problem. No matter how good your scan is, if you don't have a feel for how that simulator flies, you can't make it do what you want it to." Carollo said that a few hours in one of the large simulators will help a pilot at least develop a feel for the machine, and will teach some of the quirks of the machine. "Like when you bring the flaps from 15 to 25 on a 727. If you don't know that the nose is going to drop, you'll be pulling back on the wheel and watching the airspeed fall off. Now your scan picks up that and you jam some power in. So begins the roller coaster ride up and down the glideslope," he added.

The airlines consider a poor instrument scan and a shoddy knowledge of instrument techniques to be the biggest problem that most applicants face, although some mentioned problems with applicants simply not listening or not following instructions. While the depth of the applicant's IFR currency can be remedied by presim ride training, it won't turn a bad instrument pilot into a star.

When an applicant arrives for the simulator checkride, the preflight briefing usually runs from 15 to 20 minutes, during which the applicant receives either a verbal or written explanation of what the flight profile will look like. This is the time for the applicant to ask all the questions he or she wants before the ride begins. Possible questions might be about the operation of a particular instrument, or what power setting is best to hold a particular airspeed (Fig. 6-5).

At Federal Express, the simulator instructor gives the applicant "competent support during the ride," according to Casper. "If the applicant asks for anything that's reasonable in trying to accomplish the goal we had set out for the applicant, the nonflying pilot would go along with it." Kerry Moser took that ride with Fed-

Fig. 6-5. Airbus A-300.

eral Express and agreed about the low-key attitude. "I felt the instructors were there to help you pass the ride. You're given a two-minute warm-up period to explore power and pitch settings. It was sort of nice that you didn't have to jump in and just start flying." The rides at United and America West also allow a few minutes of practice before the ride begins.

At the UPS ride, however, an applicant reported it was "pretty much just read a couple of pieces of paper, hop in the seat, and start flying. There was no practice or anything first. You don't ask any questions during the ride either." The UPS ride is on a generic nonvisual, nonmotion AST-300 simulator.

America West does its rides a bit differently than the competition. Applicants go into the simulator in groups of three, so each pilot can watch the other pilots' rides. The trick here's to be the third pilot evaluated because you'd have seen two rides before yours.

Based on one applicant's recent report, the ride at United's Denver training center is in a generic Frasca simulator set up to represent a single-engine turbojet aircraft. The instrumentation includes an attitude direction indicator (ADI) and various turbine engine gauges such as percent of power. If you're unfamiliar with these, check out chapter 2 of the *Airline Simulator Training Manual*. This applicant reported he took the ride from the right seat. The other carriers put the applicant in the left seat. The United simulator frequently checks your progress against the actual profile and deducts points for any lack of precision. However, if you're off on an altitude at one point and don't correct it at the next check, the machine charges you double the points.

Some simulator rides might include an emergency situation or some other unusual incident. This is to see how the applicant handles pressure. For example, at one point during one ride, the instructor stood up and walked away from the simulator, an applicant reported. At another, a fire bell and warning light came on, and the airline expected the applicant to call for the warning to be silenced. It continued to ring and flash anyway during the remainder of that ILS, essentially serving as a distraction device. However, while these types of situations seem to crop up occasionally, most airlines seem to be moving away from them.

One Federal Express applicant reported his "ride was pretty straightforward. There were no takeoffs and landings. There were turns, descents, and climbs at various airspeeds. There were also vertical S maneuvers and 45-degree steep turns in the DC-10 I flew. I received an ATC clearance and flew to a holding fix. They watched to see if I slowed to the proper holding speed and when."

UPS check airman Jim Neubauer reported that "we do NDB tracking and NDB intercepts as well as VOR work before we end up with an ILS. It (the NDB work) gives us a look at how long it takes the pilot to analyze a problem." A recent UPS applicant reported an unusual problem given to him in written form only. It involved flying through a valley with a VOR at the opening and an NDB at another point in the same valley. The pilot can't climb the aircraft out of the valley. The pilot tracks a VOR radial into the valley toward the approaching NDB on a hill at the far end of the valley. He or she is told he may not pass over the beacon. Using VOR and DME (distance measuring equipment) the pilot must arc around the beacon until he or she can track away from the NDB on a specific magnetic bearing.

The vast majority of simulator rides run about 30 minutes and are subjectively hand graded by the individual instructors who give the rides. While some simulators produce a machine-drawn copy of the actual ride, only United seems to use a computer to constantly evaluate the ride's progress.

And what if you don't pass the simulator ride? Practically all the airlines allow the candidate to reapply. However, this usually means the applicant will undergo the entire interview process again, not just the simulator part.

The final decision on whether to pick up some simulator training before the ride rests with you, the applicant. You might find that $800 for a typical prehire simulator course is worth the cost, considering how much you've spent already to reach your goal. Or you might find that all you need is your confidence in your instrument skills, a brush-up on aircraft panels, plus a call to FAPA's information center for a briefing on the most recent simulator profile an airline has used. It's a judgment call.

THE SCHEDULES

Major airline schedules, as well as the pay, are the reasons why most people are interested in these jobs. Airline schedules can offer as little as 8 days off per month or as many as 20, depending again on the routes and the aircraft flown. Most major airlines operate under FAR Part 121, which prescribes a maximum of 100 flying hours per month for a pilot. That's the maximum a pilot may legally log during each calendar month. But before you run off to tell your friends how little time you'll have to work each month, if your salary guarantee is only based on 80 hours or so each month, realize that 100 flying hours means just that, the flying portion. Another important consideration is how many hours of duty, which includes preflight and postflight chores and sitting around between legs of a flight or around a hotel on an overnight.

In general, a pilot who flies ORD-HNL (Chicago, Honolulu, about a 16 hour round-trip flight) might only make the trip about 5 times a month before he or she will have flown up to that 80-hour guarantee (Fig. 6-6). The flight probably required a minimal amount of sitting time because, once off the ground, you fly until you land in HNL and go to the hotel for your rest period. On the return, it's basically the same thing back to ORD. Pretty cushy job, most likely flown in a Boeing 747 or DC-10, so the pay is good. Obviously, these routes are highly sought after because the time off is tops. This is where a high seniority number will be worth its weight in gold, for without it, anyone who's more senior will outbid you.

Fig. 6-6. Boeing 767-300.

A more average route might be ORD-HOU-MEM-DCA (Chicago, Houston, Memphis, Washington, D.C.) and then overnight and possibly DCA-ORD the next day. In a Boeing 737, for instance, the pilot will most likely have flown about seven hours in two days. What you might not notice at first glance, though, is that in

Houston, the crew sat for two hours before the flight to MEM, where they might sit for another hour and a half before heading to DCA. It can make for a pretty long day. You have various ways to choose your schedules each month, based on days off, maximum flying time, minimum flying, certain days off, certain bases, and so on. Today, the work of choosing your schedule with an airline, called bidding, has been significantly reduced because much of the tedious sorting work required years ago can now be accomplished with a personal computer (more in chapter 8).

DUTY AND TRIP RIGS

The major airlines, unlike the regionals, provide their pilots with pay from the moment they leave their base until the moment they return. Some regionals only pay their pilots when they fly. If they break down then or are weathered in somewhere, they don't get paid. Major airlines use two systems to assure proper pay to the crews, the *duty rig* and the *trip rig*.

The duty rig assures a pilot of a specific amount of pay for a certain amount of time on duty, regardless of how much actual flying was involved. For example, a 1:2 duty rig means: one hour of pay for each two hours on duty. If a pilot signs in for duty at 11 A.M. and flies one hour to the destination and sits for two hours before flying back home, he or she only flew two hours total. But, if the pilot signed off duty at 5 P.M. , he or she was on duty a total of six hours. But the pilot will be paid on a two-hours-duty-equals-one-hour-pay duty rig, so he or she will actually be paid for three hours.

A trip rig is similar in that it pays pilots a minimum amount for a given time away from their home base, regardless of how much flying was involved. If a trip rig were, say, 1:3, a pilot would be paid 1 hour of pay for every 3 hours away from base, regardless of the time flown.

Additionally, pilots are paid an hourly per diem allowance when they're away from base and are also eligible for various free-space-available passes on their own or other airlines.

THE BIG BUCKS

This is what everyone calls it. An airline job is where pilots believe they'll find their fortune, so let's take a quick look at some of the money involved in this end of the industry, with figures from the FAPA *Career Pilot* salary survey.

I've picked three airlines at random: Continental, an airline that recently emerged from bankruptcy; United, an airline currently encountering plenty of struggles as it marches ahead to cut costs and remain competitive; and Southwest, an airline that runs against the traditional hub-and-spoke concept of connecting passengers. Continental is nonunion; United is represented by ALPA, and Southwest is represented by the in-house Southwest Pilots Association (SWPA). (See Table 6-1.)

Table 6-1. Pilot salaries at selected airlines

Starting pay	Continental	United	Southwest
Per month	$ 1,895	$ 2,332	$ 2,742
Second year	$ 2,674	$ 3,509–$4,461	$ 4,627
Fifth year	$ 3,756	$ 6,543–$8,299	$ 6,228
Tenth year	$ 6,592	$ 11,816–$15,105	$ 10,149
Max pay as Captain—Annual	$102,835	$192,348	$130,704

A few things to keep in mind about the preceding scale. At Continental, the pay is the same regardless of which aircraft you fly. A B-747 first officer is paid the same as a B-737 first officer. At Southwest, the airline only operates one type of aircraft, the B-737. At United, the scales vary after year one, depending on which seat you sit in and in which type of aircraft. In year five, for instance, a United B-727 first officer is paid $6,543 per month, while the high end is limited to the B-747 first officers at $8,299 per month.

At the regionals, retirement plans, other than a 401K, are virtually unknown. At most of the majors, retirement is a very serious affair. The two major plans are the A-Fund, a defined benefit retirement plan and the B-Fund, a defined contribution retirement plan. The A-Fund pays a defined amount each year to the employee beginning at retirement based on the pilot's earnings. The B-Fund gives the pilot a monthly retirement sum based on money added to the account over the years by the company, the employee, and accrued interest (Fig. 6-7).

The choice of airlines is still substantial, although many of the old players of the industry—like Midway, Braniff, Eastern and Pan Am—have departed. While all of the jobs those carriers sucked from the aviation industry have not returned, there's hope on the horizon with the new start-up carriers. A recent list showed Kiwi, Family Air, Reno Air, Skybus and 17 airlines more flying aircraft like B-727s and MD-80s. And while individually these new carriers shouldn't pose a threat to the majors, recent figures indicate that the new start-ups combined might be taking as many as 25 percent of the passengers who normally fly on the majors. But, as I mentioned before, the rules have changed. Where some people were astonished at the thought of regional pilots paying for their own training, the captains at Kiwi, for instance, pay $50,000, while the first officers make a $35,000 investment in the airline as a part of the normal hiring process. Other start-up airlines are also requiring various sorts of financial concessions from pilots just to pick up the job too. Pilot pay at most of the start-ups is also considerably less than most major airlines.

Recently, I spoke with Peter Larratt, a Boeing 737-200 and 737-400 training captain for British Airways. I asked if he would recommend this career. "Yes," he said. "There are really several aspects of flying professionally that appeal to me. One is the initial challenge of flying large aircraft. Then, the challenge of managing the entire operation. Each day, a new job is started and you see the job through to

Fig. 6-7. Airbus A330.

a finish. Generally, too, you don't take the work home with you. You're essentially your own boss, even when you're a junior member of the crew." When I asked if he had any tips to pass on to future generations of pilots, Larratt said, "For the first few years, maintain a low profile and learn your trade well. You might be the best aircraft handler in the world, but that's a very small part of the job of a professional pilot. You can't teach experience."

LABOR ORGANIZATIONS

Finally, let's talk about an organization that you'll most likely encounter during your aviation career . . . unions. The airline industry is probably one of the most unionized of all industries. Corporations and their pilots tend not to be union, however, leaving negotiations for pay and benefits up to the individual pilots themselves, just as you'd expect in a regular job. Flight instructors also are seldom unionized, nor will you find unions in pipeline patrol, banner towing, or many other flying jobs. These tend not to have unions because the operations are just too small, often just a few pilots and aircraft. Regional airlines are mostly represented by unions, although there's more than one. One regional carrier is represented by the Air Line Pilots Association (ALPA), while another is represented by the Allied

Pilots Association (APA). At the majors, most pilots will be represented by ALPA, while some carriers like Southwest Airlines or United Parcel Service pilots have their own in-house unions. One noteworthy exception to ALPA representation is at American Airlines, where pilots are represented by APA. However you might feel about unions, if you remain in the aviation industry long enough, you're probably going to have to deal with one. That can bring on some interesting choices.

Pilots' unions and new-hire choices

by Robert Mark
Reprinted by permission, FAPA

When a new-hire pilot starts a job with a major, regional, or freight carrier, pilot unions are something he or she will most likely have to face. If pilots become employed at a union airline, should they join the union? Membership is not mandatory at carriers with an agency shop provision, although pilots who don't join still pay a monthly service charge to cover some of the costs of negotiating the contract. Most union pilots belong to agency shops. A few pilot groups, however, are closed shops, meaning a pilot must join the union to work at the carrier.

If a pilot does join a union, will it affect his or her career? Will management treat him or her differently? What are the benefits of membership? What are the pitfalls?

The airline business is one of the most unionized of industries. The Air Line Pilots Association (ALPA) represents more than 39,000 pilots at 33 airlines. The Allied Pilot's Association (APA) represents more than 10,000 American Airlines and American Eagle pilots. The Independent Pilot's Association (IPA) represents 1,200 United Parcel Service pilots, while the 1,127 pilots of Southwest Airlines pay their dues to the Southwest Pilot's Association (SWPA). Then there are many other pilots represented by other organizations such as the Teamsters union or by more informal in-house pilot unions or associations.

In his book *Flying the Line*, George Hopkins quotes Reuben Wagner, one of the early Boeing Air Transport organizers, about why they wanted to unionize this forerunner of United Airlines. "We all wanted to fly; we liked to fly. Everyone in those days was flying because they liked to fly, not for the money. But we thought we weren't getting what we should." Industrywide, there also was the question of safety, with some airline managements pushing pilots to fly in unsafe conditions or risk losing their jobs. In 1992, those words still ring as true as they did in 1931, except that today's pilots often place more emphasis on benefits and smaller issues other than pay alone.

Generally, most pilots view their contract as one of the main benefits of union membership because it sets in stone the day-to-day work rules that an airline and its pilots must follow, and it clearly outlines the recourse that both may exercise if the need arises. Often the contract is more detailed than a company-generated employee handbook. Each union contract also includes a specific grievance process to handle pilot complaints about the company without threatening the pilot's jobs.

Many pilots see membership in a union as an insurance policy against the unknown. At a nonunion regional last year, the company president left a pilot meeting and asked a small group of those pilots what they thought of his new pay policy. One pilot volunteered his opinion; he thought the policy was terrible. The pilot was fired three days later. Last week, the pilots of that company voted ALPA as their bargaining agent, with 82 percent of the vote.

Unions often help out their memberships in important ways. As one retired airline pilot put it, "I paid my dues to ALPA for 30 years and I never had an accident or an incident and the company never tried to get rid of me. But, if they did, ALPA would be there for me." (Fig. 6-8.) Former Midway Airlines pilot Dave Bear remembered that, "The union converted quite a few nonbeliever pilots after they were saved from an FAA violation by union attorneys."

Fig. 6-8. Northwest Airlines pilots are represented by ALPA.

However, a Continental pilot who came from a bankrupt ALPA carrier didn't see it the same way. "I was a little upset that after paying all those union dues for all those years, the only benefit ALPA gave us was a year's subscription to *AIR LINE PILOT*. After my old carrier went broke, it seemed we could never get anyone on the phone at ALPA. We had a job fair, but I really think it was just kind of a show thing. We were on the street, and all ALPA kept saying was,'We're sorry. We're sorry.' Maybe if we'd had some sort of national seniority list I would feel different, but the way it is today, I'm just not sold on ALPA. And I was ALPA a lot longer than I've been a nonunion pilot."

If there's a factor that makes a union more necessary for pilots than say, auto workers, it's the airman and medical certificates that pilots must maintain. When a violation of the Federal Air Regulations (FARs) occurs or when a pilot evolves into a possible medical problem, such as high blood pressure or alcohol abuse, you'd expect the company to protect the training investment they have in that employee. Some employers take the quickest route out of the problem by terminating the employee. The pilot unions are sometimes pilots' only means of keeping their jobs while they try to get such problems under control.

Pilot unions typically have services such as loss-of-license insurance plans, aeromedical staff members to help pilots reinstate their medical certificates, and management of pilot pension plans. Pilot unions also keep watch on potentially unsafe situations and monitor issues that could affect pilots' employment.

"The tangible benefits besides, obviously, the higher rate of pay, are better work rules," said one pilot who has worked for both union and nonunion airlines. "[His previous employer] had none. They did anything they wanted within the FARs."

Ken Cooksey, Master Executive Council Chairman of ALPA at Atlantic Southeast Airlines (ASA), an Atlanta-based regional carrier, said, "Before ALPA came on the property, we didn't have any work rules, so every time you turned around the rules had changed. There was just no stability." A pilot for now defunct Midway Airlines said that, before the union came to Midway, "there would be lots of confusion when you came in to work. The flight rules had changed, the pay rules had changed. The company would bend and mold the rules to make things work on a day-to-day basis. They would cut a corner here and another there, not always intentionally, but it did happen. There was a great deal of instability, mass confusion, and almost anarchy at times. Pilots would go out and fly angry."

Rich Murry, former MEC Chairman at Dallas, Texas-based Metro Airlines pinned it down, "Anger on the part of a pilot will really affect that pilot's performance in the cockpit," he said. "That can be truly dangerous. Look at the United strike in 1985. The bitterness between those who honored the picket lines and those who crossed still exists." Some United pilots report that, seven years later, those who were pro or con to the strike cockpit still limit their conversations only to things necessary to fly the aircraft effectively and safely. Hardly a friendly atmosphere.

When deciding to join or not to join, consider the union's leadership because that can have a dramatic effect on airline management as well as the pilot body. Consider the effects of a breakdown in communication between union and management and how it could affect pilots. Consider the cost. As the former union/nonunion pilot said, "It [a strike] breaks the cohesiveness of a company up. I think that other ALPA pilots and American pilots (represented by the Allied Pilots Association) for that matter, think that leaving the cockpit is the wrong thing to do. With the economy the way it is, there are plenty of pilots willing to [cross the line and] take your job."

If a strike does happen, its effects can be long-lasting. "I have mixed feelings because the strike at Eastern was different from the one at Continental," the pilot continued. "I think [Eastern pilots who crossed the picket line] got off easy from a treatment standpoint. I'm not extremely bitter . . . I can say I no longer socialize with anybody I did know that crossed the line."

And nonunion pilots who cross the picket lines develop their own reputations. "I think those guys are extremely greedy. I look at them as backstabbers, selfish . . . about every adjective in that area," the pilot said.

Then, new pilots will also want to consider the cost, about 2 percent of their salary. Some might find this a bit steep, but an American Eagle pilot said, "Pilots say they can't afford union dues, but most would never say they couldn't afford their health insurance. To me it's the same thing."

A five-year Continental Airlines pilot sees things a bit differently than his union brethren, however. Arriving at Continental after his ALPA carrier went out of business, this pilot saw massive changes erupt at Continental because of the exit of its highly publicized boss Frank Lorenzo. "The people here at Continental had the same image of what was happening to our airline as everyone out in the rest of the world did about Frank Lorenzo or Carl Ichan (Chairman of TWA), that they were just here to sell off every asset they could to line their own pockets and never put any money back into the company," he said. "Twenty years ago, Continental was the elite airline to work for. Now, again, it's really started getting better. Instead of the union, we have a pilot operations group that has had tremendous success in dealing with day-to-day problems. I believe the people here at Continental are motivated now. I see smiling employees now and not the bitterness I saw years ago."

Yet, a pilot from an ALPA carrier who recently visited a Continental crew room reported feeling like he had "just entered a very unhappy home." And a group of Continental pilots recently circulated cards to stimulate a representation election.

But a pilot from another nonunion airline said "There are lots of pilots who still believe unions are going to solve all their problems and get them right next to God, and that's just not going to happen. I think unions are designed to be a liaison between management and the pilots and nothing more."

While some people still believe there's only strength in large unions, if there's any strength at all, they need only look at the small but effective Southwest Pilot's Association (SWPA). All except three of Southwest's pilots are members of the union. SWPA's President, Don Brumbaugh, reports that the union materialized from a 1979 recommendation by Southwest's then vice president of flight operations, Don Ogden. "When Southwest's management runs into a problem with working conditions about pilots, they like to have input from the pilots before they try to implement a rule. They'd much rather work with us than against us," Brumbaugh said. On it's own too, SWPA has accomplished plenty for its members, such as the 401K retirement plan and a long-term disability and mutual aid pact that the union sponsors.

From a management viewpoint, Southwest's vice president of flight operations, Paul Sterbenz, said, "Generally speaking, we have a very good relationship with SWPA and the pilots themselves. Southwest is indeed fortunate to have a group of pilots who understand the airline business and are really supportive of management instead of working against them." The fact that SWPA signed a new five-year contract indicates just how much faith SWPA places in Southwest management.

But what if a pilot joins a carrier that's not union? He or she might find the work rules subject to change and the pay could be less than at a union carrier, although these things aren't concrete. Things might move along smoothly—or they might not. Or a generally happy pilot group might still think about a union because the company grows quickly, necessitating changes in which the pilots feel they have no input.

Robert Krzewinski, MEC Chairman at one of American's Eagle carriers said, "Most companies will do whatever they can to keep pilots from organizing because organized pilots have clout and power in bargaining for better working conditions." If the pilots think of organizing, they should be ready for some possible harassment by airline management. Management might tell pilots that the airline will shut down if a union comes on the property. ASA's Ken Cooksey reported "threats of doom and gloom from management" before ALPA came on the property.

Some companies deal with the specter of unionization by encouraging an in-house pilot organization that provides a dialogue between pilots and management without the "encumbrances" of a legally binding contract. Many pilots prefer such associations, and even formal in-house unions, because they allow the pilot group and management to focus on issues that are immediate to the carrier without the distraction of a national union agenda.

Horizon Air is a company that formed an informal pilot association. Dan Scott, Horizon's assistant to the vice president of flight operations, said the company established such a group to include the pilots in discussions about work rules, pay, and other topics, and especially to defuse issues while they're still small. While the group is not a formal union, it does meet twice a month, and Scott said the company finds that being open with the pilots works much better than not communicating with them. "We speak very frankly to our flight crews about operating margins, profitability, our competitors, and what portion of our operating revenues goes to salaries . . . They really know what's going on inside the company."

But, some pilots are uncertain of Horizon's in-house association, and they question its benefits to the pilots. One Horizon Air captain said, "This is the first experience I've had with something like this. I don't think [Horizon's in-house association] has evolved to where it's going to benefit the pilots. We don't have real bargaining power . . . and there are some loopholes, but once they're amended, we could have a better deal than the unions.

"I've always been antiunion . . . I'm kind of on the fence right now," the captain continued. "The pay is not the greatest, but it's in line with the industry standard at a regional airline. I can see where we need more bargaining power, but I'm impressed with the way management does business."

Yet another Horizon captain said that if a union representation vote happened there tomorrow, only "about 40 percent" would vote for a union because some pilots feel ALPA is an arrogant union . . . [they] feel it's counterproductive to have them represent us. ALPA doesn't represent the commuter industry well."

However, an in-house association might be ineffective if pilot concerns still aren't heeded by management. "Overall, I think pilots would rather work without a union, but they can see that the communication is one-way in regards to negotiations," the Horizon captain said.

This pilot also said there were rumors of cards circulating again among Horizon's pilots to produce a union vote. "The company definitely doesn't want a union," he said. "The pilots are dissatisfied with our situation right now because some of our FOs qualify for food stamps. Eighty to 90 percent of our pilots haven't had a raise in 10 years (some at the upper end of the scale received an increase a while back). It (negotiating) is going to be hard; there's an underlying cavalier-type attitude in our management."

John Bradley, ALPA's assistant director of representation, believes that a nonunion carrier is a thing of the past. He pointed out how some pilot groups find a union to be crucial when their carrier is bankrupt or the stockholders are considering selling the carrier. In both cases, the pilots still have some representation, even if it's only before the bankruptcy court. And union carriers can fail just as easily as nonunion carriers. It's the company's responsibility to run the airline, which often leaves pilots feeling helpless.

Sometimes, bringing the union on the property can actually be a benefit to the company. "Because Midway was lean in the early days," one pilot recalled, "they just didn't have the staff to cope with a lot of the problems the company faced on a day-to-day basis. What better outlet could we bring in than ALPA, who gave Midway management help with scheduling, pay, insurance, and safety-related problems." Still, such help couldn't keep the carrier operating.

Typically, a fresh-off-probation pilot makes application to his or her pilot group's union (if there is one), and there's a possibility that the local union council (at ALPA, the master executive council or MEC) could reject a pilot. Actions that could lead to rejection include previously violating "association policy," such as not paying dues at a prior airline employer, although this is not an automatic disqualifier. (This is different from not joining the union at a prior airline.) ALPA spokesman David Mallino said the union largely leaves the decision to the local MECs. He would not comment on whether another disqualifier is a pilot crossing a picket line at another carrier.

While union pilots often present a hostile attitude over the subject of "strike breakers," they might be a little more liberal toward pilots who just choose not to join the union. "I've always felt the pilot has the right to join or not," one pilot said. "I feel they should also not take a free ride. My belief is you should pay for the benefits (via a percentage fee, regardless of union membership, to cover the cost of negotiating the contract), but they have the right not to join the union."

If the pilot does decide to join, then he or she must consider how involved to get. "I think it's in their best interest to sit back and watch how a union is run—to view the good points and the bad points," the pilot continued.

IPA's President Bob Miller firmly believes that a union is not only a necessity but also a reality for the future of the airline business. "I think there are so many aspects of flying to deal with today that you need someone to act as your representative with the company. But more than that, the idea that we can stay in our own little world is just not a safe idea anymore. We have to get away from this isolationism. It doesn't do any airline union any good anymore to sit back and try to get more money and benefits when our whole world could be destroyed.

"We're going to have to take a more active role in things outside our own world such as the manipulation of airline capital. It's a big shell game. People like Frank Lorenzo are still involved in that money manipulation, except that now they're using the cover of *cabotage* (the right of foreign airline ownership and rights to fly in the United States) to attempt to pump that money and control into some faltering U.S. airlines." Miller added that being pro union, and trying to get the best work rules for your members, doesn't mean you're antimanagement. Both groups—pilots and management—have vested interests in seeing that their airline is successful. The two aren't mutually exclusive (Fig. 6-9).

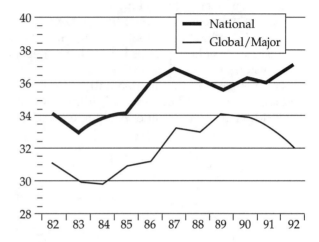

Average new-hire age
Global/Major/National airlines

Fig. 6-9. Average new-hire age.
FAPA

What then happens to pilots who either don't fly for the airlines or fly for a nonunion airline like many of the new start-up carriers. The Association of Independent Airmen (AIA) was started in 1989 in an attempt to make benefits available to today's commercially licensed aviators. Designed to reach pilots who aren't eligible for ALPA membership, AIA has grown to a group of more than 1,500 pilots. The focus on providing benefits has not shifted during the past three years, but has simply expanded to include more financial discount benefit programs.

AIA provides non-ALPA pilots with benefits that include life and loss-of-license insurance plans, two legal assistance programs, mortgage and loan programs, the AIAviator newsletter, aeromedical advice from ALPA's staff of physicians, and a subscription to *AIR LINE PILOT* magazine. AIA is also researching additional insurance plans, and training benefits for members. Priority has been put on exploring competitive benefits for members to make AIA an even more valuable professional organization. Not only is AIA a source of benefits, but also a source of safety, engineering, technology, and vital industry information.

Similarly, the Pilot Information Program (PIP) was started as an outgrowth of ALPA's education efforts. Its goal is to provide information to students and other aviation enthusiasts who are interested in the pilot profession. PIP boasts a growing membership because of ALPA's investment. PIP members become familiar with the aviation industry in general and ALPA in particular.

AIA and its sister organization, the Pilot Information Program, have begun to develop their niches in the pilot profession. First, PIP reaches out to students or other individuals who are interested in becoming pilots. For example, PIP and

ALPA sponsor the "Top Pilot" category in the National Intercollegiate Flying Association (NIFA) competitions. Then, AIA provides information and benefits to pilots who have their commercial rating. The idea is to communicate with people as they begin their careers in aviation. By the time a job with an ALPA-represented carrier is possible, these individuals are familiar with the association.

This stepping-stone approach has already produced a success story. Last year, one of ALPA's Superior Airmanship Award winners was Air Midwest pilot—and former AIA member—John Huppe.

Getting the word out about PIP and AIA begins with ALPA members, university, and high-school educators and current PIP and AIA members. The growth and sustenance of both groups is very much dependent on the support received from outside sources.

For membership information on the Association of Independent Airmen or the Pilot Information Program, call toll-free, (800) 842-2129 or write to AIA or PIP at 1625 Massachusetts Avenue, Washington, D.C. 20036.

7

More jobs

IN CASE YOU WERE BEGINNING TO THINK that the airlines have the only flying jobs in the world, let's take a look at some other opportunities.

CHARTER FLYING

There are people who believe that charter flying is only a time-builder until a real job appears. If you believe that, you could be missing out on a significant piece of the job market. A friend of mine has been flying for a charter operation at a fixed-base operator here in Chicago for 12 years, and he loves it. The operator has grown from a combined piston/turbine fleet 10 or 15 years ago to a pure turbine operator today. My buddy is typed in a Falcon 20, a Learjet, and is soon headed to Flight Safety for training in the G-III. The hours are varied, so while he knows just what days off he will have, there's always the possibility that he could be called in on his day off. But, the destinations are almost always different, as are the passengers.

While this pilot is flying jet equipment, there are hundreds of charter operators at smaller FBOs who are flying piston equipment (Navajos, Cessna 414s) and light-to-medium turbine equipment (Piper Cheyenne, Beech King Air). (See Figs. 7-1 and 7-2.) Those FBOs will also offer significant possibilities. A call to the National Air Transport Association, the FBO trade association in Washington (703-845-9000), could put you in touch with a listing of hundreds of fixed-base operators. Often, some of the more successful FBOs and their charter departments aren't necessarily located in major U.S. cities. Recently I visited an FBO in a small midwestern city and was honestly surprised to see the size of their flight department, some 23 pilots flying King Airs, Learjets, and Falcons on mostly a five-day-per-week schedule. Normally, however, charter flying tends to be an on-demand kind of service. The salary of charter pilots tends to run all over the scale, higher in the big cities and lower in smaller towns. The rate also varies with the type of aircraft you fly, but, as with life, everything is negotiable.

Fig. 7-1. Charter flying could be in a Piper Seminole.

Fig. 7-2. A Beech King Air 200 is also a popular charter aircraft.

CORPORATE FLYING

Many corporations have lost valued pilots to the airlines in recent years, but the slowdown in airline hiring has caused many of these pilots to think twice about their jobs, as have many new pilots. Corporate flying can offer not only the fine personal rewards of flying professionally, but also financial rewards that are very similar to the airlines.

The corporate scheme of operation, however, can be quite different than the airline business, and often, corporate operators aren't terribly keen on hiring former airline pilots into their flight departments. Part of the reason is that a corporation doesn't want to spend the money training an airline pilot who they believe might leave at any moment to return to an airline cockpit should a new opportunity present itself. One friend of mine flew corporate all his life and eventually moved to a chief pilot slot at a company flying a Boeing 737.

Corporately owned and operated aircraft come in all shapes and sizes, from the low end of a Piper Navajo or Beech Baron on up through King Airs, Cessna Citations, Falcons, Learjets, Gulfstreams, Challengers, to even airline equipment (Fig. 7-3). Schedules in corporate flying are sometimes a bit more unsettled than at the airlines, and somewhat similar to charter flying. Some large corporations employ a crew scheduler, and often the crews know a number of days in advance who is scheduled in what airplane to go where. Sometimes, though, the flight could be a last-minute trip scheduled because of some unforeseen business situation. Corporate flying can also involve a great deal of sitting around while you wait for the boss to complete his or her

Fig. 7-3. Corporate Learjet out west.

business. But because most corporate pilots are salaried, you're not losing money. The extra time could provide you the opportunity to catch up on your reading or even do some work for a business of your own. I never travel anywhere without my trusty notebook computer with its word processing software stored inside. Part of this book was written on a two-day layover I had during a Cessna Citation trip.

Salaries at the corporate level tend to be higher than charter flying, but there also tends to be fewer of these jobs around and, as at the airline level, the current competition is tough. Our FAPA "*CAREER PILOT* Salary Survey" shows that the range is wide and dependent on the type of aircraft and often the location of the base. Table 7-1 shows a few examples.

Table 7-1. Captain position average annual wage

BAe-1000	$120,000
Cessna Citation 3	$ 62,000
Gulfstream IV	$ 96,375
King Air 300	$ 40,133
MU-2	$ 38,381
Cheyenne I	$ 29,000
Navajo	$ 26,800
Cessna 421	$ 31,625

Rates for first officer would be a percentage of the captain wages, sometimes as little as 40 percent, often much higher, depending on whether or not the first officer is also type rated in the aircraft. Often, many of the smaller turboprop and piston aircraft fly as single-pilot operations, which can keep any pilot busy in a complex terminal area or when the weather is bad. FAPA's "Directory of Employers" could be an excellent reference here.

As you begin the search for a new job, you'll want every conceivable extra point on your side, such as possibly a type rating. But buying a type rating has become quite a controversial subject when cost versus value received is considered. Some airlines, like Southwest, require a B-737 Type Rating to even apply. Others, like Midwest Express, basically say don't bother because they're going to put you through their own training program anyway. Then airlines like United say sure, a type rating is worth something, but only if you also have a fair amount (about 500 hours) of PIC time to go along with the rating. In the corporate world, a type rating can be an asset, but if you're typed in a Learjet and the job is for a first officer on a Falcon 50, the type rating might not count for much, other than the fact that you're trainable. Let's take a closer look at type ratings.

WILL A TYPE RATING GET YOU HIRED?

by Robert Mark
reprinted by permission, FAPA

In a profession where tens of thousands of dollars can easily be spent just to land a bottom-of-the-ladder job, is an additional $10,000 to $19,000 for a type rating worth the gamble?

If a pilot's goal in picking up the type rating is to hire on with an airline, he or she should look at how the potential employer evaluates a type rating in the interview. During an airline interview, a pilot applicant is evaluated in many different areas. How pilots present themselves and how they perform on airline written exams often can be the deciding factor. If the decision is between two equally qualified pilots, one with a type rating and one without, you'd imagine that the pilot with the type rating would win out. But, because most pilots never actually learn why they were or were not hired, that premise is pretty tough to verify.

The only major or national airline that requires a type rating is Southwest. The company will not interview applicants who don't have a B-737 type rating. Southwest also operates a B-737 type rating school, and about 35 percent of the school's students get hired at Southwest after the type rating is earned.

Viewpoints from other major airlines include that of USAir spokesman Jim Popp, who said, "Our minimum requirements don't ask for a type rating. A type rating is just reviewed along with all other qualifications a pilot might have."

America West, which operates a type rating school, also doesn't require a type rating. At America West's Contract Pilot Training, Dee Rush said, "Of all the people who have gone through our type rating school, only a small portion have been hired. There are many factors that are taken into consideration when a pilot is hired."

United Airlines spokesman Joseph Hopkins said, "United is seeing an overall increase in the qualifications of its applicants, but the type rating really is evaluated along with all of a pilot's other strengths."

At regional carriers, company officials are singing the same tune as the major airlines. Glen Bergman, chief pilot at Business Express Airlines in Windsor Lock, Conn., said, "To have a type rating is important because it shows us that the pilot can pass a type rating course. We do, however, begin all new applicants now in the BE-1900, regardless of experience in other aircraft . . . I would much rather see previous turbine experience."

Drew Bedson, assistant chief pilot at PanAm Express (now out of business), said, "Possession of a type rating doesn't really affect anything in terms of being pulled for an interview. What's more important to those who do hold a type rating would be whether or not they really have used the rating as part of their job. If someone walked through the door with a type rating in a Jetstream he picked up at a school but had no practical experience flying the airplane, then he has no more experience in that machine than he would have on completion of our approved training course, so the rating wouldn't change anything."

Paul Rogers, who manages FAPA's Aviation Job Bank, said this of his corporate clients looking for pilots: "The type rating at the corporate level makes a pilot applicant look a bit better than the competition, but there are plenty of people with lots of experience who just don't present themselves well during an interview. Corporations are more interested in a well-rounded professional applicant who works well with passengers and can be an asset to the company in other ways with their education or skills."

FAPA statistics show that, in 1988, nearly 41 percent of the pilots hired by the majors were type rated (Fig. 7-4). In 1988, five out of ten pilots hired at the nation-

Fig. 7-4. A complete type rating can be obtained in a simulator.

als already were typed. But by the end of 1989, the figures dropped considerably, and only 32 percent of pilots at the majors and 45 percent at the nationals were type rated before being hired. Figures released for the first three quarters of 1990 show the numbers still declining, with 28.9 percent typed in the majors and only 40.7 percent at the nationals. It's not known how many of these type-rated pilots bought their rating and how many got the type rating from a previous employer. Also, it should be noted that all types of type ratings are included in these percentages. The type rating could be in any turbojet-powered aircraft or in any aircraft that has a maximum gross takeoff weight of more than 12,500 pounds.

Some pilot applicants believe that when their application is screened, the extra points from a type rating are what they need to get an interview or land a job. Pilot Mike Roebke said, "I bought the 737 type rating because most of my time in the last five years was in crop dusters and I didn't think anyone would look at me. I would definitely do it again if I had to." Roebke recently was hired as a B-737 first officer by America West.

Although pilot Henry Schettini was planning for the future when he paid for his type rating, he still can't find work. "I really felt my opportunities would be better if I had the type rating. I still think it's good that I have the rating, even if I don't have the job right now."

It could be just a hunch on the part of the applicant that says the type rating is worth the expense. For some it's not. As one regional airline Brasilia captain said, "I've spent enough money on this career. Another $10,000 to $15,000 just to possibly add one point in my interview score is just too much to ask."

The schools that sell air carrier type ratings believe the rating is the pragmatic way to approach the interview process. Nancy Wilson Smith, manager of customer service at Dalfort Aviation says, "Having the type rating makes a pilot more marketable. It proves you're trainable." America West's Rush said, "If you bought your own type rating, it shows you're pretty serious about your career." Aero Service's chief instructor, Steve Saunders, explained that, "Hiring on with a major is extremely competitive . . . A type rating will give you that competitive edge." Ray Brendle, owner of Kingwood, Texas-based Crew Pilot Training, said, "The airlines know that, with a type rating, the pilot has made the transition from civilian general aviation or military flying to the air carrier side."

If a pilot decides on a type rating, he should be prepared for a whopping bill, somewhere between $5,000 and $20,000. Rates vary by aircraft type and previous pilot experience. And a pilot shouldn't worry if he or she only has 2,000 hours total time. As Saunders said, "We're seeing considerably more lower-time pilots entering the type rating program . . . many from commuter operations." Pilots who never have been type rated in a turbojet aircraft will be considered an initial student by most schools. If the pilot were already typed in a turbojet, he or she would be a transition student. Pilots moving from the right seat of a B-737 to the left seat are upgrades.

An important decision for a pilot is in which aircraft to type. Currently, there are the B-707, B-727, B-737, B-747 (Fig. 7-5), DC-8, or DC-9 to choose from. A few of the schools soon will offer the B-757 too. The most prudent choice should be the aircraft that will do the pilot the most good all around. The B-707, B-727, and DC-8 were fine aircraft in their time, but they're part of an ever-decreasing portion of the aircraft fleet. Certainly, a DC-9 type rating is similar to the newer MD-80 series, but, for overall usefulness, most critics agree that the B-737 is the aircraft to fly. Crew Pilot Training's Brendle said, "The 737 is the most popular type rating in the industry because about 50 percent of all major and national airlines use the aircraft." Does this mean that a pilot's money is wasted if he or she types in a B-727? Perhaps. As Joe Marott, manager of Southwest Airlines Training Center, said, "It (a B-737 type rating) is still a requirement here at Southwest to apply for a position. Only the Boeing 737 type rating would meet our requirements for employment." So, a pilot should choose the aircraft carefully by first deciding just who it's he or she wants to work for. Many smaller aircraft type ratings also are offered, but they aren't nearly as useful or valuable.

Smart type rating students should choose a school like a good shopper buys a new car. Students should be wise, knowledgeable, and ask questions until they're satisfied. Price is only one aspect. Dalfort Aviation's manager of flight standards, Ben Williams, said, "A pilot should consider where the school does its training, how long the course will take to complete, and how long the school has been in business. Some schools will organize the ground school in one location, then ask

Fig. 7-5. Boeing 747-400.

the student to travel to a second for the simulator training and perhaps a third for the aircraft training. In this case, the cheaper school would not be a bargain."

Some apparent benefits might be intangibles too. Southwest's and America West's schools are part of those corporate structures, but both schools make it abundantly clear at the start that attending their school will not guarantee a pilot an interview with that company. On the other hand, a few private schools reportedly tell students indirectly that they have an affiliation with a particular airline. In most cases this is untrue. Keep in mind that all schools aren't created equal simply because they're FAA-approved. Consider the staff of that school too. Advanced Aviation Training's president, Robert Mencel, said, "Each instructor here is currently serving in a training capacity with a U.S. airline." At other schools, this might not be the case. Currently, if a school is designed to accomplish at least 90 percent of the training in a simulator (most are), the school must be FAA-approved. The enormous cost of aircraft training virtually assures FAA approval too, but students should ask before signing up. In most cases, an initial type rating student need only have a commercial, multiengine, and instrument rating to begin. In other phases of training such as transition, the requirements can vary, so check with the school prior to enrollment.

What can a pilot expect from a type rating program? First of all, most schools will require some form of a deposit in advance to hold a position in the class, ranging from 20 percent to the entire cost of the course. None of the schools interviewed provided any financing, so be prepared to find a loan if necessary. Most schools agreed to a specific amount of training for a specific price, but no school offered a guarantee of the rating. Additional training required will involve additional funds, which the student should ask about first. At one school, the simulator costs $375 per extra hour, while time in the B-737 goes for $45 per minute.

One bright spot on the horizon for potential type rating candidates is the new federal Veterans Training Act, the GI Bill of the 1990s. Pilots who served in the U.S. armed forces might qualify for this professional training cost assistance of up to 60 percent of the type rating bill. Pilots should contact the local Veterans Administration office for details.

According to the U.S. Master Tax Guide, a type rating may be deductible on a pilot's personal income tax return, too. The guide says that "education expenses are generally deductible if the education undertaken maintains or improves a skill required by the individual in his employment . . ." To be certain, though, pilots should check with an accountant about their specific situation before signing up.

While the price of lodging was included in the package price at only one school, all had some sort of deal with a local hotel to provide accommodations and transportation to their facilities during the student's stay. The length of that stay for the course varied considerably from two-and-one-half weeks, to the longest at six weeks. How a pilot can carve a hole in his or her schedule for that kind of training is another problem a student must solve before committing to the training.

The schools run by Southwest and America West place their contract type rating students into open slots along with their regular company pilot training classes, so students are able to talk and learn from the instructors and students already working for an airline. Southwest's Marott says, "The best thing in our school for type ratings is that we use the same manuals, the same procedures, the same simulators, airplanes, and instructors that are used to train our regular line pilots." Currently, Southwest's school teaches only the B-737-200 course to contract students. Marott said the school opened in the spring of 1987. "Since then we've graduated about 175 B-737 type-rated pilots. Of that number, approximately 60 were ultimately hired by Southwest Airlines," said Marott.

Saunders says Aero Service's B-727 type rating course includes 120 hours of actual classroom ground school. The student then moves on for 16 to 18 hours of cockpit procedures training in a nonmotion aircraft simulator. Then they'll spend 18 to 20 hours in the full-motion simulator, usually in teams with about 10 in the left seat as pilot in command and 10 in the right seat performing first-officer duties and observing. Finally, the checkride is performed both in the simulator and in an aircraft the company leases. In most cases, an initial student can't complete all the training plus the ride in the simulator only. There can be some reductions in training time for the rating, based on previous experience. These changes are made on a case-by-case basis by the FAA's Principal Operations Inspector, who oversees the school.

America West's Rush said, "The ground school lasts 12 days. This is followed by 5 days of cockpit procedures training and then the FAA oral. The student next moves to about 12 hours in the simulator and about one hour of aircraft time to finish off the takeoff and landings. America West currently is under contract with the FAA to provide all that agency's initial type training to its air carrier as well as maintenance inspectors."

Crew Pilot Training's Brendle says that, although the total amount of ground school there is similar to other schools, his "is approved for 80 hours of home study. The student must show by a test on arrival that he has completed the required work." Students receive an additional 40 hours of ground school when they reach the classroom. Brendle remarked that "some schools send you for the FAA oral right after ground school, without ever having seen the inside of the CPT or the simulator. When a student learns about an aircraft from a book only, without ever having had the chance to move a knob or switch, they give a weak oral."

Information such as ground school time, simulator time, cost, reputation of the school, along with other considerations listed previously, should be kept in mind if the pilot feels he or she needs the type rating because of qualifications required by a specific airline.

In the end, a pilot must decide if the type rating is worth the money. That decision should be based on experience as a pilot and whether the pilot feels that his or her credentials will match up to those of other candidates applying for the job, as well as whether the company to which he or she is applying requires a type rating. It's a decision that must be made at the right time under the right circumstances.

FLY FOR THE FEDERAL GOVERNMENT

An often overlooked area of flying is with the federal or state government. Positions often exist for both fixed-wing and helicopter pilots, but the search can take time because there are so many agencies to check into. The FAA, for example, uses pilots to fly its fleet of flight check aircraft, while the U.S. Customs service monitors border traffic with their aircraft. Some of the publications we've already spoken about might carry ads for government pilots, and certainly a number of flying employment services will offer publications that list flying jobs for the government. An alternative to searching the various publications for government flying jobs would be to contact the various agencies directly. A call to the Federal Information Center at 800-366-2998 should get you started with phone numbers and addresses of federal agencies.

Some of the U.S. agencies that might need pilots are:

- Department of Defense
- U.S. Customs Service
- Federal Aviation Administration
- NOAA
- Department of Transportation
- NASA
- Defense Logistics Agency

In addition, state and local governments might use pilots. Your state's department of aviation would be a good place to begin the search (Fig. 7-6).

FLYING FOR THE MILITARY

I recently spoke to a young Air Force pilot, 1st Lt. Michael Fick, about some of his experiences during his Air Force flight training since he graduated from school. I

Fig. 7-6. Many agencies of the government fly civilian aircraft.

think his answers about the training will tell you how viable this part of aviation is as a career field, although you certainly need to check into each different branch of the service for its particular requirements (see chapter 2). In 1983, the Air Force enlisted 1,590 new pilots. In 1993, that number had dropped to 700. The Air Force reports that of that current 700, 35 percent will be flying bombers and fighters while the other 65 percent will serve out their tour of duty in airlift/transport aircraft.

Q: Why did you choose the USAF, Mike? A: I had a great desire to continue my education after high school and very little money to do it with. I didn't want to be burdened for years with school loans, so I decided to apply to the U.S. Air Force Academy. My flight experience was limited prior to applying to the Academy, but my desire to fly was strong. I was turned down for the Academy my first year, but received a partial Falcon Foundation Scholarship to New Mexico Military Institute. This prep school provided me with the chance to prove my continued interest in the Academy. I graduated at the top of my class a year later and won an Academy slot.

Q: Do you plan on making the Air Force a career? A: Right now I do. But the final decision depends on how well the Air Force treats me in the future, much like any other job.

Q: Would you tell me a little about Air Force flight training? A: Sure. The training really began for me, though, at New Mexico Military Institute, where I learned about the attitude necessary to be a professional. That became even more firmly set at the Academy. My actual flight training began in the summer between my junior and senior year at the Academy, when I went through the required preliminary flight training in the T-41 (Cessna 172). Performance in the program, both my G.P.A. and M.P.A. (Military Performance Average) allowed 125 out of 600 students to apply for the Euro NATO Joint Jet Pilot Training at Sheppard AFB, TX. Forty were selected. The program ran 13 months, where standard Undergraduate Pilot Training ran 12 months. A good majority of the training revolved around fighter tactics.

Q: What aircraft did you fly in training? A: I flew the T-37 Tweety for the first six months and the T-38 Talon (Fig. 7-7) for the second six months.

Fig. 7-7. Air Force student pilot and instructor plan a T-38 flight.

Q: What effects have the military cutbacks had on your career? A: Due to the cutbacks there were very few fighter assignments when I graduated from training. Most were for tankers, transports and instructor pilots. Some of the pilots were taken out of flying for a few years first, before being given their assignments. I had the C-130s, C135s, C-12 or T-37 Instructor pilot jobs to choose from. I chose the C-12 (Beech King Air 200) assignment at Andrews AFB, MD, just across the river from Washington National Airport. This assignment should be followed by one in the C-141.

Q: What did you enjoy most about training? A: I think the two- and four-ship formation flying provided the most serious adrenalin rush, as well as two-ship low-level, where I flew at 420 knots about 500 AGL.

Q: Have you thought about your flying once you return to civilian life? A: Most definitely. One of the driving factors because I couldn't get into fighters was the flying experience that will transfer to civilian life. I'll have turboprop time, in the C-12, as well as multiengine jet time in the C-141. And the C-12 time is in some of the busiest airspace in the country to boot.

As I end this section, I'd like to give you a little food for thought in case your plans have wandered towards flying outside the United States. If you've not given that any consideration before, perhaps you should.

LANDING A FLYING JOB
OUTSIDE THE UNITED STATES

by Robert Mark
reprinted by permission, FAPA

If searching for a flying job in the ailing U.S. economy the past few years leaves you somewhere between angry and distraught, take heart. There's another source of potential work waiting to be tapped . . . flying overseas. But don't expect flying work outside the United States to be easier to find than in the States. You might find it tougher to get hired by an international carrier. You also might find yourself traveling further to work each week, sometimes thousands of miles. Residency outside the United States also will accentuate the enormous differences in living conditions and customs from those you're accustomed to.

Before you begin shipping resumés to Bahrain and Taipei, check one very important item of your personality . . . your attitude. Carefully consider the changes you might put yourself through to keep flying, especially outside the United States. Some pilots look at the possibilities and turn in their Jepp bags forever rather than endure weeks or possibly months away from home. One former PanAm pilot, a type-rated captain, found initial employment in Alaska, but complained about having to commute from Fairbanks back to his New York home each week. Then, just after he completed training, his new airline furloughed the entire class and he found himself working in the Middle East on a short-term contract with no benefits. When he returns home now, he hopes for a jump seat ride or buys a ticket, and he said he thinks the Fairbanks-Kennedy Airport trip was not such a bad ride after all.

If you're thinking of commuting 10,000 miles to work, ask yourself if this routine is practical for you. It's not difficult to pack everything you own into a few suitcases and move to Europe or the Pacific Rim if you're single, but if you have a house and family here in the United States, a cockpit job based in Hong Kong could make commuting next to impossible. If you don't take your family with you, a consideration might be how long you're willing to be away from them. How long will your marriage survive with you out of the country? One pilot, who requested anonymity, left the United States to fly freight in the Middle East with his marriage intact. After four months away from his bride, the letter came to tell him she wanted a husband who resided at least in the same country. He left Bahrain hoping to rescue the relationship, but found it was too little, too late.

Maybe a short-term overseas contract might be a better idea. You'll stay current and probably keep your family intact while you wait for times to improve in North America. Dublin, Ireland-based Parc Aviation, the pilot leasing arm of Aer Lingus, regularly uses pilots on six to nine-month overseas contracts on aircraft as small as an EMB-120. Another option could be to take your family with you to Saudi Arabia or Indonesia. But know how your family feels about this before you accept a job. How will your teenagers enjoy living in a land that doesn't have MTV or a Blockbuster Video, or where it might be impossible for them to stop with their pals at the McDonalds down the street? Some overseas positions might not provide for nor encourage you to bring your spouse or family with you because, for example, some Middle Eastern countries don't allow their women the freedoms Western women have.

And then, there are the security considerations. Americans often are in great danger in other countries merely because they're Americans. Is it a good idea to expose yourself to such conditions? If you decide the job is worth such a risk, then the job search begins.

A recent aviation magazine editorial said the time to network is before a U.S. pilot needs to look for work. If there's any single recurring theme that CAREER PILOT heard while researching this article, it was that many pilots found international work through a tip from someone else—usually another pilot—who saw an ad or heard about someone looking for crews. In 1992, a number of former Midway Commuter EMB-120 pilots found contract employment in Belgium from a tip passed on through the local Air Line Pilots Association (ALPA) office. You'll have to spend time on the phone calling airlines, leasing firms, and old pilot pals for leads. As Parc Aviation's, Tim Shattock said, "The more experience you have, though, the better your chances are."

Whether you use the FAPA "Career Pilot Job Report" for tips or connect directly with a leasing firm or airline outside the United States, expect a market that doesn't give Americans preferential treatment. And you'll have to meet international requirements that vary widely among countries and employers. Cargolux's vice president of flight operations, Graham Hurst, said the quickest way to find employment with a European Economic Community (EC) airline (Fig. 7-8) today is to "get a European passport and a European license. We don't have any restrictions to hiring U.S. pilots except that we're supposed to try to find Europeans first." France and Germany, too, are notoriously tough places for U.S. pilots to find permanent work. British Airways is quite open about not hiring any pilot who's not either a British citizen or holder of an EC passport. U.S. pilot Larry Schweitz, now a Boeing 737 captain for an Egyptian charter airline said, "I think it's as difficult to find work overseas as it is in the United States, especially with the new EC. It gives European pilots a leg up on American pilots." The EC is in the process of uniting all of Europe into a single economic and monetary unit having: a powerful central bank and a single currency by 1999, common approaches to foreign policy and defense, and centralized authority in such areas as the environment and labor

Fig. 7-8. An A320 is often flown on many international routes.

relations. The stance with labor will be for European employers to give preference in hiring to Europeans.

Besides the roadblocks the EC might create for U.S. pilots, a potential stumbling block for some could be the language requirements. While English is still the international language of air traffic control, many foreign airlines would like to hire pilots versed in another language. Former Northwest pilot Mike Henderson, now flying for KLM, said part of the requirement to fly as a permanent crew member at KLM is to "learn to speak Dutch to be able to make the normal and emergency cabin announcements." Henderson said he takes Dutch language classes at his Amsterdam crew base. Similarly, EVA Air encourages, although it doesn't require, pilot applicants to learn Mandarin Chinese.

Shattock said, "Language other than English is not normally a problem (for hiring by Parc Aviation)." Cargolux's Graham Hurst said, "If you live in Luxembourg, being able to speak French and German is an advantage." A former PanAm pilot said that, while flying for All Nippon, "I learned the Japanese numbers just so I could do the weight and balance their way. I think the other Japanese pilots really appreciated the efforts I made to learn their language too."

The pay and benefits on international jobs vary greatly. When the above-mentioned pilot began flying a B-747 on contract for All Nippon from Tokyo in 1989, the pay and benefits of more than $100,000 per year were a significant increase over what he earned at PanAm, where he was at the bottom of the B-747 pay scale. (The contract initially was between PanAm and All Nippon. When PanAm ceased operations, another outfit picked up the contract.) Henderson said his wages were about the same as what he'd been paid at Northwest.

Major medical care is available, although some contracts might not provide this benefit. Schweitz's individual short-term contract in Egypt (he heard about the job via word-of-mouth instead of a crew leasing firm) keeps him current on the 737, but, he says, "There are no benefits. Either party can cancel the contract with 30 days notice. I also have to pay my own way up and back whenever I return to the United States because I receive no pass privileges." At All Nippon, one pilot said, "The pass policy was fairly restrictive . . . but they gave us two positive space international tickets each year." As part of the basic compensation package, some international companies (such as All Nippon) provide living quarters for Americans living abroad, but many will expect you to find your own lodging at your own expense.

Because all countries require some form of work permit for noncitizens (besides a U.S. passport) Americans find it helpful that many of the international airlines and corporations assist the employees in getting their paperwork in order. Most wait until the pilot arrives at the new-duty station to complete the paperwork, although Henderson remembered KLM sending him a complete packet of material before he ever left the United States. Another pilot, however, said that when he began flying for All Nippon, "We did all the work for visas and permits on our own."

How do pilots find overseas flying work if they don't hear about it from a friend? It can be difficult. Australia's Qantas said it "only advertise[s] for pilots in the Australian press." Some airlines, like Taiwan-based EVA Air, search for pilots with ads in "internationally distributed aviation magazines." FAPA's "Pilot Job Report" and "Aviation Job Bank" are good sources for the latest news on hiring, but a pilot should also consider word-of-mouth as a supplemental source. And, Platinum- and Gold-Level FAPA members can call FAPA's Career Center directly for information about international job openings or crew-leasing operations.

Search all the aviation publications, both U.S. and international. These are usually available at the library. And don't overlook the *World Aviation Directory*, also available at most libraries. Robert Orr, who flew freight for DHL from Bahrain, said, "I think the *World Aviation Directory* would really help because it lists addresses to international carriers and leasing agencies throughout the world." Finding out whether that company is hiring or even accepting resumés is where the pilot's work really begins, however. One pilot said he believes that a pilot seeking work outside the United States "must spend the money to call people directly who are working for an airline or company you're considering."

Parc Aviation's Shattock said, "Our (contract) placement of a pilot can depend on the season of the year, a pilot's qualifications, and their experience level. A 737-400 captain, for example, needs about 500 hours PIC to be hired. Although we hire mostly captains, the first officers we do use would also need at least 500 hours plus a type rating."

For an overseas flying job, U.S. pilots usually need some type of flying certificate issued by the host country. However, it's common for the host employer to arrange and pay for the certificate. Henderson said, "In Holland, they have a B-3 license issued by the Dutch equivalent of the FAA that allows me to fly here. It requires me to maintain my FAA physical and U.S. flying currency, however." Canadian Airlines pilot Brian Rasmussen, also a former Eastern Airlines pilot, took no chances with his future. "I became dual rated with an ATP in both Canada and the United States while I was still flying for Eastern. When Canadian agreed to hire me, I was already current in Canada." To fly in Japan, one pilot said, "We had to start from scratch to qualify for a Japanese license, and the training was as tough as any I've ever been through." Because Luxembourg doesn't issue a pilot certificate higher than a private, potential Cargolux crews must obtain a Luxembourg validation to their U.S. license. Hurst says, "This means a U.S. pilot can fly a Luxembourg-registered aircraft as long as he maintains his American license and medical."

It's difficult to say whether the scale tips more toward a pilot finding international employment through a contractor or through the airline itself as a permanent employee. Cargolux's Hurst said, "We have about 30 nationalities (of pilots) working here, quite a lot of American pilots and flight engineers, about 20 out of 120 pilots." Most are permanent employees, but some are on short-term contracts. Hurst also said that, because of the large numbers of well-qualified pilots around, in 1993 "we might slow down on looking at potential pilots that don't have jet experience."

Cargolux hopefuls must have 1,500 hours minimum time, with at least 500 hours of pure turbine time. If you don't have 500 jet, 1,000 heavy turboprop time will do. The airline intends to lease a few short-term aircraft, but there's a chance it could take on more permanent crew members. Cargolux will be one of the first carriers to fly the freighter version of the Boeing 747-400. Parc Aviation or Sam Sita in Monte Carlo handles crew leasing for Cargolux. Those seeking permanent positions apply directly to Cargolux.

While most jobs outside the United States are for air-carrier-rated pilots, some agencies and companies hire corporate crews too. Houston, Texas-based Aramco, for example, hires fixed-wing and rotorcraft pilots to fly in Saudi Arabia. One crew-leasing firm manager, who requested anonymity, said he also recruited regularly for rotorcraft and fixed-wing pilots in all parts of the world. His last round of contracts were for Learjet, G-2, and G-3 rated pilots to fly in the Middle East. His firm advertised the openings in newspapers of major cities like Houston, Dallas, and Miami, but said they try to stay away from interviewing pilots from places like California because "those pilots just want more money than we can possibly offer." His last Lear pilot was paid approximately $50,000 per year, with a 30-day vacation and a one-bedroom apartment provided in Saudi Arabia. He warned pilots, however, that in places like Saudi Arabia, even though the U.S. pilots work for an American company through their contract, "over there, the Saudis call the shots."

Both you and your family must prepare for culture shock if you fly outside the United States. An All Nippon pilot said,"At least half the American pilots over here (Tokyo) wouldn't touch Japanese food . . . it just tasted different. The Japanese are a very structured society too, so in the cockpit, there's always a boss, a worker, and an elder kind of attitude. These companies also have a very different attitude towards their employees and what their employees' responsibilities are to the company. They seem to expect the employee to be grateful for having a job, so they're really not very interested in providing great travel benefits or things like that. Even the scheduling is hard set by the company. The pilots have no input."

Schweitz said, "There's a tremendous culture difference (in Egypt), and if you're not prepared to keep an open mind it can become a very difficult situation. There's a big difference in the way they treat foreigners in Egypt, too. It's a lot more than just going up in an airplane. Cairo is not Phoenix."

Certainly one of the brightest highlights of flying overseas is the tax break available to a U.S. pilot. If you maintain a permanent residence outside of the United States for more than 330 days in a year, the IRS might allow you to exclude your first $70,000 a year from U.S. taxes. That tax break can afford you a significant pay raise for a one-year contract, depending on your salary. Any money you earn will be free of U.S. taxes. However, Mike Henderson said that, while his money was free of U. S. taxes, "We'll soon be paying Dutch taxes of about 12 percent for a U.S. pilot." Pilots who are not sure if their pay is subject to taxation by the host country can get that information through the host country's U.S. embassy in Washington D.C. or through the U.S. Embassy in the host country.

A flying job outside the United States is not easy to find or sometimes maintain, but if you're the adventurous type, it can be quite profitable. If there's any advice for a U.S. pilot looking for work outside of North America, Shattock probably said it best from Dublin. "Aviation is a very cyclical business with many good and bad times. I hope we're starting to climb out of this aviation recession and that will give us a need for more pilots. Don't ever give up . . . keep on looking."

8

Final notes

THE PILOT AND THE PC

Today, pilots cannot be considered informed if they're unaware of some of the sources of information and services available through the use of a personal computer (PC). Through the online databases described in chapter 3, a PC connected through a modem in your unit can put you in touch with thousands of people who are plane nuts too, many who are professional pilots. The selection of equipment is beyond the scope of this book, but once you have a PC, you'll find yourself able to: electronically keep your logbook, run and log simulator time from a program run on a PC, or even study for your next FAA written exam through question and answer sessions that take you through the material much faster and make it more interesting. Let's take a look at some of the items that are now available.

Another name for the sometimes smaller or less sophisticated online networks is a bulletin board (BB). A bulletin board of special interest to pilots is the one run by the FAA in northern Florida. The system is inexpensive to use because it has its own 800 number, 800-645-FSDO to be exact. The system provides electronic mail messaging between registered users and any FAA representative. Also included are: a read file of North Florida Accident Prevention Programs; a listing of seminars; airshows; a database file on minimum equipment lists; advisory circulars; and the complete text of the FAA's *Aviation News* magazine, sans pictures. The bulletin board is worth a call when you put your PC and modem system online.

When I started flying 26 years ago, I don't think I realized what a pain in the neck keeping up a logbook would be. I was making entries every day or so and constantly adding numbers, often incorrectly, thereby making a mess out of my logbook. I even carried a bottle of whiteout in my flight bag to cope with the mistakes. But then one day, I was breezing through the software offered on CompuServe (Fig. 8-1) in AVSIG, and I saw a demonstration program called AEROLOG. The writer had saved a simplified version of his program on CompuServe, and anyone could download it for free through the phone lines to try it out. I did.

Within a few hours of typing in the entries from my first logbook (I had three), I saw the simplicity of it all. This computer program remembered all the tail numbers of all the aircraft I'd ever flown. When I typed N9MK the second time and the

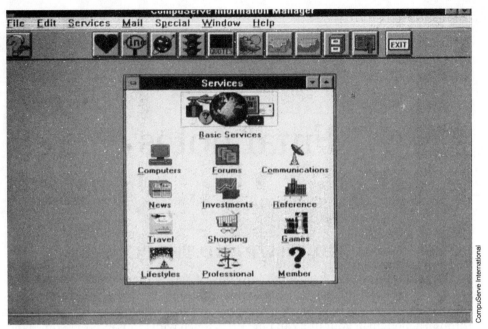

Fig. 8-1. A search of the Aviation Forum on CompuServe begins here.

102nd time, the computer did the work and put the aircraft make and model into the log entry. It added all the columns instantly. It told me in a fraction of a second how much time I had already logged in a Cessna 310 or a Piper Lance. When writing all the numbers onto the FAA's Application for Airman's Certificate (Form 8710-1), the instructor's recommendation sheet for a checkride is usually a nightmare because of the way the time must be broken down. AEROLOG (Fig. 8-2) makes this process a walk through the tulips. Certainly there are other logbook programs, but I wouldn't give up my AEROLOG computerized logbook for anything. Call AEROLOG at 800-366-1204.

Would you like to practice some IFR approaches because you're about to pick up your instrument rating? Or maybe you already own an instrument rating and need a way to keep current, normally an expensive proposition. With some of the new-generation flight simulator programs installed on your PC, however, you'll find yourself able to simulate flying aircraft, including a Cessna 172, a World War II P-51, a Learjet, and a Concorde. I've played with and enjoyed two versions of simulator programs. They both perform similar missions, but to differing degrees of realism.

Each uses a simulated cockpit that appears on the CRT of your computer. Through the use of a device called a *joystick* (which looks like the control stick from an airplane and plugs right in to your PC), you can actually fly your aircraft. Push the stick left and the craft banks left; push the stick back and up comes the nose. Want to try a loop in a P-51? Make sure you have enough airspeed first; lower the nose slightly as you pick up speed; haul back on the stick and watch the horizon out your windows turn into blue sky as you go over the top. Don't forget to pull

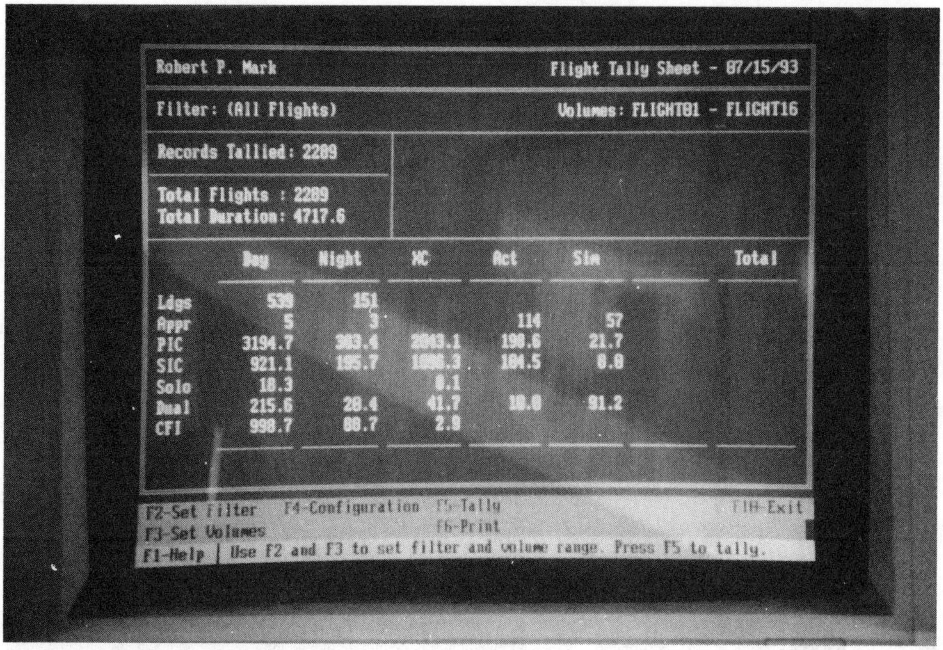

```
Robert P. Mark                          Flight Tally Sheet - 07/15/93

Filter: (All Flights)                   Volumes: FLIGHT01 - FLIGHT16

Records Tallied: 2209

Total Flights : 2209
Total Duration: 4717.6

            Day     Night    XC      Act     Sim         Total
Ldgs        539     151
Appr        5       3                 114     57
PIC         3194.7  303.4   2043.1    190.6   21.7
SIC         921.1   195.7   1006.3    104.5   0.0
Solo        18.3            0.1
Dual        215.6   28.4    41.7      10.0    91.2
CFI         998.7   80.7    2.0

F2-Set Filter   F4-Configuration  F5-Tally              F10-Exit
F3-Set Volumes                    F6-Print
F1-Help | Use F2 and F3 to set filter and volume range. Press F5 to tally.
```

Fig. 8-2. Typical AEROLOG electronic logbook screen.

the power back on the way down, or you'll tear the wings off or even pass out from the "G" load (the screen starts to turn red).

Personally, I own three of these crazy simulators. One, Chuck Yeager's Advanced Flight Trainer, allows you to not only fly the P-51 but also fly formation aerobatics, and it even includes dual flight training if you don't already know how to fly. While Yeager's aircraft are fun to fly, the scenery is rather limited, as is the aircraft. It's a VFR-only machine. But, I can't think of too many places I can check out a Spitfire for a little aerobatic practice.

Microsoft's Flight Simulator has a number of advanced features that allow you to actually fly instrument approaches and even break out of the clouds as the thunderstorm's lightning illuminates the landing airport. The view from the cockpit allows you to even change radio frequencies or listen to the marker beacon beep as you fly an ILS approach. One scenario begins at the approach end of runway 36 at Chicago Meigs, where I've flown into and out of hundreds of times. I can take off, set up the radio properly, turn northwest after departure, and fly directly to ORD and shoot the 27 right ILS instrument approach. Wait 'til you try landing one of these things. That can be the best fun.

Another program I've recently begun learning is Flight Deck Software's Instrument Flight Trainer (Fig. 8-3). What attracted me to this system was the realism of the cockpit. I can set it up to fly like the A36 Bonanza that I often pilot, but with an HSI and an RMI (two fairly sophisticated pieces of navigation equipment). Besides being able to choose a number of different aircraft and regions of the country to fly in, as well as shoot the IFR approaches, IFT will allow for easy connection of

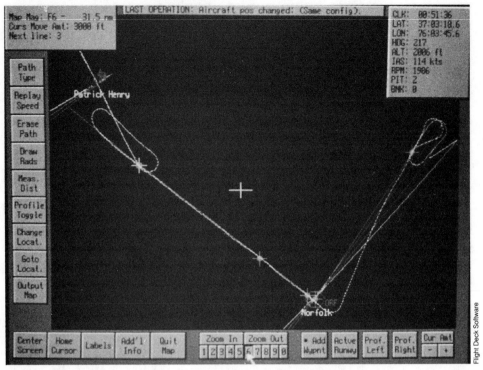

Fig. 8-3. The computer keeps track of your progress as you fly the simulator.

a control wheel in place of the joystick or a set of electrically controlled rudder pedals for even more realism. Contact Flight Deck Software at 800-955-4359.

I'd better stop here though because as these systems become more and more real, you might not want to go to the airport very often. But seriously, if you haven't made the transition to a personal computer yet, try one. They're the best for an afternoon's fun and proficiency when you can't really make it out to the airport. Also, try calling for the *FLIGHT COMPUTING CATALOG* at 800-992-7737 for a list of some of the best flight simulator and related programs and accessories.

THE END ... OR JUST THE BEGINNING?

So here you are at the end or, hopefully, the beginning (Fig. 8-4). You've had a glimpse of what lies in store for you if you decide that a career as a professional pilot is where you want to be. I've spoken about some of the jobs, as well as how to find them. I've spoken about the ratings you'll need and how to pick them up. I've discussed the schools available and how to finance your career. Best of all, I've spoken with people who have made it—people who conceived a plan and followed through on it until they reached their goal. A plan is very important, but the most important part is you must keep moving towards your goal. Don't let anything or anyone get in the way (Fig. 8-5). If someone says no, realize that means no ... today. Tomorrow it could be a maybe. If you try something and you fail along

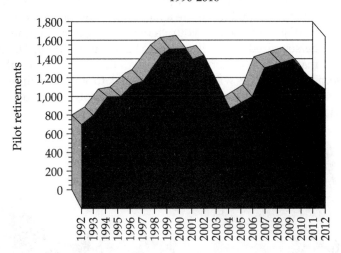

Major airline pilot retirements
(Age 60)
1990-2010

Fig. 8-4. More jobs will appear as more older pilots retire.
FAPA

Fig. 8-5. Is there a C-5 in your future?

Peter M. Bowers Collection

the way, realize that you really didn't fail. You learned something. You learned what doesn't work. If you learned something, you didn't fail. Remember, you never fail until you stop trying.

There's no doubt in my mind that as you read this, the aviation job scale might be tilting in yet another direction. No book would be complete without mentioning that layoffs, called furloughs in the airplane biz, as well as outright bankruptcies and total liquidations are a fact of life. The earlier your seniority number at an airline (Fig. 8-6), the less your chances of being furloughed. At a corporation, the last person hired is usually going to be the first laid off. The up side, though, is that in a market-driven economy like that of the United States, there's always someone, somewhere, who's willing to take the risk to start an airline or flight department of some kind. They're always going to need pilots, but you must do your homework to locate them.

Fig. 8-6. Airline seniority is everything.

Here are some final words from Lt. Michael Fick from my interview with him about the Air Force. These thoughts sum up a great many of the feelings of the other pilots I've spoken to. I asked him how much he really enjoyed what he was doing. He said, "You can't beat getting paid to fly. There's no other fun like it. Notice he didn't use the word "work" in that sentence. Flying is hardly like work (Fig. 8-7). The real work comes in those years when you're learning to become a rated pilot."

Fig. 8-7. Flying is hardly like work.

If you enjoyed this book or have suggestions for upcoming editions, please feel free to contact me on CompuServe at 73477, 3064. If you don't have a CompuServe ID yet, get your PC fired up, call 800-848-8990, and give it a try.

Good luck. Let me hear from you as you progress (Fig. 8-8).

Fig. 8-8. You can become a professional pilot.

Appendix

HERE'S THE REMAINING PORTION OF THE FARs THAT, added to those listed in chapter 2, will give you all requirements for the licenses and ratings you'll need to become a professional pilot.

PRIVATE PILOTS

61.102   APPLICABILITY

This subpart prescribes the requirements for the issuance of private pilot certificates and ratings, the conditions under which those certificates and ratings are necessary, and the general operating rules for the holders of those certificates and ratings.

61.105   AERONAUTICAL KNOWLEDGE

An applicant for a private pilot certificate must have logged ground instruction from an authorized instructor, or must present evidence showing that he has satisfactorily completed a course of instruction or home study in at least the following areas of aeronautical knowledge appropriate to the category of aircraft for which a rating is sought.

(a) *Airplanes and Rotorcraft.*
    (1) The accident reporting requirements of the National Transportation Safety Board and the Federal Aviation Regulations applicable to private pilot privileges, limitations, and flight operations for airplanes or rotorcraft, as appropriate, the use of the "Airman's Information Manual," and FAA advisory circulars.
    (2) VFR navigation, using pilotage, dead reckoning, and radio aids;

(3) The recognition of critical weather situations from the ground and in flight, the procurement and use of aeronautical weather reports and forecasts;

(4) The safe and efficient operation of airplanes or rotorcraft, as appropriate, including high density airport operations, collision avoidance precautions, and radio communication procedures;

(5) Basic aerodynamics and the principles of flight which apply to airplanes or rotorcraft, as appropriate; and

(6) Stall awareness, spin entry, spins, and spin recovery techniques for airplanes.

61.107 FLIGHT PROFICIENCY

The applicant for a private pilot certificate must have logged instruction from an authorized flight instructor in at least the following pilot operations. In addition, his logbook must contain an endorsement by an authorized flight instructor who has found him competent to perform each of those operations safely as a private pilot.

(a) *In Airplanes.*

(1) Preflight operations, including weight and balance determination, line inspection, and airplane servicing;

(2) Airport and traffic pattern operations, including operations at controlled airports, radio communications, and collision avoidance precautions;

(3) Flight maneuvering by reference to ground objects;

(4) Flight at slow airspeeds with realistic distractions, and the recognition of and recovery from stalls entered from straight flight and from turns;

(5) Normal and crosswind takeoffs and landings;

(6) Control and maneuvering an airplane solely by reference to instruments, including descents and climbs using radio aids or radar directives;

(7) Cross-country flying, using pilotage, dead reckoning, and radio aids, including one 2-hour flight;

(8) Maximum performance takeoffs and landings;

(9) Night flying, including takeoffs, landings, and VFR navigation; and

(10) Emergency operations, including simulated aircraft and equipment malfunctions.

(b) *In Helicopters.*

(1) Preflight operations, including the line inspection and servicing of helicopters;

(2) Hovering, air taxiing, and maneuvering by ground references;

(3) Airport and traffic pattern operations, including collision avoidance precautions;

(4) Cross-country flying, using pilotage, dead reckoning, and radio aids, including one 1-hour flight;

(5) Operations in confined areas and on pinnacles, rapid decelerations, landings on slopes, high-altitude takeoffs, and run-on landings;

(6) Night flying, including takeoffs, landings, and VFR navigation; and

(7) Simulated emergency procedures, including aircraft and equipment malfunctions, approaches to a hover or landing with an engine inoperative in a multiengine helicopter, or autorotational descents with a power recovery to a hover in single-engine helicopters.

61.118 PRIVATE PILOT PRIVILEGES AND LIMITATIONS: PILOT IN COMMAND

Except as provided in paragraphs (a) through (d) of this section, a private pilot may not act as pilot in command of an aircraft that is carrying passengers or property for compensation or hire; nor may he, for compensation or hire, act as pilot in command of an aircraft.

(a) A private pilot may, for compensation or hire, act as pilot in command of an aircraft in connection with any business or employment if the flight is only incidental to that business or employment and the aircraft does not carry passengers or property for compensation or hire.

(b) A private pilot may share the operating expenses of a flight with his passengers.

(c) A private pilot who is an aircraft salesman and who has at least 200 hours of logged flight time may demonstrate an aircraft in flight to a prospective buyer.

(d) A private pilot may act as pilot in command of an aircraft used in a passenger-carrying airlift sponsored by a charitable organization, and for which the passengers make a donation to the organization, if

(1) The sponsor of the airlift notifies the FAA Flight Standards District Office having jurisdiction over the area concerned, at least 7 days before the flight, and furnishes any essential information that the office requests;

(2) The flight is conducted from a public airport adequate for the aircraft used, or from another airport that has been approved for the operation by an FAA inspector;

(3) He has logged at least 200 hours of flight time;

(4) No acrobatic or formation flights are conducted;

(5) Each aircraft used is certificated in the standard category and complies with the 100-hour inspection requirement of {91.409 of this chapter; and

(6) The flight is made under VFR during the day.

For the purpose of paragraph (d) of this section, a "charitable organization" means an organization listed in *Publication No. 78 of the Department of the Treasury called the Cumulative List of Organizations described in section 170(c) of the Internal Revenue Code of 1954, as amended from time to time by published supplemental lists.

61.120 PRIVATE PILOT PRIVILEGES AND LIMITATIONS: SECOND IN COMMAND OF AIRCRAFT REQUIRING MORE THAN ONE REQUIRED PILOT

Except as provided in paragraphs (a) through (d) of {61.118 a private pilot may not, for compensation or hire, act as second in command of an aircraft that is type certificated for more than one required pilot, nor may he act as second in command of such an aircraft that is carrying passengers or property for compensation or hire.

COMMERCIAL PILOTS

61.121 APPLICABILITY

This subpart prescribes the requirements for the issuance of commercial pilot certificates and ratings, the conditions under which those certificates and ratings are necessary, and the limitations upon those certificates and ratings.

61.125 AERONAUTICAL KNOWLEDGE

An applicant for a commercial pilot certificate must have logged ground instruction from an authorized instructor, or must present evidence showing that he has satisfactorily completed a course of instruction or home study, in at least the following areas of aeronautical knowledge appropriate to the category of aircraft for which a rating is sought.

(a) *Airplanes.*
  (1) The regulations of this chapter governing the operations, privileges, and limitations of a commercial pilot, and the accident reporting requirements of the National Transportation Safety Board;
  (2) Basic aerodynamics and the principles of flight which apply to airplanes;
  (3) Airplane operations, including the use of flaps, retractable landing gears, controllable propellers, high altitude operation with and without pressurization, loading and balance computations, and the significance and use of airplane performance speeds; and
  (4) Stall awareness, spin entry, spins, and spin recovery techniques for airplanes.

(b) *Rotorcraft*

(1) The regulations of this chapter which apply to the operations, privileges, and limitations of a commercial rotorcraft pilot, and the accident reporting requirements of the National Transportation Safety Board;

(2) Meteorology, including the characteristics of air masses and fronts, elements of weather forecasting, and the procurement and use of aeronautical weather reports and forecasts;

(3) The use of aeronautical charts and the magnetic compass for pilotage and dead reckoning, and the use of radio aids for VFR navigation;

(4) The safe and efficient operation of helicopters or gyroplanes, as appropriate to the rating sought; and

(5) Basic aerodynamics and principles of flight which apply to rotorcraft and the significance and use of performance charts.

61.127 FLIGHT PROFICIENCY

The applicant for a commercial pilot certificate must have logged instruction from an authorized flight instructor in at least the following pilot operations. In addition, his logbook must contain an endorsement by an authorized flight instructor who has given him the instruction certifying that he has found the applicant prepared to perform each of those operations competently as a commercial pilot.

(a) *Airplanes.*

(1) Preflight duties, including load and balance determination, line inspection, and aircraft servicing;

(2) Flight at slow airspeeds with realistic distractions, and the recognition of a recovery from stalls entered from straight flight and from turns;

(3) Normal and crosswind takeoffs and landings, using precision approaches, flaps, power as appropriate, and specified approach speeds;

(4) Maximum performance takeoffs and landings, climbs, and descents;

(5) Operation of an airplane equipped with a retractable landing gear, flaps, and controllable propeller(s), including normal and emergency operations; and

(6) Emergency procedures, such as coping with power loss or equipment malfunctions, fire in flight, collision avoidance precautions, and engine-out procedures if a multiengine airplane is used.

(b) *Helicopters.*

(1) Preflight duties, including line inspection and helicopter servicing;

(2) Straight and level flight, climbs, turns, and descents;

(3) Air taxiing, hovering, and maneuvering by ground references;

(4) Normal and crosswind takeoffs and landings;

(5) Recognition of and recovery from imminent flight at critical/rapid descent with power (setting with power);

(6) Airport and traffic pattern operations, including collision avoidance precautions and radio communications;

(7) Cross-country flight operations;

(8) Operations in confined areas and on pinnacles, rapid decelerations, landing on slopes, high-altitude takeoffs, and run-on landings; and

(9) Simulated emergency procedures, including failure of an engine or other component or system, and approaches to a hover or landing with one engine inoperative in multiengine helicopters, or autorotational descents with a power recovery to a hover in single-engine helicopters.

61.139 COMMERCIAL PILOT PRIVILEGES AND LIMITATIONS: GENERAL

The holder of a commercial pilot certificate may:

(a) Act as pilot in command of an aircraft carrying persons or property for compensation or hire;

(b) Act as pilot in command of an aircraft for compensation or hire; and

(c) Give flight instruction in an airship if he holds a lighter-than-air category and an airship class rating, or in a free balloon if he holds a free balloon class rating.

AIRLINE TRANSPORT PILOTS

61.153 AIRPLANE RATING: AERONAUTICAL KNOWLEDGE

An applicant for an airline transport pilot certificate with an airplane rating must, after meeting the requirements of {{61.151 (except paragraph
(a) thereof) and 61.155, pass a written test on

(a) The sections of this Part relating to airline transport pilots and Part 121, Subpart C of Part 65, and {{91.1 through 91.13 and Subpart B of Part 91 of this chapter, and so much of Parts 21 and 25 of this chapter as relate to the operations of air carrier aircraft;

(b) The fundamentals of air navigation and use of formulas, instruments, and other navigational aids, both in aircraft and on the ground, that are necessary for navigating aircraft by instruments;

(c) The general system of weather collection and dissemination;

(d) Weather maps, weather forecasting, and weather sequence abbreviations, symbols, and nomenclature;

(e) Elementary meteorology, including knowledge of cyclones as associated with fronts;

(f) Cloud forms;

(g) National Weather Service Federal Meteorology Handbook No. 1, as amended;

(h) Weather conditions, including icing conditions and upper-air winds, that affect aeronautical activities;

(i) Air navigation facilities used on Federal airways, including rotating beacons, course lights, radio ranges, and radio marker beacons;

(j) Information from airplane weather observations and meteorological data reported from observations made by pilots on air carrier flights;

(k) The influence of terrain on meteorological conditions and developments, and their relation to air carrier flight operations;

(l) Radio communication procedure in aircraft operations; and

(m) Basic principles of loading and weight distribution and their effect on flight characteristics.

*Began on 61-45/61.155 AIRPLANE RATING:AERONAUTICAL EXPERIENCE

Flight time used to meet the requirements of subparagraph (1) of this paragraph may also be used to meet the requirements of subparagraph (2) of this paragraph. Also, an applicant who has made at least 20 night takeoffs and landings to a full stop for each hour of night flight time required by subparagraph (2)(ii) of this paragraph. However, not more than 25 hours of night flight time may be credited in this manner.

(c) If an applicant with less than 150 hours of pilot in-command time otherwise meets the requirements of paragraph (b)(1) of this section, his certificate will be endorsed "Holder does not meet the pilot in-command flight experience requirements of ICAO," as prescribed by *Article 39 of the "Convention on International Civil Aviation." Whenever he presents satisfactory written evidence that he has accumulated the 150 hours of pilot in-command time, he is entitled to a new certificate without the endorsement.

(d) A commercial pilot may credit the following flight time toward the 1,500 hours total flight time requirement of paragraph (b)(2) of this section.

(1) All second-in-command time acquired in airplanes required to have more than one pilot by their approved Aircraft Flight Manuals or airworthiness certificates; and

(2) Flight engineer time acquired in airplanes required to have a flight engineer by their approved Aircraft Flight Manuals, while participating at the same time in an approved pilot training program approved under Part 121 of this chapter.

However, the applicant may not credit under subparagraph (2) of this paragraph more than 1 hour for each 3 hours of flight engineer flight time so acquired, nor more than a total of 500 hours.

(e) If an applicant who credits second-in-command or flight engineer time under paragraph (d) of this section toward the 1,500 hours total flight time so acquired, nor more than a total of 500 hours.

    (1) Does not have at least 1,200 hours of flight time as a pilot including no more than 50 percent of his second-in-command time and none of his flight engineer time; but

    (2) Otherwise meets the requirements of subparagraph (b)(2) of this section, his certificate will be endorsed "Holder does not meet the pilot flight experience requirements of ICAO," as prescribed by *Article 39 of the "Convention on International Civil Aviation." Whenever he presents satisfactory evidence that he has accumulated 1,200 hours of flight time as a pilot including no more than 50 percent of his second-in-command time and none of his flight engineer time, he is entitled to a new certificate without the endorsement.

(f) Reserved.

61.157 AIRPLANE RATING: AERONAUTICAL SKILL

(a) An applicant for an airline transport pilot certificate with a single-engine or multi-engine class rating or an additional type rating must pass a practical test that includes the items set forth in Appendix A of this Part. The FAA inspector or designated examiner may modify any required maneuver where necessary for the reasonable and safe operation of the airplane being used and, unless specifically prohibited in Appendix A, may combine any required maneuvers and may permit their performance in any convenient sequence.

(b) Whenever an applicant for an airline transport pilot certificate does not already have an instrument rating he shall, as part of the oral part of the practical test, comply with {61.65(g) and, as part of the flight part, perform each additional maneuver required by {61.65(g) that is appropriate to the airplane type and not required in Appendix A of this Part.

(c) Unless the Administrator requires certain or all maneuvers to be performed, the person giving a flight test for an airline transport pilot certificate or additional airplane class or type rating may, in his discretion, waive any of the maneuvers for which a specific waiver authority is contained in Appendix A of this Part if a pilot being checked -

    (1) Is employed as a pilot by a Part 121 certificate holder; and

    (2) Within the preceding 6 calendar months, has successfully completed that certificate holder's approved training program for the airplane type involved.

(d) The items specified in paragraph (a) of this section may be performed in the airplane simulator or other training device specified in Appendix A to this part for the particular item if -

(1) The airplane simulator or other training device meets the requirements of {121.407 of this chapter; and

(2) In the case of the items preceded by an asterisk (*) in Appendix A, the applicant has successfully completed the training set forth in {121.424(d) of this chapter.

However, the FAA inspector or designated examiner may require items ii(d), V(f), or V(g) of Appendix A to this part to be performed in the airplane if he determines that action is necessary to determine the applicant's competence with respect to that maneuver.

(e) An approved simulator may be used instead of the airplane to satisfy the inflight requirements of Appendix A of this Part, if the simulator -

(1) is approved under {121.407 of this chapter and meets the appropriate simulator requirements of Appendix H of Part 121; and

(2) is used as part of an approved program that meets the training requirements of {121.424 (a) and (c) and Appendix H of Part 121 of this chapter.

(f) On and after April 15, 1991, an applicant for a type rating to be added to an airline transport pilot certificate, or for issuance of an airline transport pilot certificate in an airplane requiring a type rating, must -

(1) Have completed ground and flight training on the maneuvers and procedures of Appendix A of this part that is appropriate to the airplane for which a type rating is sought and received an endorsement from an authorized instructor in the person's logbook or training records certifying satisfactory completion of the training; or

(2) For a pilot employee of a Part 121 or Part 135 certificate holder, have completed ground and flight training that is appropriate to the airplane for which a type rating is sought and is approved under Parts 121 and 135.

61.159 ROTORCRAFT RATING: AERONAUTICAL KNOWLEDGE

An applicant for an airline transport pilot certificate with a rotorcraft category and a helicopter class rating must pass a written test on -

(a) So much of this chapter as relates to air carrier rotorcraft operations;

(b) Rotorcraft design, components, systems and performance limitations;

(c) Basic principles of loading and weight distribution and their effect on rotorcraft flight characteristics;

(d) Air traffic control systems and procedures relating to rotorcraft;

(e) Procedures for operating rotorcraft in potentially hazardous meteorological conditions;

(f) Flight theory as applicable to rotorcraft; and

(g) The items listed under paragraphs (b) through (m) of {61.153.

61.161   ROTORCRAFT RATING: AERONAUTICAL EXPERIENCE

(a) An applicant for an airline transport pilot certificate with a rotorcraft category and helicopter class rating must hold a commercial pilot certificate, or a foreign airline transport pilot or commercial pilot certificate with a rotorcraft category and helicopter class rating issued by a member of ICAO, or be a pilot in an armed force of the United States whose military experience qualifies that pilot for the issuance of a commercial pilot certificate under {61.73.

(b) An applicant must have had at least 1,200 hours of flight time as a pilot, including at least -
   (1) 500 hours of cross-country flight time;
   (2) 100 hours of night flight time, of which at least 15 hours are in helicopters;
   (3) 200 hours in helicopters, including at least 75 hours as pilot in command, or as second in command performing the duties and functions of a pilot in command under the supervision of a pilot in command, or any combination thereof; and

61.169   INSTRUCTION IN AIR TRANSPORTATION SERVICE

An airline transport pilot may instruct other pilots in air transportation service in aircraft of the category, class, and type for which he is rated. However, he may not instruct for more than 8 hours in one day nor more than 36 hours in any 7-day period. He may instruct under this section only in aircraft with functioning dual controls. Unless he has a flight instructor certificate, an airline transport pilot may instruct only as provided in this section.

61.171   GENERAL PRIVILEGES AND LIMITATIONS

An airline transport pilot has the privileges of a commercial pilot with an instrument rating. The holder of a commercial pilot certificate who qualifies for an airline transport pilot certificate retains the ratings on his commercial pilot certificate, but he may exercise only the privileges of a commercial pilot with respect to them.

FLIGHT INSTRUCTORS

61.185   AERONAUTICAL KNOWLEDGE

(a) Present evidence showing that he has satisfactorily completed a course of instruction in at least the following subjects:
   (1) The learning process.
   (2) Elements of effective teaching.

(3) Student evaluation, quizzing, and testing.
(4) Course development.
(5) Lesson planning.
(6) Classroom instructing techniques.
(b) Have logged ground instruction from an authorized ground or flight instructor in all of the subjects in which ground instruction is required for a private and commercial pilot certificate, and for an instrument rating, if an airplane or instrument instructor rating is sought.

61.187 FLIGHT PROFICIENCY

(a) An applicant for a flight instructor certificate must have received flight instruction, appropriate to the instructor rating sought in the subjects listed in this paragraph by a person authorized in paragraph (b) of this section. In addition, his logbook must contain an endorsement by the person who has given him the instruction certifying that he has found the applicant competent to pass a practical test on the following subjects:
(1) Preparation and conduct of lesson plans for students with varying backgrounds and level of experience and ability.
(2) The evaluation of student flight performance.
(3) Effective preflight and postflight instruction.
(4) Flight instructor responsibilities and certifying procedures.
(5) Effective analysis and correction of common student pilot flight errors.
(6) Performance and analysis of standard flight training procedures and maneuvers appropriate to the flight instructor rating sought. For flight instructor-airplane and flight instructor-glider applicants, this shall include the satisfactory demonstration of stall awareness, spin entry, spins, and spin recovery techniques in an aircraft of the appropriate category that is certificated for spins.
(b) The flight instruction required by paragraph (a) of this section must be given by a person who has held a flight instructor certificated during the 24 months immediately preceding the date the instruction is given, who meets the general requirements for a flight instructor certificate prescribed in {61.183, and who has given at least 200 hours of flight instruction, or 80 hours in the case of glider instruction, as a certificated flight instructor.

61.193 FLIGHT INSTRUCTOR AUTHORIZATIONS

(a) The holder of a flight instructor certificate is authorized, within the limitations of that person's flight instructor certificate and ratings, to give the -

(1) Flight instruction required by this part for a pilot certificate or rating;

(2) Ground instruction or a home study course required by this part of a pilot certificate and rating;

(3) Ground and flight instruction required by this subpart for a flight instructor certificate and rating, if that person meets the requirements prescribed in {61.187(b);

(4) Flight instruction required for an initial solo or cross-country flight;

(5) Flight review required in {61.56 in a manner acceptable to the Administrator;

(6) Instrument competency check required in {61.57(e)(2);

(7) Pilot-in-command flight instruction required under {61.101(d); and

(8) Ground and flight instruction required by this part for the issuance of the endorsements specified in paragraph (b) of this section.

(b) The holder of a flight instructor certificate is authorized within the limitations of that person's flight instructor certificate and rating, to endorse -

(1) In accordance with {{61.87(m) and 61.93(c) and (d), the pilot certificate of a student pilot the instructor has instructed authorizing the student to conduct solo or solo cross-country flights, or to act as pilot in command of an airship requiring more than one flight crew member;

(2) In accordance with {{61.87(m) and 61.93(b) and (d), the logbook of a student pilot the flight instructor has instructed, authorizing single or repeated solo flights;

(3) In accordance with {61.93(d), the logbook of a student pilot whose preparation and preflight planning for a solo cross-country flight the flight instructor has reviewed and found adequate for a safe flight under the conditions the flight instructor has listed in the logbook;

Type Rating

(3) He must pass a flight test showing competence in pilot operations under Instrument flight rules in an aircraft of the type for which the type rating is sought or, in the case of a single pilot station airplane, meet the requirements of paragraph (d)(3)(i) or (ii) of this section, whichever is applicable.

  (i) The applicant must have met the requirements of this paragraph in a multiengine airplane for which a type rating is required.

  (ii) If he does not meet the requirements of paragraph (d)(3)(i) of this section and he seeks a type rating for a single-engine airplane, he must meet the requirements of this subparagraph in either a single or multiengine airplane, and have the recent instrument experience set forth in {61.57(e) when he applies for the flight test under paragraph (d)(2) of this section.

(4) An applicant who does not meet the requirements of paragraphs (d)(1) and (3) of this section may obtain a type rating limited to "VFR only". Upon meeting these instrument requirements or the requirements of {61.73(e)(2), the "VFR only" limitation may be removed for the particular type of aircraft in which competence is shown.

(5) When an instrument rating is issued to the holder of one or more type ratings, the type ratings on the amended certificate bear the limitation described in paragraph (d)(4) of this section for each airplane type rating for which he has not shown his instrument competency under this paragraph.

(6) On and after April 15, 1991, an applicant for a type rating to be added to a pilot certificate must -

   (i) Have completed ground and flight training on the maneuvers and procedures of Appendix A of this part that is appropriate to the airplane for which a type rating is sought, and received an endorsement from an authorized instructor in the person's logbook or training records certifying satisfactory completion of the training; or

   (ii) For a pilot employee of a part 121 or part 135 certificate holder, have completed the certificate holder's approved ground and flight training that is appropriate to the airplane for which a type rating is sought.

61.65   INSTRUMENT RATING REQUIREMENTS

(b) *Ground instruction.* An applicant for the written test for an instrument rating must have received ground instruction, or have logged home study in at least the following areas of aeronautical knowledge appropriate to the rating sought.

   (1) The regulations of this chapter that apply to flight under IFR conditions, the Airman's Information Manual, and the IFR air traffic system and procedures;

   (2) Dead reckoning appropriate to IFR navigation, IFR navigation by radio aids using the VOR, ADF, and ILS systems, and the use of IFR charts and instrument approach plates;

   (3) The procurement and use of aviation weather reports and forecasts, and the elements of forecasting weather trends on the basis of that information and personal observation of weather conditions; and

   (4) The safe and efficient operation of airplanes or helicopters, as appropriate, under instrument weather conditions.

(c) *Flight instruction and Skill - Airplanes.* An applicant for the flight test for an instrument rating (airplane) must present a logbook record certified by an authorized flight instructor showing that he has received instrument flight instruction in an airplane in the following pilot operations, and has been found competent in each of them:

(1) Control and accurate maneuvering of an airplane solely by reference to instruments.

(2) IFR navigation by the use of the VOR and ADF systems, including compliance with air traffic control instructions and procedures.

(3) Instrument approaches to published minimums using the VOR, ADF, and ILS systems (instruction in the use of the ADF and ILS may be received in an instrument ground trainer and instruction in the use of the ILS glide slope may be received in an airborne ILS simulator).

(4) Cross-country flying in simulated or actual IFR conditions, on Federal airways or as routed by ATC, including one such trip of at least 250 nautical miles, including VOR, ADF, and ILS approaches at different airports.

(5) Simulated emergencies, including the recovery from unusual attitudes, equipment or instrument malfunctions, loss of communications, and engine-out emergencies if a multi-engine airplane is used, and missed approach procedures.

(d) *Instrument Instruction and Skill - (Helicopter).* An applicant for the flight test for an instrument rating (helicopter) must present a logbook record certified to by an authorized flight instructor showing that he has received instrument flight instruction in a helicopter in the following pilot operations, and has been found competent in each of them:

(1) The control and accurate maneuvering of a helicopter solely by reference to instruments.

(2) IFR navigation by the use of the VOR and ADF systems, including compliance with air traffic instructions and procedures.

(3) Instrument approaches to published minimums using the VOR, ADF, and ILS systems (instruction in the use of the ADF and ILS may be received in an instrument ground trainer, and instruction in the use of the ILS guide slope may be received in an airborne ILS simulator).

(4) Cross-country flying under simulated or actual IFR conditions, on Federal airways or as routed by ATC, including one flight of at least 100 nautical miles, including VOR, ADF, and ILS approaches at different airports.

(5) Simulated IFR emergencies, including equipment malfunctions, missed approach procedures, and deviations to unplanned alternates.

Table A-1. Aviation software

Accu-Weather, Inc.
619 W. College Ave.
State College, PA 16801
814-237-0309
Weather

Advanced Gravis, No. 111, 7400 MacPherson Ave.
Burnaby, BC Canada V5J, 5B6
604-431-5020
Flight simulators

Air Routing International
2925 Briar Park
6th Floor
Houston, TX 77042
800-231-5787
Databases, Weather

AirDigital Corporation
3923 E. Thunderbird Road
#26
Phoenix, AZ 85032
602-996-8332
Business, Logbooks

AOPA Online (PC Access software)
Attn. Seth Golby
421 Aviation Way
Frederick, MD 21701
800-462-2672
Databases, DUATS, Weather

Aus-Ex Corporation
1807 Airport Drive
San Marcos, TX 78666
512-754-8200
Fax: 512-754-8202
Flight simulators

Aviontek
20783 Non Pariel Way
Groveland, CA 95321
209-962-6596
DUATS

AzureSoft
1250 Aviation Ave.
Suite 240
San Jose, CA 95110
408-947-1121
Flight simulators

Beattle Enterprises
PO Box 50154
Clayton, MO 63105
314-727-7721
Navigation

Black Hawk Aviation
4117 White Pine Dr.
Raleigh, NC 27612
919-840-0333
Flight planners, Flight simulators

Bullseye Software
PO Drawer 7900
Incline Village, NY 89452
702-831-2523
Flight simulators

Cape Cod Connection
21 Pleasant View Ave.
Falmouth, MA 02540
508-457-0739
Flight simulators

Cara Comp.
7108 SW 112th Place
Miami, FL 33173
800-962-7217
Flight instruction

Castle Information Agency
2124-B Gateway Dr.
#101
PO Box 6010
Grand Forks, ND 58206-6010
701-594-2381
Logbooks

CAVU Companies
12411 Osborne St.
Suite 107
Hansen Hills, CA 91331
818-897-6569
Fax: 818-897-6569, ext. 99
Business

CH Products
970 Park Center Drive
Vista, CA 92083
619-598-2518
Flight simulators

Charlot Aviation Training Services, Inc.
333 Cherie Court
Fort Walton Beach, FL 32548-4127
800-CATS INC
Flight instruction

ComAir Aviation Academy
2700 Flightline Ave.
Sanford, FL 32772
800-822-6359
Fax: 407-323-3817
Flight instruction

CompuFlight
48 Harbor Park Dr.
Port Washington, NY 11050
516-625-0202
Flight planners, weather

CompuServe
PO Box 20212
5000 Arlington Center Blvd.
Columbus, OH 43220
614-457-8600
800-848-8199 (service line)
Flight planners, Flight simulators, Weather, Miscellaneous

Computer Pilots Association of America
PO Box 580608
Houston, TX 77258-0608
713-333-4698
Fax: 713-333-4685
Flight simulators

Computer Training Systems
580 Sylvan Ave.
Englewood Cliffs, NJ 07632
201-567-5639
Fax: 201-567-3202
Flight instruction

Countstone, Inc.
PO Box 391
Chesterfield, MO 63006
800-325-9226
Logbooks

Daedalus Software
915 Highland Ave.
Pelham, NY 10803
914-738-8768
Flight instruction, Logbook

Data Transformation Corp. (DTC)
108-D Greentree Rd.
Turnersville, NJ 08012
800-AID-DUAT
DUATS

Dave Brown Products
4560 Layhigh Road
Hamilton, OH 45013
513-738-1576
Flight simulators

DKP Software, Inc.
PO Box 5292
Katy, TX 77492
713-232-5255
Business, Logbooks

EasySoft Software Company/AvTools Software
3646 Autumn Ridge Parkway
Marietta, GA 30066
800-336-0482
Business, Databases, Flight planners, Miscellaneous

EMI Aerocorp., Inc.
7 N. Brentwood Blvd.
St. Louis, MO 63105
314-727-9600
Flight planners

Excel Software Corporation
12280 Saratoga-Sunnyvale Road
Suite 212
Saratoga, CA 95070
408-446-5512
Fax: 408-446-5513
Flight planners

E-Z Flight Software
12021 Wilshire Blvd.
Suite 172
Los Angeles, CA 90025
818-997-7444
Flight planners

Flight Data Centers, Inc.
34 South River St.
Wilkes-Barre, PA 18702-2406
800-451-DATA
DUATS, Weather

Flight Deck Software
PO Box 425
Williamsburg, VA 23187
800-955-4359
Fax: 804-229-8516
BBS: 804-229-1571
Flight simulators

Flight Link
Chico Municipal Airport
290 Airpark Blvd.
Suite 6
Chico, CA 95936
916-891-5987
Flight simulators

Flightmaster
421 W Jefferson Blvd.
Dallas, TX 75208
214-264-3652
Flight simulators

Global Weather Dynamics, Inc.
2400 Garden Rd.
Monterey, CA 93940
408-649-4500
Weather

GTE Federal Systems DUATS
15000 Conference Center Dr.
Chantilly, VA 22021-3808
800-345-DUAT
703-818-5404
DUATS, Flight planners

IGS International
130 Redwood Place
Scotts Valley, CA 95066
408-438-2276
Flight planners

Jeppesen Sanderson
55 Inverness Dr. E.
Englewood, CO 80112-5498
303-799-9090
Flight instruction

JR SAR Software
1600 West Kitt Hawk Way
Tucson, AZ 85737
Flight planners

King Flight Schools
3840 Calle Fortunada
San Diego, CA 92123
619-541-2200
Fax: 619-541-2201
Flight instruction

Kraft Systems, Inc.
450 W. California Ave.
Vista, CA 92083
619-724-7146
Flight simulators

Maxximum Company
205 South 20th St.
Nampa, ID 83686
800-766-6299
208-465-4606
Flight simulators

McKenna Service Co.
901 East Orchard
Unit J
Mundelein, IL 60060
708-566-1120
Flight simulators

MDM Systems, Inc.
756 Tywola Road
Suite 105
Charlotte, NC 28217
704-523-7400
Flight simulators

Mentor Plus Software, Inc.
22775 Airport Rd. N.E.
PO Box 0356
Aurora, OR 97002-0356
800-448-3852, ext. 12
503-678-1431
Flight instruction, Navigation

Merritt-Dempsey, Inc.
PO Box 89822
Sioux Falls, SD 57105
605-335-1339
Logbooks

Microcomputer Software Design
PO Box 1006
Bloomington, IL 61702-1006
309-662-5176
Flight planners, Navigation

MicroProse Software, Inc.
180 Lakefront Drive
Hunt Valley, MD 21030
410-771-1151
Flight simulators

Microsoft Corporation
One Microsoft Way
Redmond, WA 98052-6399
800-227-4679
800-451-1261
Flight simulators

NT Systems
572 Royal Palm Dr.
Melbourne, FL 32935
407-254-6484
Flight simulators

Polaris Microsystems
PO Box 804
Woodbury, NJ 08096
800-336-1204
609-848-1043
Logbook

Precision Approach
PO Box 122
Prophetstown, IL 61277
708-456-5907
Flight simulators

Precision Flight Controls
7031 Forbes
Citrus Heights, CA 95610
916-721-7613
Flight simulators

RMS - Technology, Inc.
124 Berkley Ave.
PO Box 249
Molalla, OR 97038
800-533-3211
503-829-6166
Flight planners, Flight instruction

Sierra On-Line
PO Box 485
Coarse Gold, CA 93614
800-326-5543
Flight simulators

Simutech Corporation
PO Box 274112
Tampa, FL 33688 or
46 Harbor Lake Circle
Safety Harbor, FL 34695
800-226-7820
Flight simulators

Soft Ventures
113 Parkwood Place, S.E.
Calgary, Alberta, Canada T2J 3X1
403-278-1681
Business logbooks

Sporty's Pilot Shop
Clermont Airport
Batavia, OH 45103
800-543-8033
513-732-2411

subLOGIC
501 Kenyon Road
Champaign, IL 61820
217-359-8482
Flight simulators

Sunrise Software
411 Tonelli Trail
Lockport, IL 60441
815-838-4260
800-383-0970
Logbooks

Sunshine Unlimited, Inc.
PO Box 471
Lindsborg, KS 67456
913-227-3880
Business, Databases, Flight Planners,
Logbooks, Miscellaneous

S.W. Enterprises
PO Box 5432
Norman, OK 73070
405-527-7368
Flight simulators

T-34 Microsystems
1950 Prudential Drive
Suite 300
Jacksonville, FL 32207
904-396-2785
Fax: 904-396-0926
Flight simulators

TekMate
15307 Parkville
Houston, TX 77068
713-440-5542
Flight simulators

Glossary

No technical book would be complete without a glossary. So here's a list of the terms I really think you need to be familiar with in order to become an effective professional pilot. Don't worry about the size of the list, however. You won't need to know all of the terminology for your first job.

abbreviated IFR flight plans An authorization by ATC requiring pilots to submit only that information needed for the purpose of ATC. The abbreviated IFR flight plans include only a small portion of the usual IFR flight plan information. In certain instances, this might be only aircraft identification, location, and pilot request. Other information might be requested if needed by ATC for separation/control purposes. It's frequently used by aircraft that are airborne and desire an instrument approach or by aircraft that are on the ground and desire a climb to VFR-on-top. (See VFR-On-Top.) (Refer to AIM.)

abeam An aircraft is "abeam" a fix, point, or object when that fix, point, or object is approximately 90 degrees to the right or left of the aircraft track. Abeam indicates a general position rather than a precise point.

abort To terminate a preplanned aircraft maneuver: e.g., an aborted takeoff.

ACDO (See Air Carrier District Office.)

acknowledge Let me know that you've received my message.

active runway (See Runway In Use/Active Runway/Duty Runway.)

additional services Advisory information provided by ATC that includes but is not limited to the following:

- Traffic advisories.
- Vectors, when requested by the pilot, to assist aircraft that's receiving traffic advisories to avoid observed traffic.
- Altitude deviation information of 300 feet or more from an assigned altitude as observed on a verified (reading correctly) automatic altitude readout (Mode C).
- Advisories that traffic is no longer a factor.

- Weather and chaff information.
- Weather assistance.
- Bird activity information.
- Holding pattern surveillance.

Additional services are provided to the extent possible, contingent only on the controller's ability to fit them into the performance of higher priority duties and on the basis of limitations of the radar, volume of traffic, frequency congestion, and controller work load. The controller has complete discretion for determining if he or she is able to provide or continue to provide a service in a particular case. The controller's reason not to provide or continue to provide a service in a particular case is not subject to question by the pilot and need not be made known to him or her. (See Traffic Advisories.) (Refer to AIM.)

advise intentions Tell me what you plan to do.

advisory Advice and information provided to assist pilots in the safe conduct of flight and aircraft movement. (See Advisory Service.)

advisory frequency The appropriate frequency to be used for airport advisory service. (See Local Airport Advisory, Unicom.) (Refer to Advisory Circular 90-42, AIM.)

advisory service Advice and information provided by a facility to assist pilots in the safe conduct of flight and aircraft movement. (See Local Airport Advisory, Traffic Advisories, Safety Alert, Additional Services, Radar Advisory, En Route Flight Advisory Service.) (Refer to AIM.)

aerodrome A defined area on land or water (including any buildings, installations, and equipment) intended to be used either wholly or in part for the arrival, departure, and movement of aircraft.

aeronautical chart A map used in air navigation containing all or part of the following: topographic features, hazards and obstructions, navigation aids, navigation routes, designated airspace, and airports. Commonly used aeronautical charts are:

- Sectional Charts, 1:500,000. Designed for visual navigation of slow- or medium-speed aircraft. Topographic information on these charts features the portrayal of relief and a judicious selection of visual checkpoints for VFR flight. Aeronautical information includes visual and radio aids to navigation, airports, controlled airspace, restricted areas, obstructions, and related data.

- VFR Terminal Area Charts, 1:250,000. Depict terminal control area (TCA) airspace that provides for the control or segregation of all the aircraft within the TCA. The chart depicts topographic information and aeronautical information that includes visual and radio aids to navigation, airports, controlled airspace, restricted areas, obstructions, and related data.

- World Aeronautical Charts (WACs), 1:1,000,000. Provide a standard series of aeronautical charts covering land areas of the world at a size and scale convenient for navigation by moderate-speed aircraft. Topographic information includes cities and towns, principal roads, railroads, distinctive landmarks, drainage, and relief. Aeronautical information includes visual and radio aids to navigation, airports, airways, restricted areas, obstructions, and other pertinent data.

- En route Low-altitude Charts Provide aeronautical information for en route instrument navigation (IFR) in the low-altitude stratum. Information includes the portrayal of airways, limits of controlled airports, minimum route and frequencies of radio aids, selected airports, minimum route and minimum obstruction clearance altitudes, airway distances, reporting points, restricted areas, and related data. Area charts, which are a part of this series, furnish terminal data at a larger scale in congested areas.
- En route High-altitude Charts Provide aeronautical information for en route instrument navigation (IFR) in the high-altitude stratum. Information includes the portrayal of jet routes, identification and frequencies of radio aids, selected airports, distances, time zones, special-use airspace, and related information.
- U.S. Terminal Procedures Publication (TPP) Combines instrument approach procedure (IAP) charts, standard terminal arrival (STAR) charts, and standard instrument departure (SID) charts. IAPs portray the aeronautical data that's required to execute an instrument approach to an airport. These charts depict the procedures, including all related data, and the airport diagram. Each procedure is designated for use with a specific type of electronic navigation system including NDB, tacan, VOR, ILS/MLS, and RNAV. These charts are identified by the type of navigational aid(s) that provides final approach guidance. SIDs are designed to expedite clearance delivery and to facilitate transition between takeoff and en route operations. Each SID procedure is presented as a separate chart and might serve a single airport or more than one airport in a given geographical location. STARs are designed to expedite ATC arrival procedures and to facilitate transition between en route and instrument approach operations. Each STAR procedure is presented as a separate chart and might serve a single airport or more than one airport in a given geographical location.
- Airport Taxi Charts Designed to expedite the efficient and safe flow of ground traffic at an airport. These charts are identified by the official airport name; e.g., Washington National Airport.

affirmative Yes.

air carrier A person who undertakes directly by lease, or other arrangement, to engage in air transportation.

Air Carrier District Office (ACDO) An FAA field office serving an assigned geographical area, staffed with Flight Standards personnel serving the aviation industry and the general public on matters related to the certification and operation of scheduled air carriers and other large aircraft operations.

aircraft approach category A grouping of aircraft based on a speed of 1.3 times the stall speed in the landing configuration at maximum gross landing weight. An aircraft shall fit in only one category. If it's necessary to maneuver at speeds in excess of the upper limit of a speed range for a category, the minimums for the next higher category should be used. For example, an aircraft that falls in Category A, but is circling to land at a speed in excess of 91 knots, should use the approach Category B minimums when circling to land. The categories are as follows:

- Category A. Speed less than 91 knots.
- Category B. Speed 91 knots or more but less than 121 knots.
- Category C. Speed 121 knots or more but less than 141 knots.
- Category D. Speed 141 knots or more but less than 166 knots.
- Category E. Speed 166 knots or more.

airmet (WA) In-flight weather advisories issued only to amend the area forecast concerning weather phenomena that are of operational interest to all aircraft and potentially hazardous to aircraft having limited capability because of lack of equipment, instrumentation, or pilot qualifications. Airmets concern weather of less severity than that covered by sigmets or convective sigmets. Airmets cover moderate icing, moderate turbulence, sustained winds of 30 knots or more at the surface, widespread areas of ceilings less than 1,000 feet and/or visibility less than 3 miles, and extensive mountain obscurement. (See Severe Weather Forecast Alerts, Sigmet, Convective Sigmet, Center Weather Advisory.) (Refer to AIM.)

airport An area on land or water that's used or intended to be used for the landing and takeoff of aircraft and includes its buildings and facilities, if any.

airport advisory area The area within 10 miles of an airport without a control tower or where the tower is not in operation, and on which an FSS is located. (See Local Airport Advisory.) (Refer to AIM.)

airport lighting Various lighting aids that might be installed on an airport. Types of airport lighting include:

- Approach Light System (ALS). An airport lighting facility that provides visual guidance to landing aircraft by radiating light beams in a directional pattern by which the pilot aligns the aircraft with the extended centerline of the runway on his final approach for landing. Condenser-Discharge Sequential Flashing Lights/Sequenced Flashing Lights might be installed in conjunction with the ALS at some airports. Types of approach light systems are:

  a. ALSF-1. ALS with Sequenced Flashing Lights in ILS Cat-I configuration.

  b. ALSF-2. ALS with Sequenced Flashing Lights in ILS Cat-I configuration.

  c. SSALF. Simplified Short ALS with Sequenced Flashing Lights.

  d. SSALR. Simplified Short ALS with Runway Alignment Indicator Lights.

e. MALSF. Medium-intensity ALS with Sequenced Flashing Lights.

f. MALSR. Medium-intensity ALS with Runway Alignment Indicator Lights.

g. LDIN. Lead-in-light system: Consists of one or more series of flashing lights installed at or near ground level that provides positive visual guidance along an approach path, either curving or straight, where special problems exist with hazardous terrain, obstructions, or noise abatement procedures.

h. RAIL. Runway Alignment Indicator Lights (Sequenced Flashing Lights that are installed only in combination with other light systems).

i. ODALS. Omnidirectional ALS consist of seven omnidirectional flashing lights located in the approach area of a nonprecision runway. Five lights are located on the runway centerline extended with the first light located 300 feet from the threshold and extending at equal intervals up to 1,500 feet from the threshold. The other two lights are located, one on each side of the runway threshold, at a lateral distance of 40 feet from the runway edge, or 75 feet from the runway edge when installed on a runway equipped with a VASI. (Refer to Order 6850.2A).

- Runway Lights/Runway Edge Lights. Lights having a prescribed angle of emission used to define the lateral limits of a runway. Runway lights are uniformly spaced at intervals of approximately 200 feet, and the intensity might be controlled or preset.

- Touchdown Zone Lighting. Two rows of transverse light bars located symmetrically about the runway centerline, normally at 100-foot intervals. The basic system extends 3,000 feet along the runway.

- Runway Centerline Lighting. Flush centerline lights spaced at 50-foot intervals beginning 75 feet from the landing threshold and extending to within 75 feet of the opposite end of the runway.

- Threshold Lights. Fixed green lights arranged symmetrically left and right of the runway centerline, identifying the runway threshold.

- Runway End Identifier Lights (REIL). Two synchronized flashing lights, one on each side of the runway threshold, that provide rapid and positive identification of the approach end of a particular runway.

- Visual Approach Slope Indicator (VASI). An airport lighting facility providing vertical visual approach slope guidance to aircraft during approach to landing by radiating a directional pattern of high-intensity red-and-white focused light beams that indicate to pilots that they are "on path" if they see red/white, "above path" if white/white, and "below path" if red/red. Some airports serving large aircraft have three-bar VASIs that provide two visual glidepaths to the same runway.

- Boundary Lights. Lights defining the perimeter of an airport or landing area. (Refer to AIM.)

airport marking aids Markings used on runway and taxiway surfaces to identify a specific runway, a runway threshold, a centerline, a hold line, etc. A runway should be marked in accordance with its present usage, such as:

- Visual.
- Nonprecision instrument.
- Precision instrument.

(Refer to AIM.)

airport radar service area (ARSA) (See Controlled Airspace.)

airport surface detection equipment (ASDE) Radar equipment specifically designed to detect all principal features on the surface of an airport, including aircraft and vehicular traffic, and to present the entire image on a radar indicator console in the control tower. Used to augment visual observation by tower personnel of aircraft and/or vehicular movements on runways and taxiways.

airport surveillance radar (ASR) Approach control radar used to detect and display an aircraft's position in the terminal area. ASR provides range and azimuth information but doesn't provide elevation data. Coverage of the ASR can extend up to 60 miles.

airport traffic area Unless otherwise specifically designated in FAR Part 93, that airspace within a horizontal radius of 5 statute miles from the geographical center of any airport at which a control tower is operating, extending from the surface up to, but not including, an altitude of 3,000 feet above the elevation of an airport. Unless otherwise authorized or required by ATC, no person may operate an aircraft within an airport traffic area except for the purpose of landing at or taking off from an airport within that area. ATC authorizations might be given as individual approval of specific operations or might be contained in written agreements between airport users and the tower concerned. (Refer to FAR Parts 1 and 91.)

Air Route Traffic Control Center (ARTCC) A facility established to provide ATC service to aircraft operating on IFR flight plans within controlled airspace and principally during the en route phase of flight. When equipment capabilities and controller work load permit, certain advisory/assistance services might be provided to VFR aircraft. (See NAS Stage A, En route Air Traffic Control Services.) (Refer to AIM.)

airspeed The speed of an aircraft relative to its surrounding air mass. The unqualified term "airspeed" means one of the following:

- Indicated Airspeed. The speed shown on the aircraft airspeed indicator. This is the speed used in pilot/controller communications under the general term "airspeed." (Refer to FAR Part 1.)

- True Airspeed. The airspeed of an aircraft relative to undisturbed air. Used primarily in flight planning and the en route portion of flight. When used in pilot/controller communications, it's referred to as "true airspeed" and not shortened to "airspeed."

air traffic clearance An authorization by ATC for an aircraft to proceed under specified traffic conditions within controlled airspace. Issued for the purpose of preventing collision between known aircraft. (See ATC Instructions, ICAO Air Traffic Control Clearance.)

airway A control area or portion thereof established in the form of a corridor, the centerline of which is defined by radio navigational aids. (See Low-altitude Airway Structure.) (Refer to FAR Part 71, AIM.)

alternate airport An airport at which an aircraft may land if a landing at the intended airport becomes inadvisable. (See ICAO Alternate Aerodrome.)

altimeter setting The barometric pressure reading used to adjust a pressure altimeter for variations in existing atmospheric pressure or to the standard altimeter setting (29.92). (Refer to FAR Part 91, AIM.)

altitude readout An aircraft's altitude, transmitted via the Mode C transponder feature, that's visually displayed in 100-foot increments on a radarscope having readout capability. (See Automated Radar Terminal Systems, NAS Stage A, Alphanumeric Display.) (Refer to AIM.)

altitude restriction An altitude or altitudes, stated in the order flown, that are to be maintained until reaching a specific point or time. Altitude restrictions might be issued by ATC due to traffic, terrain, or other airspace considerations.

approach clearance Authorization by ATC for a pilot to conduct an instrument approach. The type of instrument approach for which a clearance and other pertinent information is provided in the approach clearance when required. (See Instrument Approach Procedure, Cleared Approach.) (Refer to AIM, FAR Part 91.)

Approach Control Facility A terminal ATC facility that provides approach control service in a terminal area. (See Approach Control Service, Radar Approach Control Facility.)

Approach Control Service ATC service provided by an approach control facility for arriving and departing VFR/IFR aircraft and, on occasion, en route aircraft. At some airports not served by an approach control facility, the ARTCC provides limited approach control service. (See ICAO Approach Control Service.) (Refer to AIM.)

approach gate An imaginary point used within ATC as a basis for vectoring aircraft to the final approach course. The gate will be established along the final approach course one mile from the outer marker (or the fix used in lieu of the outer marker) on the side away from the airport for precision approaches and one mile from the final approach fix on the side away from the airport for nonprecision approaches. In either case, when measured along the final approach course, the gate will be no closer than five miles from the landing threshold.

approach speed The recommended speed contained in aircraft manuals used by pilots when making an approach to landing. This speed will vary for different segments of an approach as well as for aircraft weight and configuration.

area navigation (RNAV) A method of navigation that permits aircraft operation on any desired course within the coverage of station-referenced navigation signals or within the limits of a self-contained system capability.

Random area navigation routes are direct routes, based on area navigation capability, between waypoints defined in terms of latitude/longitude coordinates, degree/distance fixes, or offsets from published or established routes/airways at a specified distance and direction. The major types of equipment are:

- Vortac-referenced or Course Line Computer (CLC) systems, which account for the greatest number of RNAV units in use. To function, the CLC must be within the service range of a vortac.
- Omega/VLF, although two separate systems, can be considered as one operationally. A long-range navigation system based on very low frequency radio signals transmitted from a total of 17 stations worldwide.
- Inertial (INS) systems, which are totally self-contained and require no information from external references. They provide aircraft position and navigation information in response to signals resulting from inertial effects on components within the system.
- MLS area navigation (MLS/RNAV), which provides area navigation with reference to an MLS ground facility.
- Loran C is a long-range radio navigation system that uses ground waves transmitted at low frequency to provide user position information at ranges of up to 600 to 1,200 nautical miles at both en route and approach altitudes. The usable signal coverage areas are determined by the signal-to-noise ratio, the envelope-to-cycle difference, and the geometric relationship between the positions of the user and the transmitting stations. (See ICAO Area Navigation.)

ARINC An acronym for Aeronautical Radio, Inc., a corporation largely owned by a group of airlines. Arinc is licensed by the FCC as an aeronautical station and contracted by the FAA to provide communications support for ATC and meteorological services in portions of international airspace.

ATC advises Used to prefix a message of noncontrol information when it's relayed to an aircraft by other than an air traffic controller. (See Advisory.)

ATC instructions Directives issued by ATC for the purpose of requiring a pilot to take specific actions; e.g., "Turn left heading two-five-zero," "Go around," "Clear the runway." (Refer to FAR Part 91.)

autoland approach An autoland approach is a precision instrument approach to touchdown and, in some cases, through the landing rollout. An autoland approach is performed by the aircraft autopilot that's receiving position information and/or steering commands from onboard navigation equipment. (See Coupled Approach.) *Note:* Autoland and coupled approaches are flown in VFR and IFR. It's common for carriers to require their crews to fly coupled approaches and autoland approaches (if certified) when the weather conditions are less than approximately 4,000 RVR.

automated radar terminal systems (ARTS) The generic term for the ultimate in functional capability afforded by several automation systems. Each differs in functional capabilities and equipment. ARTS plus a suffix Roman numeral denotes a specific system. A following letter indicates a major modification to that system. In general, an ARTS displays for the terminal controller aircraft identification, flight plan data, and other flight-associated information: e.g., altitude, speed, and aircraft position symbols in conjunction with radar presentation. Normal radar coexists with the alphanumeric display. In addition to enhancing visualization of the air traffic situation, ARTS facilitates intra/interfacility transfer and coordination of flight information. These capabilities are enabled by specially designed computers and subsystems tailored to the radar and communications equipment and operational requirements of each automated facility. Modular design permits adoption of improvements in computer software and electronic technologies as they become available while retaining the characteristics unique to each system:

- ARTS II. A programmable, nontracking, computer-aided display subsystem capable of modular expansion. ARTS II systems provide a level of automated ATC capability at terminals having low-to-medium activity. Flight identification and altitude might be associated with the display of secondary radar targets. The system has the capability of communicating with ARTCCs and other ARTS II, IIA, III, and IIIA facilities.

- ARTS IIA. A programmable radar-tracking computer subsystem capable of modular expansion. The ARTS IIA detects, tracks, and predicts secondary radar targets. The targets are displayed by means of computer-generated symbols, groundspeed, and flight plan data. Although it doesn't track primary radar targets, they're displayed coincident with the secondary radar as well as the symbols and alphanumerics. The system has the capability of communicating with ARTCCs and other ARTS II, IIA, III, and IIIA facilities.

- ARTS III. The Beacon Tracking Level (BTL) of the modular, programmable automated radar terminal system in use at medium- to high-activity terminals. ARTS III detects, tracks, and predicts secondary radar-derived aircraft targets. These are displayed by means of computer-generated symbols and alphanumeric characters depicting flight identification, aircraft altitude, groundspeed, and flight plan data. Although it doesn't track primary targets, they're displayed coincident with the secondary radar as well as the symbols and alphanumerics. The system has the capability of communicating with ARTCCs and other ARTS III facilities.

- ARTS IIIA. The Radar Tracking and Beacon Tracking Level (RT&BTL) of the modular, programmable ARTS, ARTS IIIA detects, tracks, and predicts primary as well as secondary radar-derived aircraft targets. This more sophisticated computer-driven system upgrades the existing ARTS III system by providing improved tracking, continuous data recording, and fail-safe capabilities.

automatic direction finder (ADF) An aircraft radio navigation system that senses and indicates the direction to an L/MF nondirectional radio beacon (NDB) ground transmitter. Direction is indicated to the pilot as a magnetic bearing or as a relative bearing to the longitudinal axis of the aircraft, depending on the type of indicator installed in the aircraft. In certain applications, such as military, ADF operations might be based on airborne and ground transmitters in the VHF/UHF frequency spectrum. (See Bearing, Nondirectional Beacon.)

automatic terminal information service (ATIS) The continuous broadcast of recorded noncontrol information in selected terminal areas. Its purpose is to improve controller effectiveness and to relieve frequency congestion by automating the repetitive transmission of essential but routine information: e.g., "Los Angeles information Alfa. One-three-zero-zero Coordinated Universal Time. Weather, measured ceiling two thousand overcast, visibility three, haze, smoke, temperature seven-one, dew point five-seven, wind two-five-zero at five, altimeter two-niner-niner-six. ILS Runway Two-five Left approach in use, Runway Two-five Right closed, advise you have Alfa." (See ICAO Automatic Terminal Information Service.) (Refer to AIM.)

aviation safety reporting program A voluntary reporting program that invites pilots, controllers, maintenance people, and others directly involved in aviation to contribute to the FAA's efforts to promote safety by reporting actual or potential safety discrepancies or deficiencies. NASA handles receipt, processing, and analysis of raw data under its Aviation Safety Reporting System.

below minimums Weather conditions below the minimums prescribed by regulation for the particular action involved: e.g., landing minimums, takeoff minimums.

braking action (good, fair, poor, or nil) A report of conditions on the airport movement area providing a pilot with a degree/quality of braking that he or she might expect. Braking action is reported in terms of good, fair, poor, or nil. (See Runway Condition Reading.)

braking action advisories When tower controllers have received runway braking action reports that include the terms "poor" or "nil," or whenever weather conditions are conducive to deteriorating or rapidly changing runway braking conditions, the tower will include on the ATIS broadcast the statement, "Braking action advisories are in effect." During that time, braking action reports for the runway in use are issued to each arriving and departing aircraft. Pilots should be prepared for deteriorating braking conditions and should request current runway-condition information if not volunteered by controllers. Pilots should also be prepared to provide a descriptive runway-condition report to controllers after landing.

category (1) As used with respect to the certification, ratings, privileges, and limitations of airmen, means a broad classification of aircraft. Examples include: airplane, rotorcraft, glider, and lighter-than-air; and (2) As used with respect to the certification of aircraft, means a grouping of aircraft based on intended use or operating limitations. Examples include: Transport, Normal, Utility, Acrobatic, Limited, Restricted, and Provisional.

category A With respect to Transport category rotorcraft, means multiengine rotorcraft designed with engine and system isolation features specified in FAR Part 29 and using scheduled takeoff and landing operations under a crucial engine failure concept that assures adequate designated surface area and adequate performance capability for continued safe flight in the event of engine failure.

category B With respect to Transport category rotorcraft, means single-engine or multiengine rotorcraft that don't fully meet all Category A standards. Category B rotorcraft have no guaranteed stay-up ability in the event of engine failure, and unscheduled landing is assumed.

category II operations With respect to the operation of aircraft, means a straight-in ILS approach to the runway of an airport under a Category II ILS instrument approach procedure issued by the Administrator or other appropriate authority.

category III operations With respect to the operation of aircraft, means an ILS approach to, and landing on, the runway of an airport using a Category III ILS instrument approach procedure issued by the Administrator or other appropriate authority.

center weather advisory (CWA) An unscheduled weather advisory issued by Center Weather Service Unit meteorologists for ATC use to alert pilots of existing or anticipated adverse weather conditions within the next two hours. A CWA might modify or redefine a sigmet. (See Severe Weather Forecast Alerts, Sigmet, Convective Sigmet, Airmet.) (Refer to AIM.)

charted visual flight procedure (CVFP) approach An approach wherein a radar-controlled aircraft on an IFR flight plan, operating in VFR conditions and having an ATC authorization, might proceed to the airport of intended landing via visual landmarks and altitudes depicted on a CVFP.

circle-to-land maneuver A maneuver initiated by the pilot to align the aircraft with a runway for landing when a straight-in landing from an instrument approach is not possible or is not desirable. This maneuver is made only after ATC authorization has been obtained and the pilot has established required visual reference to the airport. (See Circle to Runway, Landing Minimums.) (Refer to AIM.)

circle to runway (runway number) Used by ATC to inform the pilot that he or she must circle to land because the runway in use is other than the runway aligned with the instrument approach procedure. When the direction of the circling maneuver in relation to the airport/runway is required, the controller will state the direction (eight cardinal compass points) and specify a left or right downwind or base leg as appropriate: e.g., "Cleared VOR Runway Three-six approach circle to Runway Two-two," or "Circle northwest of the airport for a right downwind to Runway Two-two." (See Circle-to-Land Maneuver, Landing Minimums.) (Refer to AIM.)

class (1) As used with respect to the certification, ratings, privileges, and limitations of airmen, means a classification of aircraft within a category having similar operating characteristics. Examples include: single-engine, multiengine, land, water, gyroplane, helicopter, airship, and free balloon; and (2) As used with respect to the certification of aircraft, means a broad grouping of aircraft having similar characteristics or propulsion, flight, or landing. Examples include: airplane, rotorcraft, glider, balloon, landplane, and seaplane.

clear-air turbulence (CAT) Turbulence encountered in air where no clouds are present. This term is commonly applied to high-level turbulence associated with wind shear. CAT is often encountered in the vicinity of the jet stream. (See Wind Shear, Jet Stream.)

clearance limit The fix, point, or location to which an aircraft is cleared when issued an air traffic clearance. (See ICAO Clearance Limit.)

clearance void if not off by (time) Used by ATC to advise an aircraft that the departure clearance is automatically canceled if takeoff is not made prior to a specified time. The pilot must obtain a new clearance or cancel his or her IFR flight plan if not off by the specified time. (See ICAO Clearance Void Time.)

cleared approach ATC authorization for an aircraft to execute any standard or special instrument approach procedure for that airport. Normally, an aircraft will be cleared for a specific instrument approach procedure. (See Cleared [Type Of] Approach, Instrument Approach Procedure.) (Refer to AIM, FAR Part 91.)

cleared (type of) approach ATC authorization for an aircraft to execute a specific instrument approach procedure to an airport: e.g., "Cleared for ILS Runway Three-six approach." (See Approach Clearance, Instrument Approach Procedure.) (Refer to AIM, FAR Part 91.)

cleared as filed Means the aircraft is cleared to proceed in accordance with the route of flight filed in the flight plan. This clearance doesn't include the altitude, SID, or SID transition. (See Request Full Route Clearance.) (Refer to AIM.)

cleared for takeoff ATC authorization for an aircraft to depart. It's predicated on known traffic and known physical airport conditions.

cleared for the option ATC authorization for an aircraft to make a touch-and-go, low-approach, missed approach, stop-and-go, or full-stop landing at the discretion of the pilot. It's normally used in training so that an instructor can evaluate a student's performance under changing situations. (See Option Approach.) (Refer to AIM.)

cleared through ATC authorization for an aircraft to make intermediate stops at specified airports without refiling a flight plan while en route to the clearance limit.

cleared to land ATC authorization for an aircraft to land. It's predicated on known traffic and known physical airport conditions.

commercial operator A person who, for compensation or hire, engages in the carriage by aircraft in air commerce of persons or property, other than as an air carrier or foreign air carrier or under the authority of FAR Part 375. Where it's doubtful that an operation is for "compensation or hire," the test applied is whether the carriage by air is merely incidental to the person's other business or is, in itself, a major enterprise for profit.

common traffic advisory frequency (CTAF) A frequency designed for the purpose of carrying out airport advisory practices while operating to or from an uncontrolled airport. The CTAF might be a unicom, multicom, FSS, or tower frequency and is identified in appropriate aeronautical publications. (Refer to AC 90-42.)

commuter pilot A seldom-used term to describe pilots who fly for smaller airlines in turboprop aircraft, usually seating less than 70 passengers. See also Regional Pilot.

compass heading (CH) Heading flown by reference to the magnetic compass. Magnetic heading corrected for compass deviation is compass heading.

compass locator A low-power, low- or medium-frequency (L/MF) radio beacon installed at the site of the outer or middle marker of an instrument landing system (ILS). It can be used for navigation at distances of approximately 15 miles or as authorized in the approach procedure.

- Outer Compass Locator (LOM) A compass locator installed at the site of the outer marker of an ILS. (See Outer Marker.)

- Middle Compass Locator (LMM) A compass locator installed at the site of the middle marker of an ILS. (See Middle Marker.) (See ICAO Locator.)

compulsory reporting points Reporting points that must be reported to ATC. They're designated on aeronautical charts by solid triangles or filed in a flight plan as fixes selected to define direct routes. These points are geographical locations that are defined by navigation aids/fixes. Pilots should discontinue position reporting over compulsory reporting points when informed by ATC that their aircraft is in "radar contact."

contact approach An approach wherein an aircraft on an IFR flight plan (having an ATC authorization, operating clear of clouds with at least one mile flight visibility and a reasonable expectation of continuing to the destination airport in those conditions) may deviate from the instrument approach procedure and proceed to the destination airport by visual reference to the surface. This approach will only be authorized when requested by the pilot and the reported ground visibility at the destination airport is at least one statute mile. (Refer to AIM.)

controlled airspace Airspace designated as a control zone, airport radar service area, terminal control area, transition area, control area, continental control area, and positive control area within which some or all aircraft might be subject to ATC. (Refer to AIM, FAR Part 71.) There are several types of controlled airspace. *Note:* The airspace reclassification rule goes into effect on September 16, 1993. The rule changes the names of types of airspace to letter designations. (See illustration of current and new airspace classification and the individual airspace descriptions in Section 4, "Airspace Structure and Air Traffic Control" for operating rule changes that will take effect on September 16, 1993. Also, see Section 12, "Regulations and Advisories.") The letter designations are:

- A. Positive control areas (PCAs), including jet routes and area high routes.
- B. Terminal control areas (TCAs).
- C. Airport radar service areas (ARSAs).
- D. Control zone/airport traffic areas (ATAs).

- E. Control zone/nontower airports and controlled airspace, including Victor airways, transition areas, and control areas.
- G. Uncontrolled airspace.

1. Control Zone. Controlled airspace that extends upward from the surface of the earth and terminates at the base of the continental control area. Control zones that don't underline the continental control area have no upper limit. A control zone might include one or more airports and is normally a circular area with a radius of 5 statute miles and any extensions necessary to include instrument approach and departure paths.

2. Airport Radar Service Area (ARSA). Regulatory airspace surrounding designated airports wherein ATC provides radar vectoring and sequencing on a full-time basis for all IFR and VFR aircraft. The service provided in an ARSA is called ARSA service, which includes: IFR/IFR-standard IFR separation, IFR/VFR-traffic advisories and conflict resolution, and VFR/VFR-traffic advisories and, as appropriate, safety alerts. The AIM contains an explanation of ARSA. The ARSAs are depicted on VFR aeronautical charts. (See Conflict Resolution, Outer AREA.) (Refer to AIM, the A/FD, FAR Part 91.)

3. Terminal Control Area (TCA). Controlled airspace extending upward from the surface or higher to specified altitudes, within which all aircraft are subject to operating rules and pilot and equipment requirements specified in FAR Part 91. TCAs are depicted on sectional, world aeronautical, en route low-altitude, DOD FLIP, and TCA charts. (Refer to FAR Part 91, AIM.)

4. Transition Area. Controlled airspace extending upward from 700 feet or more above the surface of the earth when designated in conjunction with an airport for which an approved instrument approach procedure has been prescribed, or from 1,200 feet or more above the surface of the earth when designated in conjunction with airway route structures or segments. Unless otherwise specified, transition areas terminate at the base of the overlying controlled airspace. Transition areas are designed to contain IFR operations in controlled airspace during portions of the terminal operation and while transiting between the terminal and en route environment.

5. Control Area. Airspace designated as colored federal airways, VOR federal airways, control areas associated with jet routes outside the continental control area (FAR 71.161), additional control areas (FAR 71.163), control area extensions (FAR 71.165), and area low routes. Control areas don't include the continental control area, but unless otherwise designated, they do include the airspace between a segment of a main VOR federal airway and its associated alternate segments with the vertical extent of the area corresponding to the vertical extent of the related segment of the main airway. The vertical extent of the various categories of airspace contained in control areas is defined in FAR Part 71.

6. Continental Control Area. The airspace of the 48 contiguous states, the District of Columbia, and Alaska, excluding the Alaska Peninsula west of

longitude 160°00'00" W, at and above 14,500 feet msl, but doesn't include: (a) the airspace less than 1,500 feet above the surface of the earth; or (b) prohibited and restricted areas, other than the restricted areas listed in FAR Part 71.

7. Positive Control Area (PCA). Airspace designated in FAR Part 71 within which there's positive control of aircraft. Flight in PCA is normally conducted under IFR. PCA is designated throughout most of the conterminous United States, and its vertical extent is from 18,000 feet msl to and including Flight Level 600. In Alaska, PCA doesn't include the airspace less than 1,500 feet above the surface of the earth nor the airspace over the Alaska Peninsula west of Longitude 160° West. Rules for operating in PCA are found in FARs 91.135 and 91.215. (See ICAO Controlled Airspace.)

convective sigmet A weather advisory concerning convective weather significant to the safety of all aircraft. Convective sigmets are issued for tornadoes, lines of thunderstorms, embedded thunderstorms of any intensity level, areas of thunderstorms greater than or equal to VIP Level 4 with an area coverage of four tenths (40 percent) or more and hail three-fourths inch or greater. (See Severe Weather Forecast Alerts, Sigmet, Center Weather Advisory, Airmet.) (Refer to AIM.)

coupled approach A coupled approach is an instrument approach performed by the aircraft autopilot that's receiving position information and/or steering commands from onboard navigation equipment. In general, coupled nonprecision approaches must be discontinued and flown manually at altitudes lower than 50 feet below the minimum descent altitude, and coupled precision approaches must be flown manually below 50 feet agl. (See Autoland Approach.) *Note:* Coupled and autoland approaches are flown in VFR and IFR. It's common for carriers to require their crews to fly coupled approaches and autoland approaches (if certified) when the weather conditions are less than approximately 4,000 RVR.

crash pad An apartment or room in a pilot's base city when his permanent home is in another location. Pilots will often share one apartment, making the monthly crash pad cost very low.

crew member A person assigned to perform duty in an aircraft during flight time.

critical altitude The maximum altitude at which, in standard atmosphere, it's possible to maintain at a specified rotational speed, a specified power, or a specified manifold pressure. Unless otherwise stated, the critical altitude is the maximum altitude at which it's possible to maintain, at the maximum continuous rotational speed, one of the following: (1) The maximum continuous power, in the case of engines for which this power rating is the same at sea level and at the rated altitude; (2) The maximum continuous rated manifold pressure; in the case of engines, the maximum continuous power, which is governed by a constant manifold pressure.

critical engine The engine that, on failure, would most adversely affect the performance or handling qualities of an aircraft.

cross (fix) at (altitude) Used by ATC when a specific altitude restriction at a specific fix is required.

cross (fix) at or above (altitude) Used by ATC when an altitude restriction at a specified fix is required. It doesn't prohibit the aircraft from crossing the fix at a higher altitude than specified; however, it must be at or above the minimum IFR altitude. (See Altitude Restriction, Minimum IFR Altitudes.) (Refer to FAR Part 91.)

cruise Used in an ATC clearance to authorize a pilot to conduct flight at any altitude from the minimum IFR altitude up to and including the altitude specified in the clearance. The pilot might level off at any intermediate altitude within this block of airspace. Climb/descent within the block is to be made at the discretion of the pilot. However, once the pilot starts descent and verbally reports leaving an altitude in the block, he or she may not return to that altitude without additional ATC clearance. Further, it's approval for the pilot to proceed to and make an approach at the destination airport and can be used in conjunction with:

- An airport clearance limit at locations with a standard/special instrument approach procedure. The FARs require that if an instrument letdown to an airport is necessary, the pilot shall make the letdown in accordance with a standard/special instrument approach procedure for that airport.

- An airport clearance limit at locations that are within/below/outside controlled airspace and without a standard/special instrument approach procedure. Such a clearance is not authorization for the pilot to descend under IFR conditions below the applicable minimum IFR altitude, nor does it imply that ATC is exercising control over aircraft in uncontrolled airspace; however, it provides a means for the aircraft to proceed to the destination airport, descend, and land in accordance with applicable FARs governing VFR flight operations. Also, this provides search-and-rescue protection until such time as the IFR flight plan is closed. (See Instrument Approach Procedure.)

dead reckoning Dead reckoning, as applied to flying, is the navigation of an airplane solely by means of computations based on airspeed, course, heading, wind direction, and speed, groundspeed, and elapsed time.

decision height (DH) With respect to the operation of aircraft, means the height at which a decision must be made during an ILS, MLS, or PAR instrument approach to either continue the approach or to execute a missed approach. (See IACO Decision Altitude/Decision Height.)

departure control A function of an approach control facility providing ATC service for departing IFR and, under certain conditions, VFR aircraft. (See Approach Control Facility.) (Refer to AIM.)

deviations (1) A departure from a current clearance, such as an off-course maneuver, to avoid weather or turbulence. (2) Where specifically authorized in the FARs and requested by the pilot, ATC might permit pilots to deviate from certain regulations. (Refer to AIM.)

direct Straight-line flight between two navigational aids, fixes, points, or any combination thereof. When used by pilots in describing off-airway routes, points defining direct route segments become compulsory reporting points unless the aircraft is under radar contact.

discrete code As used in the ATC radar beacon system (ATCRBS), any one of the 4,096 selectable Mode 3/A aircraft transponder codes except those ending in zero-zero; e.g., discrete codes: 0010,1201,2317,7777; nondiscrete codes: 0100,1200,7700. Nondiscrete codes are normally reserved for radar facilities that aren't equipped with discrete decoding capability and for other purposes such as emergencies (7700), VFR aircraft (1200), etc. (See Radar.) (Refer to AIM.)

discrete frequency A separate radio frequency for use in direct pilot-controller communications in ATC that reduces frequency congestion by controlling the number of aircraft operating on a particular frequency at one time. Discrete frequencies are normally designated for each control sector in en route/terminal ATC facilities. Discrete frequencies are listed in the Airport/Facility Directory and the DOD FLIP IFR En route Supplement. (See Control Sector.)

displaced threshold A threshold that's located at a point on the runway other than the designated beginning of the runway. (See Threshold.) (Refer to AIM.)

distance measuring equipment (DME) Equipment (airborne and ground) used to measure, in nautical miles, the slant-range distance of an aircraft from the DME navigational aid. (See Tactical Air Navigation, Vortac, Microwave Landing System.)

DME fix A geographical position determined by reference to a navigational aid that provides distance and azimuth information. It's defined by a specific distance in nautical miles and a radial, azimuth, or course (i.e., localizer) in degrees magnetic from that aid. (See Distance Measuring Equipment, Fix, Microwave Landing System.)

downburst A strong downdraft that induces an outburst of damaging winds on or near the ground. Damaging winds, either straight or curved, are highly divergent. The sizes of downbursts vary from one-half mile or less to more than ten miles. An intense downburst often causes widespread damage. Damaging winds, lasting 5 to 30 minutes, could reach speeds as high as 120 knots.

EFIS Electronic Flight Instrument System replaces the basic mechanical attitude and heading indicator with CRTs and electronic representations of the mechanical instruments.

emergency locator transmitter (ELT) A radio transmitter attached to the aircraft structure that operates from its own power source on 121.5 MHz and 243.0 MHz. It aids in locating downed aircraft by radiating a downward sweeping audio tone, two to four times per second. It's designed to function without human action after an accident. (Refer to AIM, FAR 91.3.)

empty weight The weight of the basic airplane: the structure, powerplant, fixed equipment, all fixed ballast and unusable fuel, undrainable oil, and hydraulic fluid.

estimated time en route (ETE) The estimated flying time from departure point to destination (liftoff to touchdown).

estimated time of arrival (ETA) The time the flight is estimated to arrive at the gate (scheduled operators) or the actual runway on times for nonscheduled operators.

execute missed approach Instructions issued to a pilot making an instrument approach that direct the pilot to continue inbound to the missed approach point and execute the missed approach procedure as described on the instrument approach procedure chart or as previously assigned by ATC. The pilot may climb immediately to the altitude specified in the missed approach procedure on making a missed approach. No turns should be initiated prior to reaching the missed approach point. When conducting an ASR or PAR approach, execute the assigned missed approach procedure immediately on receiving instructions to "execute missed approach." (Refer to AIM.)

expected departure clearance time (EDCT) The runway release time assigned to an aircraft in a controlled departure time program and shown on the flight progress strip as an EDCT.

expect further clearance (time) (EFC) The time a pilot can expect to receive clearance beyond a clearance limit.

extended over-water operation (1) With respect to aircraft other than helicopters, an operation over water at a horizontal distance of more than 50 nautical miles from the nearest shoreline; and (2) With respect to helicopters, an operation over water at a horizontal distance of more than 50 nautical miles from the nearest shoreline and more than 50 nm from an offshore heliport structure.

feathered propeller A propeller whose blades have been rotated so that the leading and trailing edges are nearly parallel with the aircraft flight path to stop or minimize drag and engine rotation. Normally used to indicate shutdown of a reciprocating or turboprop engine due to malfunction.

ferry flight A flight for the purpose of:

- Returning an aircraft to base.
- Delivering an aircraft from one location to another.
- Moving an aircraft to and from a maintenance base.

Ferry flight, under certain conditions, may be conducted under terms of a special flight permit.

filed flight plan The flight plan as filed with an ATS unit by the pilot or his or her designated representative without any subsequent changes or clearances.

final Commonly used to mean that an aircraft is on the final approach course or is aligned with a landing area. (See Final Approach Course, Final Approach-IFR, Traffic Pattern, Segments of an Instrument Approach Procedure.)

final approach course A published MLS course, a straight-line extension of a localizer, a final approach radial/bearing, or a runway centerline all without regard to distance. (See Final Approach-IFR, Traffic Pattern.)

final approach fix (FAF) The fix from which the final approach (IFR) to an airport is executed and that identifies the beginning of the final approach segment. It's designated on government charts by the Maltese cross symbol for nonprecision approaches and the lightning bolt symbol for precision approaches; when

ATC directs a lower-than-published glideslope/path intercept altitude, it's the resultant actual point of the glideslope/path intercept. (See Final Approach Point, Glideslope Intercept Altitude, Segments of an Instrument Approach Procedure.)

final approach-IFR The flight path of an aircraft that's inbound to an airport on a final instrument approach course, beginning at the final approach fix or point and extending to the airport or the point where a circle-to-land maneuver or a missed approach is executed. (See Final Approach Fix, Final Approach Course, Final Approach Point, Segments of an Instrument Approach Procedure, ICAO Final Approach.)

flag A warning device incorporated in certain airborne navigation and flight instruments indicating that:

- Instruments are inoperative or otherwise not operating satisfactorily, or
- Signal strength or quality of the received signal falls below acceptable values.

flameout Unintended loss of combustion in turbine engines resulting in the loss of engine power.

flap extended speed The highest speed permissible with wing flaps in a prescribed extended position.

flight level A level of constant atmospheric pressure related to a reference datum of 29.92 inches of mercury. Each is stated in three digits that represent hundreds of feet. For example, Flight Level 250 represents a barometric altimeter indication of 25,000 feet; Flight Level 255, an indication of 25,500 feet. (See ICAO Flight Level.)

flight management systems A computer system that uses a large database to allow routes to be preprogrammed and fed into the system by means of a data loader. The system is constantly updated with respect to position accuracy by reference to conventional navigation aids. The sophisticated program and its associated database ensures that the most appropriate aids are automatically selected during the information-update cycle.

flight path A line, course, or track along which an aircraft is flying or is intended to be flown. (See Course, Track.)

flight plan Specified information relating to the intended flight of an aircraft that's filed orally or in writing with an FSS or an ATC facility. (See Fast File, Filed.) (Refer to AIM.)

flight recorder A general term applied to any instrument or device that records information about the performance of an aircraft in flight or about conditions encountered in flight. Flight recorders might make records of airspeed, outside air temperature, vertical acceleration, engine rpm, manifold pressure, and other pertinent variables for a given flight. (See ICAO Flight Recorder.)

Flight Standards District Office (FSDO) An FAA field office serving an assigned geographical area and staffed with Flight Standards personnel who serve the aviation industry and the general public on matters relating to the certification and operation of air carrier and general aviation aircraft. Activities include general surveillance of operational safety, certification of airmen, and aircraft accident prevention, investigation, enforcement, etc.

flight time The time from the moment the aircraft first moves under its own power for the purpose of flight until the moment it comes to rest at the next point of landing. ("Block-to-block time".)

flow control Measures designed to adjust the flow of traffic into a given airspace, along a given route, or bound for a given aerodrome (airport) so as to ensure the most effective use of the airspace. (See Quota Flow Control.) (Refer to A/FD.)

fly heading (degrees) Informs the pilot of the heading he or she should fly. The pilot might have to turn to, or continue on, a specific compass direction in order to comply with the instructions. The pilot is expected to turn in the shorter direction to the heading unless otherwise instructed by ATC.

fuel dumping Airborne release of usable fuel. This doesn't include the dropping of fuel tanks. (See Jettisoning of External Stores.)

fuel remaining A phrase used by either pilots of controllers when relating to the fuel remaining on board until actual fuel exhaustion. When transmitting such information in response to either a controller question or pilot-initiated cautionary advisory to ATC, pilots will state the approximate number of minutes the flight can continue with the fuel remaining. All reserve fuel should be included in the time stated, as should an allowance for established fuel gauge system error.

gate hold procedures Procedures at selected airports to hold aircraft at the gate or other ground location whenever departure delays exceed or are anticipated to exceed 15 minutes. The sequence for departure will be maintained in accordance with initial call-up unless modified by flow control restrictions. Pilots should monitor the ground control/clearance delivery frequency for engine start/taxi advisories or new proposed start/taxi time if the delay changes. (See Flow Control.)

General Aviation District Office (GADO) An FAA field office serving a designated geographical area and staffed with Flight Standards personnel who have the responsibility for serving the aviation industry and the general public on all matters relating to the certification and operation of general aviation aircraft.

glideslope Provides vertical guidance for aircraft during approach and landing. The glideslope/glidepath is based on the following:

- Electronic components emitting signals that provide vertical guidance by reference to airborne instruments during instrument approaches such as ILS/MLS.

- Visual ground aids, such as VASI, that provide vertical guidance for a VFR approach or for the visual portion of an instrument approach and landing.

- PAR. Used by ATC to inform an aircraft making a PAR approach of its vertical position (elevation) relative to the descent profile. (See ICAO Glidepath.)

global positioning system A space-based radio positioning, navigation, and time-transfer system being developed by the Department of Defense. When fully deployed, the system is intended to provide highly accurate position and velocity information, and precise time, on a continuous global basis, to an unlimited number of properly equipped users. The system will be unaffected by weather and will provide a worldwide common grid reference system. The GPS concept is predicated on accurate and continuous knowledge of the spatial position of each satellite in the system with respect to time and distance from a transmitting satellite to the user. The GPS receiver automatically selects appropriate signals from the satellites in view and translates these into a three-dimensional position, velocity, and time. Predictable system accuracy for civil users is projected to be 100 meters horizontally. Performance standards and certification criteria are being developed.

go around Instructions for a pilot to abandon his or her approach to landing. Additional instructions might follow. Unless otherwise advised by ATC, a VFR aircraft or an aircraft conducting visual approach should overfly the runway while climbing to traffic pattern altitude and enter the traffic pattern via the crosswind leg. A pilot on an IFR flight plan making an instrument approach should execute the published missed approach procedure or proceed as instructed by ATC: e.g., "Go around" (additional instructions if required.) (See Low Approach, Missed Approach.)

gross weight Empty weight plus useful load is the gross weight of the airplane at takeoff. When an airplane is carrying the maximum load for which it's certificated, the takeoff weight is called the maximum allowable gross weight.

ground delay The amount of delay attributed to ATC, encountered prior to departure, usually associated with a CDT (controlled departure time) program.

groundspeed The speed of an aircraft relative to the surface of the earth.

hand-off An action taken to transfer the radar identification of an aircraft from one controller to another if the aircraft will enter the receiving controller's airspace and if radio communications with the aircraft will be transferred.

hazardous in-flight weather advisory service (HIWAS) Continuous recorded hazardous in-flight weather broadcast to airborne pilots over selected VOR outlets defined as a HIWAS Broadcast Area.

hazardous weather information Summary of significant meteorological information (sigmet/WS), convective significant meteorological information (convective sigmet/WST), urgent pilot weather reports (urgent pirep/UUA), center weather advisories (CWA), airmen's meteorological information (airmet/WA), and any other weather such as isolated thunderstorms that are rapidly developing and increasing in intensity, or low ceilings and visibilities that are becoming widespread and are considered significant and aren't included in a current hazardous weather advisory.

height above landing (HAL) The height above a designated helicopter landing area used for helicopter instrument approach procedures. (Refer to FAR Part 97.)

height above touchdown (HAT) The height of the decision height or minimum descent altitude above the highest runway elevation in the touchdown zone (first 3,000 feet of the runway). HAT is published on instrument approach charts in conjunction with all straight-in minimums. (See Decision Height, Minimum Descent Altitude.)

heliport An area of land, water, or structure used or intended to be used for the landing and takeoff of helicopters and includes its buildings and facilities, if any.

high-speed taxiway A long-radius taxiway designed and provided with lighting or marking to define the path of aircraft traveling at high speed (up to 60 knots) from the runway center to a point on the center of a taxiway. Also referred to as long-radius exit or turnoff taxiway. The high-speed taxiway is designed to expedite aircraft turning off the runway after landing, thus reducing runway occupancy time.

hold for release Used by ATC to delay an aircraft for traffic management reasons: i.e., weather, traffic volume, etc. Hold-for-release instructions (including departure delay information) are used to inform a pilot or a controller (either directly or through an authorized relay) that a departure clearance is not valid until a release time or additional instructions have been received. (See ICAO Holding Point.)

holding fix A specified fix, identifiable to a pilot by navaids or visual reference to the ground, used as a reference point in establishing and maintaining the position of an aircraft while holding. (See Fix, Visual Holding.) (Refer to AIM.)

how do you hear me? A question relating to the quality of the transmission or to determine how well the transmission is being received.

Hz (See Hertz.)

IAF (See Initial Approach Fix.)

IAP (See Instrument Approach Procedure.)

ICAO (See International Civil Aviation Organization.)

ident A request for a pilot to activate the aircraft transponder identification feature. This will help the controller to confirm an aircraft identity or to identify an aircraft. (Refer to AIM.)

IFR takeoff minimums and departure procedures FAR Part 91 prescribes standard takeoff rules for certain civil users. At some airports, obstructions or other factors require the establishment of nonstandard takeoff minimums, departure procedures, or both to assist pilots in avoiding obstacles during climb to the minimum en route altitude. Those airports are listed in NOS/DOD instrument approach charts (IAPs) under a section titled "IFR Takeoff Minimums and Departure Procedures." The NOS/DOD IAP chart legend illustrates the symbol used to alert the pilot to nonstandard takeoff minimums and departure procedures. When departing IFR from such airports, or from any airports where there are no departure procedures, SIDs, or ATC facilities available, pilots should advise ATC of any departure limitations. Controllers might query a pilot to determine acceptable departure directions, turns, or headings after takeoff. Pilots should be familiar with the departure procedures and must assure that their aircraft can meet or exceed any specified climb gradients.

ILS categories (1) ILS CAT I. An ILS approach procedure that provides for approach to a height above touchdown of not less than 200 feet and with runway visual range of not less than 1,800 feet. (2) ILS CAT II. An ILS approach procedure that provides for approach to a height above touchdown of not less than 100 feet and with runway visual range of not less than 1,200 feet. (3) ILS CAT III. (a) IIIA. An ILS approach procedure that provides for approach without a decision height minimum and with runway visual range of not less than 700 feet. (b) IIIB. An ILS approach procedure that provides for approach without a decision height minimum and with runway visual range of not less than 150 feet. (c) IIIC. An ILS approach procedure that provides for approach without a decision height minimum and without runway visual range minimum.

immediately Used by ATC when such action compliance is required to avoid an imminent situation.

indicated airspeed The speed of an aircraft as shown on its pilot-static airspeed indicator calibrated to reflect standard atmosphere adiabatic compressible flow at sea level, uncorrected for airspeed system errors.

inertial navigation system (INS) An RNAV system that's a form of self-contained navigation. (See Area Navigation.)

initial approach fix (IAF) The fixes depicted on instrument approach procedure charts that identify the beginning of the initial approach segments(s). (See Fix, Segments of an Instrument Approach Procedure.)

inner marker (IM) A marker beacon used with an ILS CAT II precision approach located between the middle marker and the end of the ILS runway, transmitting a radiation pattern keyed at six dots per second and indicating to the pilot, both aurally and visually, that he or she is at the designated decision height (DH), normally 100 feet above the touchdown zone elevation, on the ILS CAT II approach. It also marks progress during a CAT III approach. (See Instrument Landing System.) (Refer to AIM.)

instrument approach procedure (IAP) A series of predetermined maneuvers for the orderly transfer of an aircraft under instrument flight conditions from the beginning of the initial approach to a landing or to a point from which a landing might be made visually. It's prescribed and approved for a specific airport by competent authority. (See Segments of an Instrument Approach Procedure.) (Refer to AIM, FAR Part 91.)

- U.S. civil standard IAPs are approved by the FAA as prescribed under FAR Part 97 and are available for public use.

- U.S. military standard IAPs are approved and published by the Department of Defense.

- Special IAPs are approved by the FAA for individual operators but aren't published in FAR Part 97 for public use. (See IACO Instrument Approach Procedure.)

instrument flight rules (IFR) Rules governing the procedures for conducting instrument flight. Also a term used by pilots and controllers to indicate type of flight plan. (See Instrument Meteorological Conditions, Visual Flight Rules,

Visual Meteorological Conditions, ICAO Instrument Flight Rules.) (Refer to AIM.)

instrument landing system (ILS) A precision instrument approach system that normally consists of the following electronic components and visual aids:

- Localizer (See Localizer.)
- Glideslope (See Glideslope.)
- Outer Marker (See Outer Marker.)
- Middle Marker (See Middle Marker.)
- Approach lights (See Airport Lighting.)

(Refer to FAR Part 91, AIM.)

intersecting runways Two or more runways that cross or meet within their lengths. (See Intersection.)

intersection (1) A point defined by any combination of courses, radials, or bearings of two or more navigational aids. (2) Used to describe the point where two runways, a runway and a taxiway, or two taxiways cross or meet.

intersection departure A departure from any runway intersection except the end of the runway. (See Intersection.)

landing gear extended speed The maximum speed at which an aircraft can be safely flown with the landing gear extended.

landing gear operating speed The maximum speed at which the landing gear can be safely extended or retracted.

landing minimums The minimum visibility prescribed for landing a civil aircraft while using an instrument approach procedure. The minimum applies with other limitations set forth in FAR Part 91 with respect to the minimum descent altitude (MDA) or decision height (DH) prescribed in the instrument approach procedures as follows:

- Straight-in landing minimums. A statement of MDA and visibility, or DH and visibility, required for a straight-in landing on a specified runway.
- Circling minimums. A statement of MDA and visibility required for the circle-to-land maneuver.

Descent below the established MDA or DH is not authorized during an approach unless the aircraft is in a position from which a normal approach to the runway of intended landing can be made and adequate visual reference to required visual cues is maintained. (See Circle-to-Land Maneuver, Decision Heights, Minimum Descent Altitude, Visibility, Instrument Approach Procedure, Straight-in Landing.) (Refer to FAR Part 91.)

landing roll The distance from the point of touchdown to the point where the aircraft can be brought to a stop or can exit the runway.

large aircraft Aircraft of more than 12,500 pounds maximum certificated takeoff weight.

load factor The ratio of a specified load to the total weight of the aircraft. The specified load is expressed in terms of any of the following: aerodynamic forces, inertia forces, or ground or water reactions.

localizer The component of an ILS that provides course guidance to the runway. (See Instrument Landing System, ICAO Localizer Course.) (Refer to AIM.)

localizer type directional aid (LDA) A navaid used for nonprecision instrument approaches with utility and accuracy comparable to a localizer but which is not a part of a complete ILS and is not aligned with the runway. (Refer to AIM.)

loran An electronic navigational system by which hyperbolic lines of position are determined by measuring the difference in the time of reception of synchronized pulse signals from two fixed transmitters. Loran A operates in the 1,750- to 1,950-kHz frequency band. Loran C and D operate in the 100- to 110-kHz frequency band. (Refer to AIM.)

lost communications Loss of the ability to communicate by radio. Aircraft are sometimes referred to as Nordo (no radio). Standard pilot procedures are specified in FAR Part 91. Radar controllers issue procedures for pilots to follow in the event of lost communications during a radar approach when weather reports indicate that an aircraft will likely encounter IFR weather conditions during the approach. (Refer to AIM, FAR Part 91.)

low approach An approach over an airport or runway following an instrument approach or a VFR approach, including the go-around maneuver where the pilot intentionally doesn't make contact with the runway. (Refer to AIM.)

low frequency (LF) The frequency band between 30 and 300 kHz. (Refer to AIM.)

mach number The ratio of true airspeed to the speed of sound: e.g., Mach 0.82, Mach 1.6. (See Airspeed.)

magnetic course (MC) Proposed flight path direction relative to magnetic north. Victor airways are plotted on aeronautical charts as magnetic courses.

magnetic heading (MH) Actual heading of an aircraft in flight relative to magnetic north.

maintain (1) Concerning altitude/flight level, the term means to remain at the altitude/flight level specified. The phrase "climb and" or "descend and" normally precedes "maintain" and the altitude assignment: e.g., "descend and maintain 5,000." (2) Concerning other ATC instructions, the term is used in its literal sense: e.g., maintain VFR.

make short approach Used by ATC to inform a pilot to alter his or her traffic pattern so as to make a short final approach. (See Traffic Pattern.)

manifold pressure Absolute pressure as measured at the appropriate point in the induction system and usually expressed in inches of mercury.

marker beacon An electronic navigation facility transmitting a 75-MHz vertical fan or bone-shaped radiation pattern. Marker beacons are identified by their modulation frequency and keying code, and when received by compatible airborne equipment, indicate to the pilot, both aurally and visually, that he or she is passing over the facility. (See Inner Marker, Middle Marker, Outer Marker.) (Refer to AIM.)

metering fix A fix along an established route from which aircraft will be metered prior to entering terminal airspace. Normally, this fix should be established at a distance from the airport that will facilitate a profile descent 10,000 feet above airport elevation (AAE) or above.

microburst A small downburst with outbursts of damaging winds extending 2.5 miles or less. In spite of its small horizontal scale, an intense microburst could induce wind speeds as high as 150 knots. (Refer to AIM.)

microwave landing system (MLS) A precision instrument approach system operating in the microwave spectrum that normally consists of the following components:

- Azimuth station.
- Elevation station.
- Precision distance measuring equipment.

(See MLS Categories.)

middle marker (MM) A marker beacon that defines a point along the glideslope of an ILS normally located at or near the point of decision heights (ILS Category I). It's keyed to transmit alternate dots and dashes, with the alternate dots and dashes keyed at the rate of 95 dot/dash combinations per minute on a 1,300-Hz tone, which is received aurally and visually by compatible airborne equipment. (See Marker Beacon, Instrument Landing System.) (Refer to AIM.)

minimum crossing altitude (MCA) The lowest altitude at certain fixes at which an aircraft must cross when proceeding in the direction of a higher minimum en route IFR altitude (MEA). (See Minimum En Route IFR Altitude.)

minimum descent altitude (MDA) The lowest altitude, expressed in feet above mean sea level, to which descent is authorized on final approach or during circle-to-land maneuvering in execution of a standard instrument approach procedure where no electronic glideslope is provided. (See Nonprecision Approach Procedure.)

minimum en route IFR altitude (MEA) The lowest published altitude between radio fixes that assures acceptable navigational signal coverage and meets obstacle clearance requirements between those fixes. The MEA prescribed for a federal airway or segment thereof, area navigation low or high route, or other direct route, applies to the entire width of the airway, segment, or route between the radio fixes defining the airway, segment, or route. (Refer to AIM; FAR Parts 91 and 95.)

minimum fuel Indicates that an aircraft's fuel supply has reached a state where, on reaching the destination, it can accept little or no delay. This is not an emergency situation but merely indicates that an emergency situation is possible should any undue delay occur. (Refer to AIM.)

minimum IFR altitudes (MIA) Minimum altitudes for IFR operations as prescribed in FAR Part 91. These altitudes are published on aeronautical charts and prescribed in FAR Part 95 for airways and routes and in FAR Part 97 for standard instrument approach procedures. If no applicable minimum altitude is prescribed in FAR Part 95 or 97, the following minimum IFR altitude applies:

- In designated mountainous areas, 2,000 feet above the highest obstacle within a horizontal distance of 4 nautical miles from the course to be flown.
- Other than mountainous areas, 1,000 feet above the highest obstacle within a horizontal distance of 4 nautical miles from the course to be flown.
- As otherwise authorized by the Administrator or assigned by ATC.

(See Minimum En Route IFR Altitude, Minimum Obstruction Clearance Altitude, Minimum Crossing Altitude, Minimum Safe Altitude, Minimum Vectoring Altitude.) (Refer to FAR Part 91.)

minimum obstruction clearance altitude (MOCA) The lowest published altitude in effect between radio fixes on VOR airways, off-airway routes, or route segments that meets obstacle clearance requirements for the entire route segment and that assures acceptable navigational signal coverage within 25 statute (22 nautical) miles of a VOR. (Refer to FAR Parts 91 and 95.)

minimum reception altitude (MRA) The lowest altitude at which an intersection can be determined. (Refer to FAR Part 95.)

minimum vectoring altitude (MVA) The lowest msl altitude at which an IFR aircraft will be vectored by a radar controller, except as otherwise authorized for radar approaches, departures, and missed approaches. The altitude meets IFR obstacle clearance criteria. It may be lower than the published MEA along an airway or J-route segment. It may be used for radar vectoring only on the controller's determination that an adequate radar return is being received from the aircraft being controlled. Charts depicting minimum vectoring altitudes are normally available only to the controllers and not to pilots. (Refer to AIM.)

missed approach (1) A maneuver conducted by a pilot when an instrument approach can't be completed to a landing. The route of flight and altitude are shown on IAP charts. A pilot executing a missed approach prior to the missed approach point (MAP) must continue along the final approach to the MAP. The pilot may climb immediately to the altitude specified in the missed approach procedure. (2) A term used by the pilot to inform ATC that he or she is executing the missed approach. (3) At locations where ATC radar service is provided, the pilot should conform to radar vectors when provided by ATC in lieu of the published missed approach procedure. (See Missed Approach Point.) (Refer to AIM.)

movement area The runways, taxiways, and other areas of an airport/heliport that are used for taxiing/hover taxiing, air taxiing, takeoff, and landing of aircraft, exclusive of loading ramps and parking areas. At those airports/heliports with a tower, specific approval for entry onto the movement area must be obtained from ATC. (See ICAO Movement Area.)

multiple runways The use of a dedicated arrival runway(s) for departures and a dedicated departure runway(s) for arrivals when feasible to reduce delays and enhance capacity.

navaid classes VOR, vortac, and tacan aids are classed according to their operational use. The three classes of navaids are:

- T—Terminal.
- L—Low altitude.
- H—High altitude.

The normal service range for T, L, and H class aids is found in the AIM. Certain operational requirements make it necessary to use some of these aids at greater service ranges than specified. Extended range is made possible through flight inspection determinations. Some aids also have lesser service range due to location, terrain, frequency protection, etc. Restrictions to service range are listed in the Airport/Facility Directory.

negative contact Used by pilots to inform ATC that:

- Previously issued traffic is not in sight. It might be followed by the pilot's request for the controller to provide assistance in avoiding the traffic.
- They were unable to contact ATC on a particular frequency.

no gyro approach A radar approach/vector provided in case of a malfunctioning gyrocompass or directional gyro. Instead of providing the pilot with headings to be flown, the controller observes the radar track and issues control instructions "turn right/left" or "stop turn" as appropriate. (Refer to AIM.)

nonapproach control tower Authorizes aircraft to land or take off at the airport controlled by the tower or to transit the airport traffic area. The primary function of a nonapproach control tower is the sequencing of aircraft in the traffic pattern and on the landing area. Nonapproach control towers also separate aircraft operating under instrument flight rules clearances from approach controls and centers. They provide ground control services to aircraft, vehicles, personnel, and equipment on the airport movement area.

nonprecision approach procedure A standard instrument approach procedure in which no electronic glideslope is provided: e.g., VOR, tacan, NDB, LOC, ASR, LDA, or SDF approaches.

nonradar Precedes other terms and generally means without the use of radar, such as:

- Nonradar Approach. Used to describe instrument approaches for which course guidance on final approach is not provided by ground-based precision or surveillance radar. Radar vectors to the final approach course might or might not be provided by ATC. Examples of nonradar approaches are VOR, NDB, tacan, and ILS/MLS approaches. (See Final Approach-IFR, Final Approach Course, Radar Approach, Instrument Approach Procedure.)
- Nonradar Approach Control. An ATC facility providing approach control service without the use of radar. (See Approach Control Service, Approach Control Facility.)

- Nonradar Arrival. An aircraft arriving at an airport without radar service or at an airport served by a radar facility and radar contact has not been established or has been terminated due to a lack of radar service to the airport. (See Radar Arrival, Radar Service.)

- Nonradar Route. A flight path or route over which the pilot is performing his or her own navigation. The pilot might be receiving radar separation, radar monitoring, or other ATC services while on a nonradar route. (See Radar Route.)

- Nonradar Separation. The spacing of aircraft in accordance with established minima without the use of radar: e.g., vertical, lateral, or longitudinal separation. (See Radar Service, ICAO Nonradar Separation.)

notice to airmen (NOTAM) A notice containing information (not known sufficiently in advance to publicize by other means) concerning the establishment, condition, or change in any component (facility, service, procedure of, or hazard in the National Airspace System), the timely knowledge of which is essential to personnel concerned with flight operations.

- Notam(D). A notam given (in addition to local dissemination) distant dissemination beyond the area of responsibility of the FSS. These notams will be stored and available until canceled.

- Notam(L). A notam given local dissemination by voice and other means (such as TelAutograph and telephone) to satisfy local user requirements.

- FDC Notam. A notam that's regulatory in nature, transmitted by USNOF, and given systemwide dissemination.

(See ICAO Notam.)

numerous targets vicinity (location) A traffic advisory issued by ATC to advise pilots that targets on the radarscope are too numerous to issue individually. (See Traffic Advisories.)

off-route vector A vector by ATC that takes an aircraft off a previously assigned route. Altitudes assigned by ATC during such vectors provide required obstacle clearance.

omega An RNAV system designed for long-range navigation based on ground-based electronic navigational aid signals.

opposite direction aircraft Aircraft are operating in opposite directions when:

- They're following the same track in reciprocal directions.
- Their tracks are parallel and the aircraft are flying in reciprocal directions.
- Their tracks intersect at an angle of more than 135 degrees.

option approach An approach requested and conducted by a pilot that will result in either a touch-and-go, missed-approach, low-approach, stop-and-go, or full-stop landing. (See Cleared for the Option.) (Refer to AIM.)

outer area (associated with ARSA) Nonregulatory airspace surrounding designated ARSA airports wherein ATC provides radar vectoring and sequencing on a full-time basis for all IFR and participating VFR aircraft. The service provided in the outer area is called ARSA service, which includes: IFR/IFR-standard IFR separation; IFR/VFR-traffic advisories and conflict resolution; VFR/VFR-traffic advisories and, as appropriate, safety alerts. The normal radius will be 20 nautical miles with some variations based on site-specific requirements. The outer area extends outward from the primary ARSA airport and extends from the lower limits of radar/radio coverage up to the ceiling of the approach control's delegated airspace, excluding the ARSA and other airspace as appropriate. (See Controlled Airspace-Airport Radar Service Area, Conflict Resolution.)

outer marker (OM) A marker beacon at or near the glideslope intercept altitude of an ILS approach. It's keyed to transmit two dashes per second on a 400-Hz tone, which is received aurally and visually by compatible airborne equipment. The OM is normally located four to seven miles from the runway threshold on the extended centerline of the runway. (See Instrument Landing System, Marker Beacon.) (Refer to AIM.)

overrun An area beyond the takeoff runway that's no less wide than the runway and centered on the extended centerline of the runway, able to support the airplane during an aborted takeoff (without causing structural damage to the airplane) and designated by the airport authorities for use in decelerating the airplane during an aborted takeoff. (Stopway is a term used for civilian airports.)

over-the-top Above the layer of clouds or other obscuring phenomena forming the ceiling.

pan-pan The international radiotelephony urgency signal. When repeated three times, indicates uncertainty or alert, followed by the nature of the urgency. (See Mayday.) (Refer to AIM.)

PAR (See Precision Approach Radar.)

parallel ILS approaches Approaches to parallel runways by IFR aircraft that, when established inbound toward the airport on the adjacent final approach courses, are radar-separated by at least two miles. (See Final Approach Course, Simultaneous ILS Approaches.)

parallel runways Two or more runways at the same airport whose centerlines are parallel. In addition to runway number, parallel runways are designated as L (left) and R (right) or, if three parallel runways exist, L (left), C (center), and R (right).

pilotage Navigation by visual reference to landmarks.

pilot in command The pilot responsible for the operation and safety of an aircraft during flight time. (Refer to FAR Part 91.)

pilots automatic telephone weather answering service (PATWAS) A continuous telephone recording containing current and forecast weather information for pilots. (See Flight Service Station.) (Refer to AIM.)

pilot's discretion When used is conjunction with altitude assignments, means that ATC has offered the pilot the option of starting climb or descent whenever he or she wants and conducting the climb or descent at any rate he or she wants. He might temporarily level off at any intermediate altitude. However, once he has vacated an altitude, he or she may not return to that altitude.

practice instrument approach   An instrument approach procedure conducted by a VFR or an IFR aircraft for the purpose of pilot training or proficiency demonstrations.

precision approach radar (PAR)   Radar equipment in some ATC facilities operated by the FAA and/or the military services at joint-use civil/military locations and separate military installations to detect and display azimuth, elevation, and range of aircraft on the final approach course to a runway. This equipment might be used to monitor certain nonradar approaches, but is primarily used to conduct a precision instrument approach wherein the controller issues guidance instructions to the pilot based on the aircraft's position in relation to the final approach course (azimuth), the glidepath (elevation), and the distance (range) from the touchdown point on the runway as displayed on the radarscope. (See Glideslope-PAR.) (Refer to AIM.)

preferential routes   Preferential routes (PDRs, PARs, and PDARs) are adapted in ARTCC computers to accomplish inter/intrafacility controller coordination and to assure that flight data is posted at the proper control positions. Locations having a need for these specific inbound and outbound routes normally publish such routes in local facility bulletins, and their use by pilots minimizes flight plan route amendments. When the work load or traffic situation permits, controllers normally provide radar vectors or assign requested routes to minimize circuitous routing. Preferential routes are usually confined to one ARTCC's area and are referred to by the following names or acronyms:

- Preferential Departure Route (PDR). A specific departure route from an airport to terminal area to an en route point where there's no further need for flow control. PDR might be included in a standard instrument departure (SID) or a preferred IFR route.

- Preferential Arrival Route (PAR). A specific arrival route from an appropriate en route point to an airport or terminal area. PAR might be included in a standard terminal arrival route (STAR) or a preferred IFR route. The abbreviation "PAR" is used primarily within the ARTCC and shouldn't be confused with the abbreviation for precision approach radar.

- Preferential Departure and Arrival Route (PDAR). A route between two terminals that are within or immediately adjacent to one ARTCC's area. PDARs aren't synonymous with preferred IFR routes but might be listed as such as they do accomplish essentially the same purpose. (See NAS Stage A, Preferred IFR Routes.)

procedure turn (PT)   The maneuver prescribed when it's necessary to reverse direction to establish an aircraft on the intermediate approach segment or final approach course. The outbound course, direction of turn, distance within which the turn must be completed, and minimum altitude are specified in the procedure. However, unless otherwise restricted, the point at which the turn might be commenced and the type and rate of turn are left to the discretion of the pilot.

procedure turn inbound That point of a procedure turn maneuver where course reversal has been completed and an aircraft is established inbound on the intermediate approach segment or final approach course. A report of "procedure turn inbound" is normally used by ATC as a position report for separation purposes. (See Final Approach Course, Procedure Turn, Segments of an Instrument Approach Procedure.)

profile descent An uninterrupted descent (except where level flight is required for speed adjustment: e.g., 250 knots are 10,000 feet msl) from cruising altitude/level to interception of a glideslope or to a minimum altitude specified for the initial or intermediate approach segment of a nonprecision instrument approach. The profile descent normally terminates at the approach gate or where the glideslope or other appropriate minimum altitude is intercepted.

progressive taxi Precise taxi instructions given to a pilot who's unfamiliar with the airport or issued in stages as the aircraft proceeds along the taxi route.

prohibited area (See Special-use Airspace, ICAO Prohibited Area.)

(ICAO) prohibited area An airspace of defined dimensions above the land areas or territorial waters of a state, within which the flight of aircraft is prohibited.

radar A device that, by measuring the time interval between transmission and reception or radio pulses and correlating the angular orientation of the radiated antenna beam or beams in azimuth and/or elevation, provides information on range, azimuth, and/or elevation of objects in the path of the transmitted pulses.

- Primary Radar. A radar system in which a minute portion of a radio pulse transmitted from a site is reflected by an object and then received back at that site for processing and display at an ATC facility.

- Secondary Radar/Radar Beacon (ATCRBS). A radar system in which the object to be detected is fitted with cooperative equipment in the form of a radio receiver/transmitter (transponder). Radar pulses transmitted from the searching transmitter/receiver (interrogator) site are received in the cooperative equipment and used to trigger a distinctive transmission from the transponder. This reply transmission, rather than a reflected signal, is then received back at the transmitter/receiver site for processing and display at an ATC facility. (See Transponder, Interrogator, ICAO Radar.) (Refer to AIM.)

radar approach An instrument approach procedure that uses precision approach radar (PAR) or airport surveillance radar (ASR). (See Surveillance Approach, Airport Surveillance Radar, Precision Approach Radar, Instrument Approach Procedure, ICAO Radar Approach.) (Refer to AIM.)

radar contact (1) Used by ATC to inform an aircraft that it's identified on the radar display and radar flight following will be provided until radar identification is terminated. Radar service might also be provided within the limits of necessity and capability. When a pilot is informed of "radar contact," he or she automatically discontinues reporting over compulsory reporting points. (See Radar Flight Following, Radar Contact Lost, Radar Service, Radar Service Terminated.) (Refer to AIM.) (2) The term used to inform the controller that the aircraft is identified and approval is granted for the aircraft to enter the receiving controller's airspace. (See ICAO Radar Contact.)

radar contact lost Used by ATC to inform a pilot that radar identification of his or her aircraft has been lost. The loss might be attributed to several things, including the aircraft's merging with weather or ground clutter, the aircraft's flying below radar line of sight, the aircraft's entering an area of poor radar return, or a failure of the aircraft transponder or the ground radar equipment. (See Clutter, Radar Contact.)

radar environment An area in which radar service can be provided. (See Radar Contact, Radar Service, Additional Services, Traffic Advisories.)

radar flight following The observation of the progress of radar-identified aircraft (whose primary navigation is being provided by the pilot) wherein the controller retains and correlates the aircraft identity with the appropriate target or target symbol displayed on the radarscope. (See Radar Contact, Radar Service.) (Refer to AIM.)

radar identification The process of ascertaining that an observed radar target is the radar return from a particular aircraft. (See Radar Contact, Radar Service, ICAO Radar Identification.)

radar-identified aircraft An aircraft, the position of which has been correlated with an observed target or symbol on the radar display. (See Radar Contact, Radar Contact Lost.)

radar service A term that encompasses one or more of the following radar services based that can be provided by a controller to a pilot of a radar-identified aircraft.

- Radar Monitoring. The radar flight following of aircraft (whose primary navigation is being performed by the pilot) to observe and note deviations from its authorized flight path, airway, or route. When being applied specifically to radar monitoring of instrument approaches: e.g., with precision approach radar (PAR) or radar monitoring of simultaneous ILS/MLS approaches, it includes advice and instructions whenever an aircraft nears or exceeds the prescribed PAR safety limit or simultaneous ILS/MLS no-transgression zone. (See Additional Services, Traffic Advisories.)

- Radar Navigational Guidance. Vectoring aircraft to provide course guidance.

- Radar Separation. Radar spacing of aircraft in accordance with established minima. (See ICAO Radar Service.)

radar weather echo intensity levels Existing radar systems can't detect turbulence. However, there's a direct correlation between the degree of turbulence and other weather features associated with thunderstorms; there's also a correlation between radar weather features associated with thunderstorms and the radar weather echo intensity for precipitation. This intensity is classified into six levels. These levels are sometimes expressed during communications as "VIP Level" one through six (derived from the component of the weather radar that produces the information—Video Integrator and Processor). The following list gives the "VIP Levels" in relation to the precipitation intensity within a thunderstorm:

- Level 1—Weak.
- Level 2—Moderate.
- Level 3—Strong.
- Level 4—Very strong.
- Level 5—Intense.
- Level 6—Extreme.

(See AC 00-45.)

radio altimeter Aircraft equipment that makes use of the reflection of radio waves from the ground to determine the height of the aircraft above the surface.

radio magnetic indicator (RMI) An aircraft navigational instrument coupled with a gyro compass or similar compass that indicates the direction of a selected navaid and indicates bearing with respect to the heading of the aircraft.

rated takeoff power With respect to reciprocating, turboprop, and turboshaft engine type certification, means the approved brake horsepower that's developed statically under standard sea-level conditions, within the engine operating limitations established under FAR Part 33, and limited in use to periods of not more than five minutes for takeoff operation.

rated takeoff thrust With respect to turbojet engine type certification, means the approved jet thrust that's developed statically under standard sea-level conditions, without fluid injection and without the burning of fuel in a separate combustion chamber, within the engine operating limitations established under FAR Part 33 and limited in use to periods of not more than five minutes for takeoff operation.

regional pilot New term for commuter pilot (see commuter pilot).

release time A departure time restriction issued to a pilot by ATC (either directly or through an authorized relay) when necessary to separate a departing aircraft from other traffic. (See ICAO Release Time.)

reporting point A geographical location in relation to which the position of an aircraft is reported. (See Compulsory Reporting Points, ICAO Reporting Point.) (Refer to AIM.)

request full route clearance (FRC) Used by pilots to request that the entire route of flight be read verbatim in an ATC clearance. Such request should be made to preclude receiving an ATC clearance based on the original filed flight plan when a filed IFR flight plan has been revised by the pilot, company, or operations prior to departure.

restricted area (See Special-use Airspace, ICAO Restricted Area.)

(ICAO) restricted area An airspace of defined dimensions (above the land areas or territorial waters of a state) within which the flight of aircraft is restricted in accordance with certain specified conditions.

resume own navigation Used by ATC to advise a pilot to resume his or her own navigational responsibility. It's issued after completion of a radar vector or when radar contact is lost while the aircraft is being radar vectored. (See Radar Contact Lost, Radar Service Terminated.)

RNAV waypoint (WP) A predetermined geographical position used for route or instrument approach definition or progress reporting purposes that's defined relative to a vortac station position.

runway heading The magnetic direction that corresponds with the runway centerline extended, not the painted runway number. When cleared to "fly or maintain runway heading," pilots are expected to fly or maintain the heading that corresponds with the extended centerline of the departure runway. Drift correction shall not be applied: e.g., Runway 4, actual magnetic heading of the runway centerline 044, fly 044.

runway is use/active runway/duty runway Any runway or runways currently being used for takeoff or landing. When multiple runways are used, they're all considered active runways. In the metering sense, a selectable adapted item that specifies the landing runway configuration or direction of traffic flow. The adapted optimum flight plan from each transition fix to the vertex is determined by the runway configuration for arrival-metering processing purposes.

runway use program A noise abatement runway selection plan designed to enhance noise abatement efforts with regard to airport communities for arriving and departing aircraft. These plans are developed into runway use programs and apply to all turbojet aircraft of 12,500 pounds or heavier; turbojet aircraft less than 12,500 pounds are included only if the airport proprietor determines that the aircraft creates a noise problem. Runway use programs are coordinated with FAA offices, and safety criteria used in these programs are developed by the Office of Flight Operations. Runway use programs are administered by the air traffic service as "formal" or "informal" programs.

- Formal Runway Use Program. An approved noise abatement program that's defined and acknowledged in a letter of understanding between flight operations, air traffic service, the airport proprietor, and the users. Once established, participation in the program is mandatory for aircraft operators and pilots as provided for in FAR 91.129.

- Informal Runway Use Program. An approved noise abatement program that doesn't require a letter of understanding, and participation in the program is voluntary for aircraft operators/pilots.

safety alert A safety alert issued by ATC to aircraft under their control if ATC is aware the aircraft is at an altitude which, in the controller's judgment, places the aircraft in unsafe proximity to terrain, obstructions, or other aircraft. The controller may discontinue the issuance of further alerts if the pilot advises that he or she is taking action to correct the situation or has the other aircraft in sight.

- Terrain/Obstruction Alert. A safety alert issued by ATC to aircraft under their control if ATC is aware the aircraft is at an altitude which, in the controller's judgment, places the aircraft in unsafe proximity to terrain/obstructions: e.g., "Low-altitude alert, check your altitude immediately."

- Aircraft Conflict Alert. A safety alert issued by ATC to aircraft under their control if ATC is aware of an aircraft that's not under their control at an altitude which, in the controller's judgment, places both aircraft in unsafe proximity to each other. With the alert, ATC will offer the pilot an alternate course of action when feasible: e.g., "Traffic alert, advise you turn right heading zero-niner-zero or climb to eight thousand immediately."

The issue of a safety alert is contingent on the capacity of the controller to have an awareness of an unsafe condition. The course of action provided will be predicated on other traffic under ATC control. Once the alert is issued, it's solely the pilot's prerogative to determine what course of action, if any, he or she will take.

say again Used to request a repeat of the last transmission. Usually specifies transmission or portion thereof not understood or received: e.g., "Say again all after Abram VOR."

say altitude Used by ATC to ascertain an aircraft's specific altitude/flight level. When the aircraft is climbing or descending, the pilot should state the indicated altitude rounded to the nearest 100 feet.

say heading Used by ATC to request an aircraft heading. The pilot should state the actual heading of the aircraft.

second in command A pilot who is designated to be second in command of an aircraft during flight time.

segments of an instrument approach procedure An instrument approach procedure might have as many as four separate segments, depending on how the approach procedure is structured.

- Initial Approach. The segment between the initial approach fix and the intermediate fix or the point where the aircraft is established on the intermediate course or final approach course. (See ICAO Initial Approach Segment.)

- Intermediate Approach. The segment between the intermediate fix or point and the final approach fix. (See ICAO Intermediate Approach Segment.)

- Final Approach. The segment between the final approach fix or point and the runway, airport, or missed approach point. (See ICAO Final Approach Segment.)

- Missed Approach. The segment between the missed approach point or the point of arrival at decision height and the missed approach fix at the prescribed altitude. (See ICAO Missed Approach Procedure.) (Refer to FAR Part 97.)

severe weather avoidance plan (SWAP) An approved plan to minimize the effect of severe weather on traffic flows in impacted terminal and/or ARTCC areas. SWAP is normally implemented to provide the least disruption to the ATC system when flight through portions of airspace is difficult or impossible due to severe weather.

short-range clearance A clearance issued to a departing IFR flight that authorizes IFR flight to a specific fix short of the destination while ATC facilities are coordinating and obtaining the complete clearance.

short takeoff and landing (STOL) aircraft An aircraft that, at some weight within its approved operating weight, is capable of operating from a STOL runway in compliance with the applicable STOL characteristics, airworthiness, operations, noise, and pollution standards. (See Vertical Takeoff and Landing Aircraft.)

sidestep maneuver A visual maneuver accomplished by a pilot at the completion of an instrument approach to permit a straight-in landing on a parallel runway not more than 1,200 feet to either side of the runway to which the instrument approach was conducted. (Refer to AIM.)

sigmet (WS) A weather advisory issued concerning weather significant to the safety of all aircraft. Sigmet advisories cover severe and extreme turbulence, severe icing, and widespread dust storms or sandstorms that reduce visibility to less than three miles. (See Severe Weather Forecast Alerts, Convective Sigmet, Center Weather Advisory, Airmet, ICAO Sigmet Information.) (Refer to AIM.)

simultaneous ILS approaches An approach system permitting simultaneous ILS/MLS approaches to airports having parallel runways separated by at least 4,300 feet between centerlines. Integral parts of a total system are ILS/MLS, radar, communications, ATC procedures, and appropriate airborne equipment. (See Parallel Runways.) (Refer to AIM.)

special-use airspace Airspace of defined dimensions identified by an area on the surface of the earth wherein activities must be confined because of their nature and/or wherein limitations might be imposed on aircraft operations that aren't a part of those activities. Types of special-use airspace are:

- Alert Area. Airspace that might contain a high volume of pilot training activities or an unusual type of aerial activity, or that's hazardous to aircraft. Alert areas are depicted on aeronautical charts for the information of non-participating pilots. All activities within an alert area are conducted in accordance with FARs, and pilots of participating aircraft as well as pilots transiting the area are equally responsible for collision avoidance.

- Controlled Firing Area. Airspace wherein activities are conducted under conditions so controlled as to eliminate hazards to nonparticipating aircraft and to ensure the safety of persons and property on the ground.

- Military Operations Area (MOA). An MOA is an airspace assignment of defined vertical and lateral dimensions established outside positive control areas to separate/segregate certain military activities from IFR traffic and to identify for VFR traffic where these activities are conducted. (Refer to AIM.)

- Prohibited Area. Designated airspace within which the flight of aircraft is prohibited. (Refer to En route Charts, AIM.)
- Restricted Area. Airspace designated under FAR Part 73, within which the flight of aircraft, while not wholly prohibited, is subject to restriction. Most restricted areas are designated joint use, and IFR/VFR operations in the area may be authorized by the controlling ATC facility when it's not being used by the using agency. Restricted areas are depicted on en route charts. Where joint use is authorized, the name of the ATC controlling facility is also shown. (Refer to AIM, FAR Part 73.)
- Warning Area. Airspace that might contain hazards to nonparticipating aircraft in international airspace.

special VFR operations   Aircraft operating in accordance with clearances within control zones in weather conditions less than the basic VFR weather minima. Such operations must be requested by the pilot and approved by ATC. (See Special VFR Conditions, ICAO Special VFR Flight.)

speed adjustment   An ATC procedure used to request pilots to adjust aircraft speed to a specific value for the purpose of providing desired spacing. Pilots are expected to maintain a speed of plus or minus 10 knots or 0.02 Mach number of the specified speed. Examples of speed adjustments are:

- "Increase/reduce speed to Mach point [number]."
- "Increase/reduce speed to [speed in knots]," or "Increase/reduce speed [number of knots] knots."

taxi into position and hold   Used by ATC to inform a pilot to taxi onto the departure runway in takeoff position and hold. It's not authorization for takeoff. It's used when takeoff clearance can't immediately be issued because of traffic or other reasons. (See Cleared for Takeoff.)

TCAS I   A TCAS that uses interrogations of, and replies from, airborne radar beacon transponders and provides traffic advisories to the pilot.

TCAS II   A TCAS that uses interrogations of, and replies from, airborne radar beacon transponders and provides traffic advisories and resolution advisories in the vertical plane.

TCAS III   A TCAS that uses interrogations of, and replies from, airborne radar beacon transponders and provides traffic advisories and resolution advisories in the vertical and horizontal planes to the pilot.

terminal radar program   A national program instituted to extend the terminal radar services-provided IFR aircraft to VFR aircraft. Pilot participation in the program is urged but is not mandatory. The program is divided into two parts and referred to as Stage II and Stage III. The stage service provided at a particular location is contained in the Airport/Facility Directory.

- Stage 1 originally was composed of two basic radar services (traffic advisories and limited vectoring to VFR aircraft). These services are provided by all commissioned terminal radar facilities, but the term "Stage 1" has been deleted from use.

- Stage II/Radar Advisory and Sequencing for VFR Aircraft provides, in addition to the basic radar services, vectoring and sequencing on a full-time basis to arriving VFR aircraft. The purpose is to adjust the flow of arriving IFR and VFR aircraft into the traffic pattern in a safe and orderly manner and to provide traffic advisories to departing VFR aircraft.
- Stage III/Radar Sequencing and Separation Service for VFR Aircraft provides, in addition to the basic radar services and Stage II, separation between all participating VFR aircraft. The purpose is to provide separation between all participating VFR aircraft and all IFR aircraft operating within the airspace defined as a terminal radar service area (TRSA) or terminal control area (TCA). (See Terminal Radar Service Area, Controlled Airspace.) (Refer to AIM; the A/FD.)

terminal radar service area (TRSA) Airspace surrounding designated airports wherein ATC provides radar vectoring, sequencing, and separation on a full-time basis for all IFR and participating VFR aircraft. Service provided in a TRSA is called Stage III service. The AIM contains an explanation of TRSA. TRSAs are depicted on VFR aeronautical charts. Pilot participation is urged but is not mandatory. (See Terminal Radar Program.) (Refer to AIM, the A/FD.)

touchdown zone The first 3,000 feet of the runway beginning at the threshold. The area is used for determination of touchdown zone elevation in the development of straight-in landing minimums for instrument approaches. (See ICAO Touchdown Zone.)

tower A terminal facility that uses air/ground communications, visual signaling, and other devices to provide ATC services to aircraft operating in the vicinity of an airport or on the movement area. Authorizes aircraft to land or take off at the airport controlled by the tower or to transit the airport traffic area regardless of flight plan or weather conditions (IFR or VFR). A tower may also provide approach control services (radar or nonradar). (See Airport Traffic Area, Airport Traffic Control Service, Approach Control Facility, Approach Control Service, Movement Area, Tower En route Control Service, ICAO Aerodrome Control Tower.) (Refer to AIM.)

tower en route control service The control of IFR en route traffic within delegated airspace between two or more adjacent approach control facilities. This service is designed to expedite traffic and reduce control and pilot communication requirements.

traffic (1) A term used by a controller to transfer radar identification of an aircraft to another controller for the purpose of coordinating separation action. Traffic is normally issued (a) in response to a hand-off or point out, (b) in anticipation of a hand-off or point out, or (c) in conjunction with a request for control of an aircraft. (2) A term used by ATC to refer to one or more aircraft.

traffic advisories Advisories issued to alert pilots to other known or observed air traffic that might be in such proximity to the position or intended route of flight of their aircraft to warrant their attention. Such advisories might be based on:

- Visual observation.
- Observation of radar-identified and nonidentified aircraft targets on an ATC radar display, or
- Verbal reports from pilots or other facilities.

The word "traffic" followed by additional information, if known, is used to provide such advisories: e.g., "Traffic, two o'clock, one-zero miles, southbound, eight thousand." Traffic advisory service will be provided to the extent possible, depending on higher priority duties of the controller or other limitations: e.g., radar limitations, volume of traffic, frequency congestion, or controller work load. Radar/nonradar traffic advisories don't relieve the pilot of his or her responsibility to see and avoid other aircraft. Pilots are cautioned that there are many times when the controller is not able to give traffic advisories concerning all traffic in the aircraft's proximity; in other words, when a pilot requests or is receiving traffic advisories, he or she shouldn't assume that all traffic will be issued. (Refer to AIM.)

transcribed weather broadcast (TWEB) A continuous recording of meteorological and aeronautical information that's broadcast on L/MF and VOR facilities for pilots. (Refer to AIM.)

transmissometer An apparatus used to determine visibility by measuring the transmission of light through the atmosphere. It's the measurement source for determining runway visual range (RVR) and runway visibility value (RVV). (See Visibility.)

transponder The airborne radar beacon receiver/transmitter portion of the ATC radar beacon system (ATCRBS) that automatically receives radio signals from interrogators on the ground and selectively replies with a specific reply pulse or pulse group only to those interrogations being received on the mode to which it's set to respond. (See Interrogator, ICAO Transponder.) (Refer to AIM.)

true airspeed (TAS) The airspeed of an aircraft relative to undisturbed air.

true course (TC) Proposed flight path direction relative to the north.

true heading (TH) Actual aircraft heading in flight relative to true north. True heading is the true course plus or minus wind correction angle.

turbojet aircraft An aircraft having a jet engine in which the energy of the jet operates a turbine that in turn operates the air compressor.

turboprop aircraft An aircraft having a jet engine in which the energy of the jet operates a turbine that drives the propeller.

uncontrolled airspace Uncontrolled airspace is that portion of the airspace that has not been designated as continental control area, control area, control zone, terminal control area, or transition area and within which ATC has neither the authority nor the responsibility for exercising control over air traffic. (See Controlled Airspace.)

under the hood Indicates that the pilot is using a hood to restrict visibility outside the cockpit while simulating instrument flight. An appropriately rated pilot is required in the other control seat while this operation is being conducted. (Refer to FAR Part 91.)

useful load The weight of pilot, passengers, baggage, usable fuel, and drainable oil.

vector A heading issued to an aircraft to provide navigational guidance by radar. (See ICAO Radar Vectoring.)

verify Request confirmation of information: e.g., "Verify assigned altitude."

very high frequency (VHF) The frequency band between 30 and 300 MHz. Portions of this band, 108 to 118 MHz, are used for certain navaids; 118 to 136 MHz are used for civil air/ground voice communications. Other frequencies in this band are used for purposes not related to ATC.

VFR conditions Weather conditions equal to or better than the minimum for flight under VFR. The term may be used as an ATC clearance/instruction only when:

- An IFR aircraft requests a climb/descent in VFR conditions.
- The clearance will result in noise abatement benefits where part of the IFR departure route doesn't conform to an FAA-approved noise abatement route or altitude.
- A pilot has requested a practice instrument approach and is not on an IFR flight plan.

All pilots receiving this authorization must comply with the VFR visibility and distance from cloud criteria in FAR Part 91. Use of the term doesn't relieve controllers of their responsibility to separate aircraft in TCAs/TRSAs as required by FAA Order 7110.65. When used as an ATC clearance/instruction, the term may be abbreviated "VFR": e.g., "Maintain VFR," "Climb/descend VFR," etc.

VFR-on-top ATC authorization for an IFR aircraft to operate in VFR conditions at any appropriate VFR altitude (as specified in FARs and as restricted by ATC). A pilot receiving this authorization must comply with the VFR visibility, distance from cloud criteria, and the minimum IFR altitudes specified in FAR Part 91. The use of this term doesn't relieve controllers of their responsibility to separate aircraft in TCAs/TRSAs as required by FAA Order 7110.65.

VFR-over-the-top With respect to the operation of aircraft, means the operation of an aircraft over-the-top under VFR when it's not being operated on an IFR flight plan.

visibility The ability, as determined by atmospheric conditions and expressed in units of distance, to see and identify prominent unlighted objects by day and prominent lighted objects by night. Visibility is reported as statute miles, hundreds of feet, or meters. (Refer to FAR Part 91, AIM.)

- Flight Visibility. The average forward horizontal distance, from the cockpit of an aircraft in flight, at which prominent unlighted objects might be seen and identified by day and prominent lighted objects might be seen and identified by night.

- Ground Visibility. Prevailing horizontal visibility near the earth's surface as reported by the U.S. National Weather Service or an accredited observer.

- Prevailing Visibility. The greatest horizontal visibility equaled or exceeded throughout at least half the horizon circle that need not necessarily be continuous.

- Runway Visibility Value (RVV). The visibility determined for a particular runway by a transmissometer. A meter provides a continuous indication of the visibility (reported in miles or fractions of miles) for the runway. RVV is used in lieu of prevailing visibility in determining minimums for a particular runway.

- Runway Visual Range (RVR). An instrumentally derived value, based on standard calibrations, that represents the horizontal distance a pilot will see down the runway from the approach end. It's based on the sighting of either high-intensity runway lights or on the visual contrast of other targets, whichever yields the greater visual range. RVR, in contrast to prevailing or runway visibility, is based on what a pilot in a moving aircraft should see looking down the runway. RVR is horizontal visual range, not slant visual range. It's based on the measurement of a transmissometer made near the touchdown point of the instrument runway and is reported in hundreds of feet. RVR is used in lieu of RVV and/or prevailing visibility in determining minimums for a particular runway.

    a. Touchdown RVR. The RVR visibility readout values obtained from RVR equipment serving the runway touchdown zone.

    b. Mid-RVR. The RVR readout values obtained from RVR equipment located midfield of the runway.

    c. Rollout RVR. The RVR readout values obtained from RVR equipment located nearest the rollout end of the runway.

(See ICAO Visibility.)

visual approach An approach wherein an aircraft on an IFR flight plan, operating in VFR conditions under the control of an ATC facility and having an ATC authorization, may proceed to the airport of destination in VFR conditions. (See ICAO Visual Approach.)

visual descent point (VDP) A defined point on the final approach course of a non-precision straight-in approach procedure from which normal descent from the MDA to the runway touchdown point may be commenced, provided the approach threshold of that runway, or approach lights, or other markings identifiable with the approach end of that runway are clearly visible to the pilot.

visual separation A means employed by ATC to separate aircraft in terminal areas. There are two ways to effect this separation:

- The tower controller sees the aircraft involved and issues instructions, as necessary, to ensure that the aircraft avoid each other.

- A pilot sees the other aircraft involved and, on instructions from the controller, provides his or her own separation by maneuvering his or her aircraft as necessary to avoid the other aircraft. This might involve following another aircraft or keeping it in sight until it's no longer a factor. (See and Avoid.) (Refer to FAR Part 91.)

vortices Circular patterns of air created by the movement of an airfoil through the air when generating lift. As an airfoil moves through the atmosphere in sustained flight, an area of low pressure is created above it. The air flowing from the high pressure area to the low pressure area around and about the tips of the airfoil tends to roll up into two rapidly rotating vortices, cylindrical in shape. These vortices are the most predominant parts of aircraft wake turbulence, and their rotational force is dependent on the wing loading, gross weight, and speed of the generating aircraft. The vortices from medium to heavy aircraft can be of extremely high velocity and hazardous to smaller aircraft. (See Aircraft Classes, Wake Turbulence.) (Refer to AIM.)

wake turbulence Phenomena resulting from the passage of an aircraft through the atmosphere. The term includes vortices, thrust-stream turbulence, jet blast, jet wash, propeller wash, and rotor wash both on the ground and in the air. (See Jet Blast, Aircraft Classes, Vortices.) (Refer to AIM.)

waypoint A predetermined geographical position used for route/instrument approach definition (or progress-reporting purposes) that's defined relative to a vortac station or in terms of latitude/longitude coordinates.

when able When used in conjunction with ATC instructions, gives the pilot the latitude to delay compliance until a condition or event has been reconciled. Unlike "pilot discretion," when instructions are prefaced "when able," the pilot is expected to seek the first opportunity to comply. Once a maneuver has been initiated, the pilot is expected to continue until the specifications of the instructions have been met. "When able" shouldn't be used when expeditious compliance is required.

wind shear A change in wind speed and/or wind direction in a short distance, resulting in a tearing or shearing effect. It can exist in a horizontal or vertical direction and occasionally in both.

Index

Employers, Directory of, 72
exams, written, 32-33

F

FAA, 7
FAA predictions, 13-14, **14**
FAA written exams, 32-33
Falcon 2000, 15
FAPA Career Pilot, 130
FAPA job search firm, 71-73
   Aviation Job Bank, 72
   Career Pilot magazine, 72
   Directory of Employers,
      72
   Pilot Job Report, 72
   Pilot Salary Survey, 72
   resume services, 73
FAPA publication, 120
FAR, 5, 167-188
   Part 61, 29
   Part 121, 129
   Part 135 Air Taxi rules, 5
   Part 141, 29
      classroom, **30**
FAR Part 61 vs. Part 141,
   29-31
FAR 61.73, 18
FARs, private pilots, 167-
   170
Federal Aviation Adminis-
   tration, 150
federal government jobs,
   150
   agencies, 150
ferrying aircraft, 80-85, **81**
final notes, 162-166
financing, 41-42
   student loans, 41-42
   training, 41-42
first steps, 14
Flight Computing Catalog,
   162
Flight Deck Software, 162
flight experience, instrument rating, 18
flight instructor certificate,
   20
flight instructor, logbooks,
   21
flight instructors, 4, 176-180

aeronautical knowledge,
   176-177
authorizations, 177-180
   rating, 178-179
flight proficiency, 176
rating requirements, 179-
   180
flight proficiency, 168-169
flight training, 25-49
   AB INITIO, 36
   Alpha Eta Rhoe Aviation
      society, 44-46
   commercial schools, 33-36
   cost, 31-32
   exams, written, 32-33
   FAR Part 61 and Part 141,
      29-31
   financing, 41-42
   GI Bill, 42
   instructor and school,
      choosing, 28-29
   internships, 42-44
   military, 46-49
   what to expect, 25-27
Flight Training magazine,
   68-69, 77
FlightSafety F-100 simulator cockpit, **123**
Flying publication, 66
flying, history, 1-3
Fokker 50 specs, 102-103
Fokker 50, 102-103
Fokker 70, 101-102, **102**
forest fire tanker pilot, 5
Form 8710-1, 54
Form 8710-1 (*see* Application for Airman's Cer-
   tificate), 54
Fortune 500, 4
freight flying, 89-92
future plans, 12

G

G-V, Corporate, 13
General Aviation News &
   Flyer, 77
General Aviation News and
   Flyer, 68
GI Bill, 42
glossary, 190-232

goal, 10
ground operations, Com-
   mercial Flight Test, 56

H

Helicopter Association International, 76
helicopter cockpit, **76**
helicopter jobs, 75-77
   Caprock Helicopters, 77
   General Aviation News &
      Flyer, 77
   Helicopter Annual, 76
   Trade-a-Plane, 77
helicopter pilot, 5
helicopter private pilot,
   aeronautical experience,
   16
helicopter, 5, 19
   commercial at work, **5, 19**
hiring chart, majors, **119**
history, 1-3
Hopkins, George, 133

I

Independent Pilot's Association (IPA), 133
information service num-
   bers, military training, 48
instructor, choosing, 28-29
instrument rating, 17-18
   flight experience, 18
instrument time, logbooks,
   21
international jobs, 153-158
internships, 42-44
   United Flight Operations
      College Relations pro-
      gram, 43-44
interview, majors, 121-123
   majors, number hired in
      1992, **122**
ISA-21 (*see* Society of
   Women Airline Pilots)

J

Jean Haley's story, 22-24
Jetstream 41, **11**
job hunt, 62-64
   goals, 62
   on your own, 62-64

About the author

Robert Mark is an airline transport pilot with more than 5000 hours logged in 37 different aircraft. Mark, a former airline pilot, still holds current Instrument and Multiengine Flight Instructor Ratings. Also a former air traffic controller, Robert Mark has been a writer for twenty years. He is the author of *The Joy of Flying*, 3rd Edition, and numerous magazine articles for *Career Pilot, Flying, Airline Pilot, Professional Pilot, AOPA Pilot, Aviation International News* and the *Chicago Tribune*. He writes the monthly flight instructor column for *General Aviation News & Flyer*. Robert Mark lives in Chicago with his wife Nancy.

Other Bestsellers of Related Interest

The classic you've been searching for . . .
**STICK AND RUDDER: An Explanation of
the Art of Flying**—Wolfgang Langewiesche

Students, certificated pilots, and instructors alike have praised this book as *"the most useful guide to flying ever written."* The book explains the important phases of the art of flying, in a way the learner can use. It shows precisely what the pilot does when he flies, just how he does it, and why. 400 pages, 88 illustrations. Book No. 3820, $19.95 hardcover only

**THE PILOT'S AIR TRAFFIC CONTROL
HANDBOOK—2nd Edition**—Paul E. Illman

Keep up with the most recent changes in rules and regulations and gain an understanding of why air traffic control is essential for both safe and legal flight with this handbook. It familiarizes you with the national airspace system, the federal facilities that comprise the ATC system, and the operating procedures required to use the system properly—including a close-up look at the new airspace designations currently being implemented. 240 pages, 88 illustrations. Book No. 4232, $18.95 paperback, $28.95 hardcover

**STANDARD AIRCRAFT HANDBOOK
—5th Edition**—Edited by Larry Reithmaier, originally compiled and edited by Stuart Leavell and Stanley Bungay

Now updated to cover the latest in aircraft parts, equipment, and construction techniques, this classic reference provides practical information on FAA-approved metal airplane hardware. Techniques are presented in step-by-step fashion and explained in shop terms without unnecessary theory and background. All data on materials and procedures is derived from current reports by the nation's largest aircraft manufacturers. 240 pages, 213 illustrations. Book No. 3634, $11.95 paperback only

Prices Subject to Change Without Notice.

Look for These and Other TAB Books at Your Local Bookstore

To Order Call Toll Free 1-800-822-8158
(24-hour telephone service available.)

or write to TAB Books, Blue Ridge Summit, PA 17294-0840.

Title	Product No.	Quantity	Price

☐ Check or money order made payable to TAB Books

Charge my ☐ VISA ☐ MasterCard ☐ American Express

Acct. No. _____ Exp. _____

Signature: _____

Name: _____

Address: _____

City: _____

State: _____ Zip: _____

Subtotal	$ _____
Postage and Handling ($3.00 in U.S., $5.00 outside U.S.)	$ _____
Add applicable state and local sales tax	$ _____
TOTAL	$ _____

TAB Books catalog free with purchase; otherwise send $1.00 in check or money order and receive $1.00 credit on your next purchase.

Orders outside U.S. must pay with international money in U.S. dollars drawn on a U.S. bank.

TAB Guarantee: If for any reason you are not satisfied with the book(s) you order, simply return it (them) within 15 days and receive a full refund.

BC